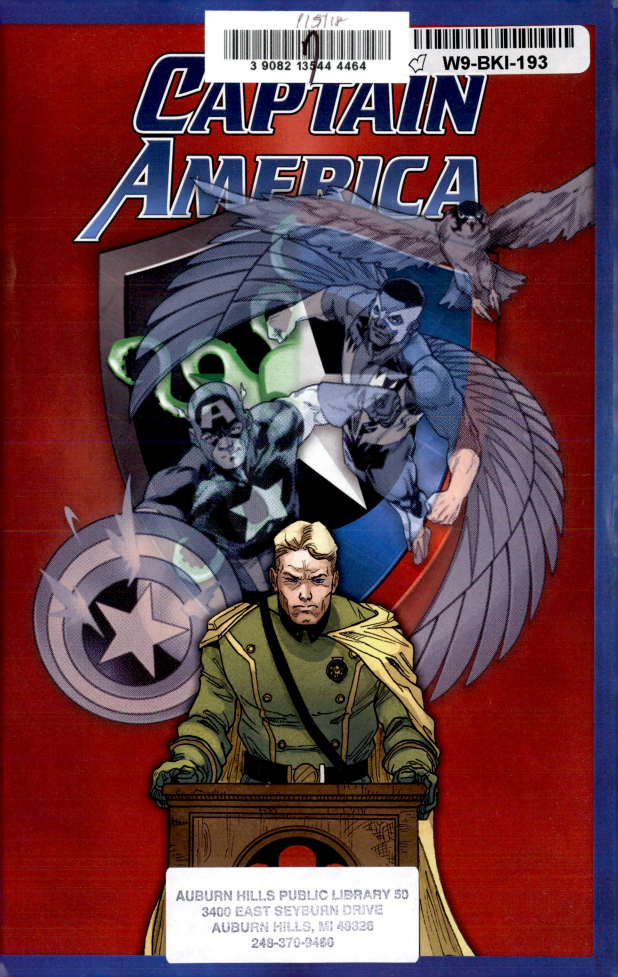

CAPTAIN AMERICA

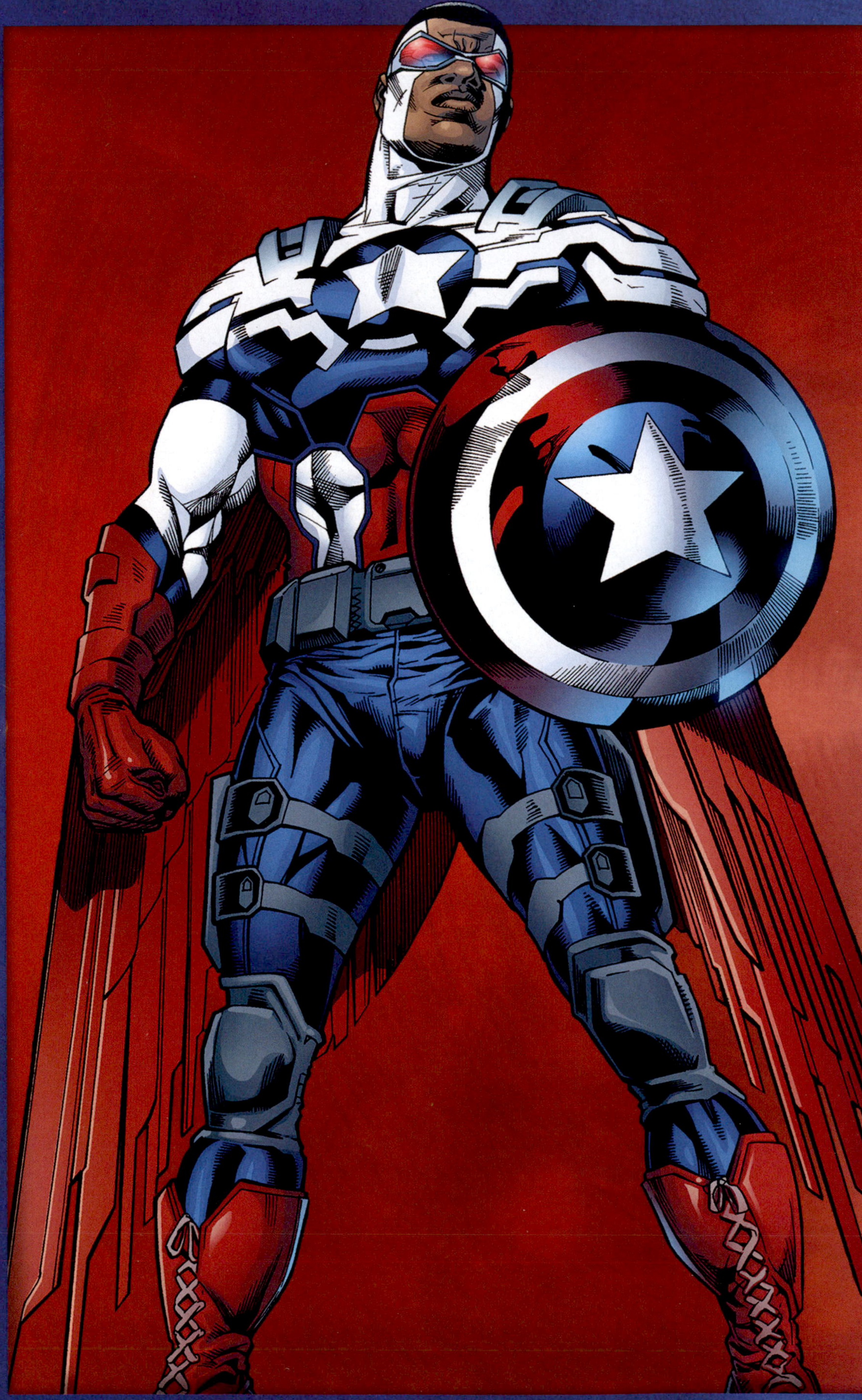

CAPTAIN AMERICA
SECRET EMPIRE

Nick Spencer with
Donny Cates [*Steve Rogers #18-19, Sam Wilson #24*]
WRITERS

SAM WILSON — CAPTAIN AMERICA

Sean Izaakse [#22] and
Joe Bennett & **Joe Pimentel** [#23-24]
ARTISTS

Nolan Woodard [#22] and
Matt Yackey [#23-24]
COLOR ARTISTS

STEVE ROGERS — CAPTAIN AMERICA

Andres Guinaldo & **Ramón Bachs** [#17] and
Javier Pina & **Andres Guinaldo** [#18-19]
ARTISTS

Rachelle Rosenberg
COLOR ARTIST

Elizabeth Torque [*Sam Wilson #22-24, Steve Rogers #17-18*] & **Jesús Saiz** [*Steve Rogers #19*]
COVER ART

VC's Joe Caramagna
LETTERER

Alanna Smith
ASSISTANT EDITOR

Tom Brevoort
EDITOR

COLLECTION EDITOR **Mark D. Beazley**
ASSISTANT EDITOR **Caitlin O'Connell**
ASSOCIATE MANAGING EDITOR **Kateri Woody**
SENIOR EDITOR, SPECIAL PROJECTS **Jennifer Grünwald**
VP PRODUCTION & SPECIAL PROJECTS **Jeff Youngquist**
SVP PRINT, SALES & MARKETING **David Gabriel**

BOOK DESIGNER **Adam Del Re**

EDITOR IN CHIEF **Axel Alonso**
CHIEF CREATIVE OFFICER **Joe Quesada**
PRESIDENT **Dan Buckley**
EXECUTIVE PRODUCER **Alan Fine**

CAPTAIN AMERICA
CREATED BY
JOE SIMON & JACK KIRBY

CAPTAIN AMERICA: SECRET EMPIRE. Contains material originally published in magazine form as CAPTAIN AMERICA: STEVE ROGERS #17-19 and CAPTAIN AMERICA: SAM WILSON #22-24. First printing 2017. ISBN# 978-1-302-90849-2. Published by MARVEL WORLDWIDE, INC., a subsidiary of MARVEL ENTERTAINMENT, LLC. OFFICE OF PUBLICATION: 135 West 50th Street, New York, NY 10020. **Printed in Canada.** DAN BUCKLEY, President, Marvel Entertainment; JOE QUESADA, Chief Creative Officer; TOM BREVOORT, SVP of Publishing; DAVID BOGART, SVP of Business Affairs & Operations, Publishing & Partnership; C.B. CEBULSKI, VP of Brand Management & Development, Asia; DAVID GABRIEL, SVP of Sales & Marketing, Publishing; JEFF YOUNGQUIST, VP of Production & Special Projects; DAN CARR, Executive Director of Publishing Technology; ALEX MORALES, Director of Publishing Operations; SUSAN CRESPI, Production Manager; STAN LEE, Chairman Emeritus. For information regarding advertising in Marvel Comics or on Marvel.com, please contact Vit DeBellis, Integrated Sales Manager, at vdebellis@marvel.com. For Marvel subscription inquiries, please call 888-511-5480. **Manufactured between 7/28/2017 and 8/29/2017 by SOLISCO PRINTERS, SCOTT, QC, CANADA.**

10 9 8 7 6 5 4 3 2 1

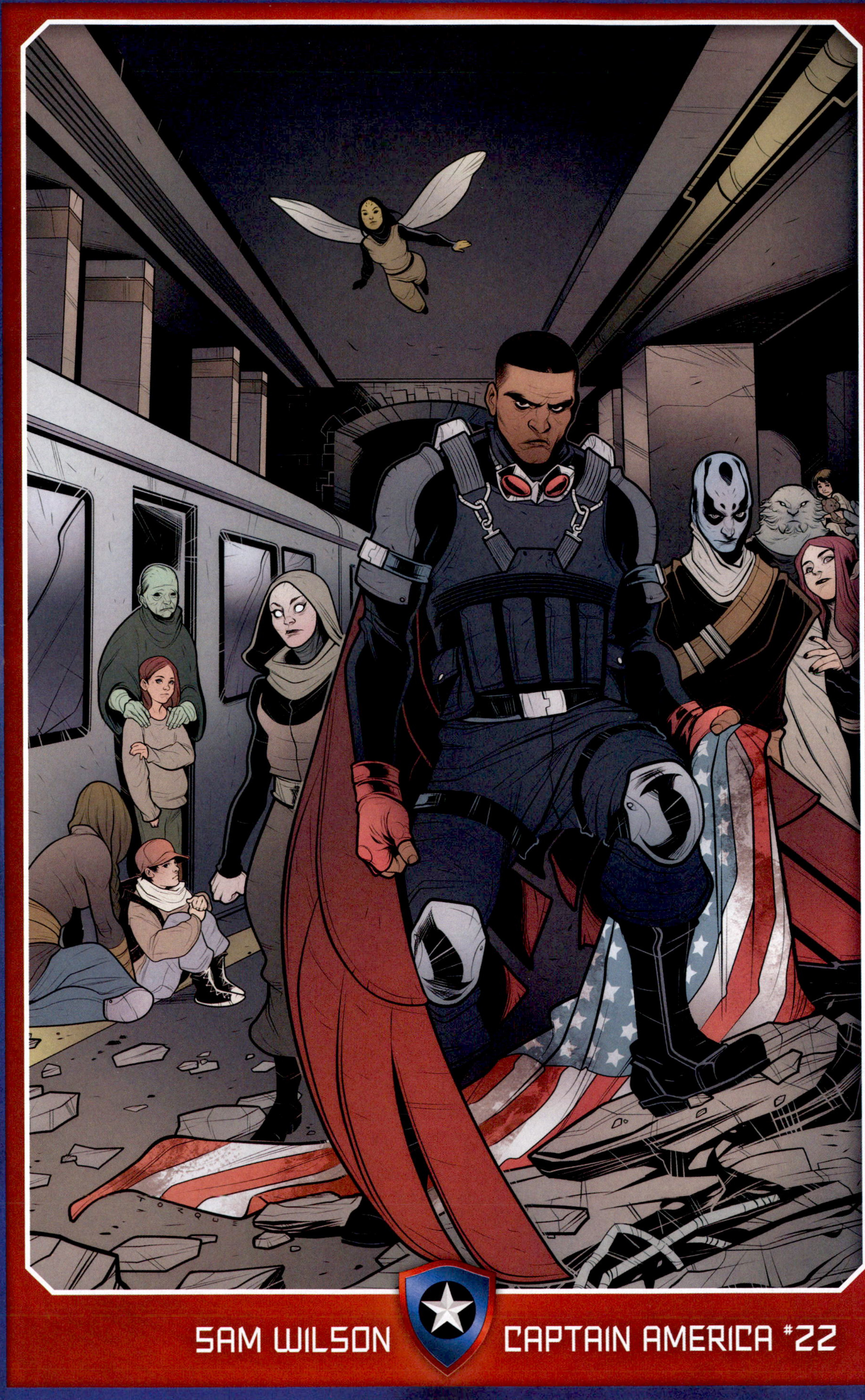
SAM WILSON
CAPTAIN AMERICA #22

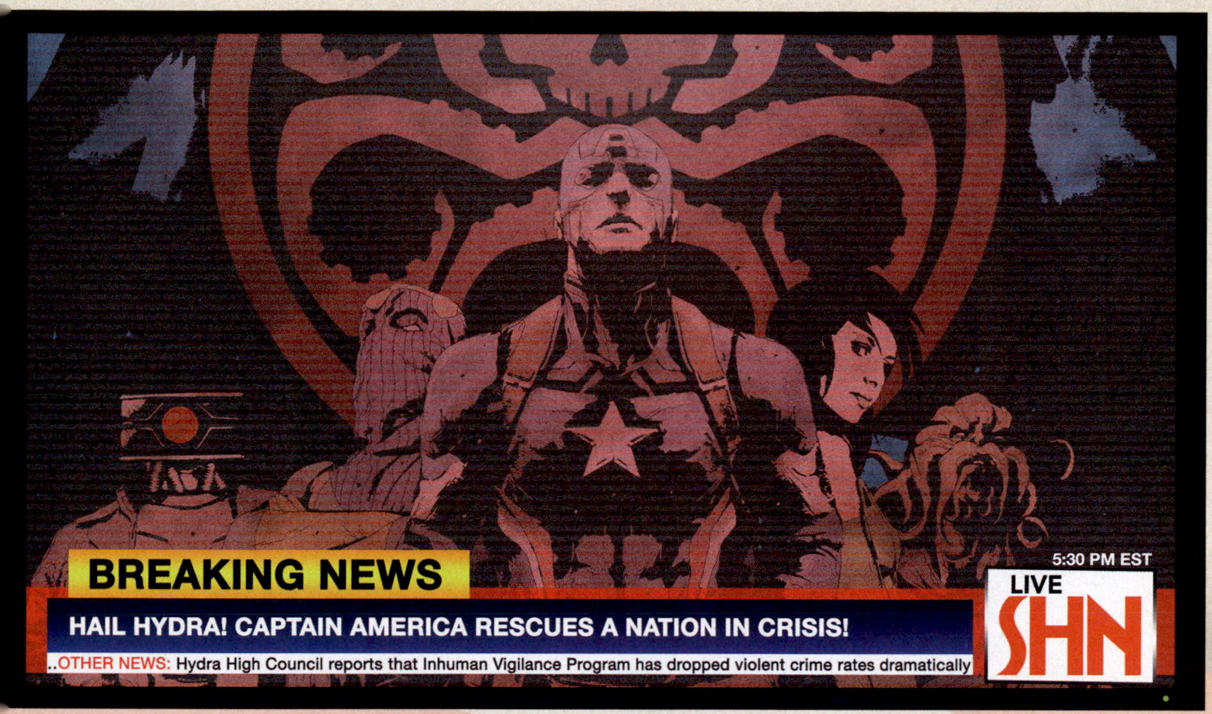
BREAKING NEWS
HAIL HYDRA! CAPTAIN AMERICA RESCUES A NATION IN CRISIS!
..OTHER NEWS: Hydra High Council reports that Inhuman Vigilance Program has dropped violent crime rates dramatically
5:30 PM EST
LIVE
SHN

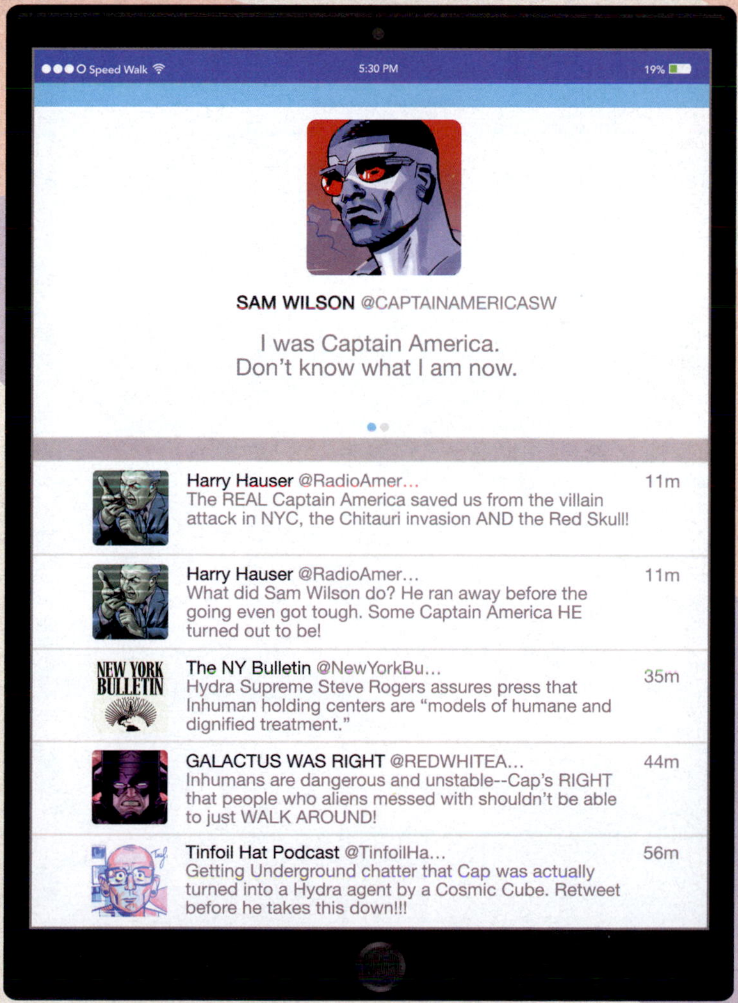
Speed Walk
5:30 PM
19%
SAM WILSON @CAPTAINAMERICASW
I was Captain America.
Don't know what I am now.
Harry Hauser @RadioAmer... 11m
The REAL Captain America saved us from the villain attack in NYC, the Chitauri invasion AND the Red Skull!
Harry Hauser @RadioAmer... 11m
What did Sam Wilson do? He ran away before the going even got tough. Some Captain America HE turned out to be!
NEW YORK BULLETIN
The NY Bulletin @NewYorkBu... 35m
Hydra Supreme Steve Rogers assures press that Inhuman holding centers are "models of humane and dignified treatment."
GALACTUS WAS RIGHT @REDWHITEA... 44m
Inhumans are dangerous and unstable--Cap's RIGHT that people who aliens messed with shouldn't be able to just WALK AROUND!
Tinfoil Hat Podcast @TinfoilHa... 56m
Getting Underground chatter that Cap was actually turned into a Hydra agent by a Cosmic Cube. Retweet before he takes this down!!!

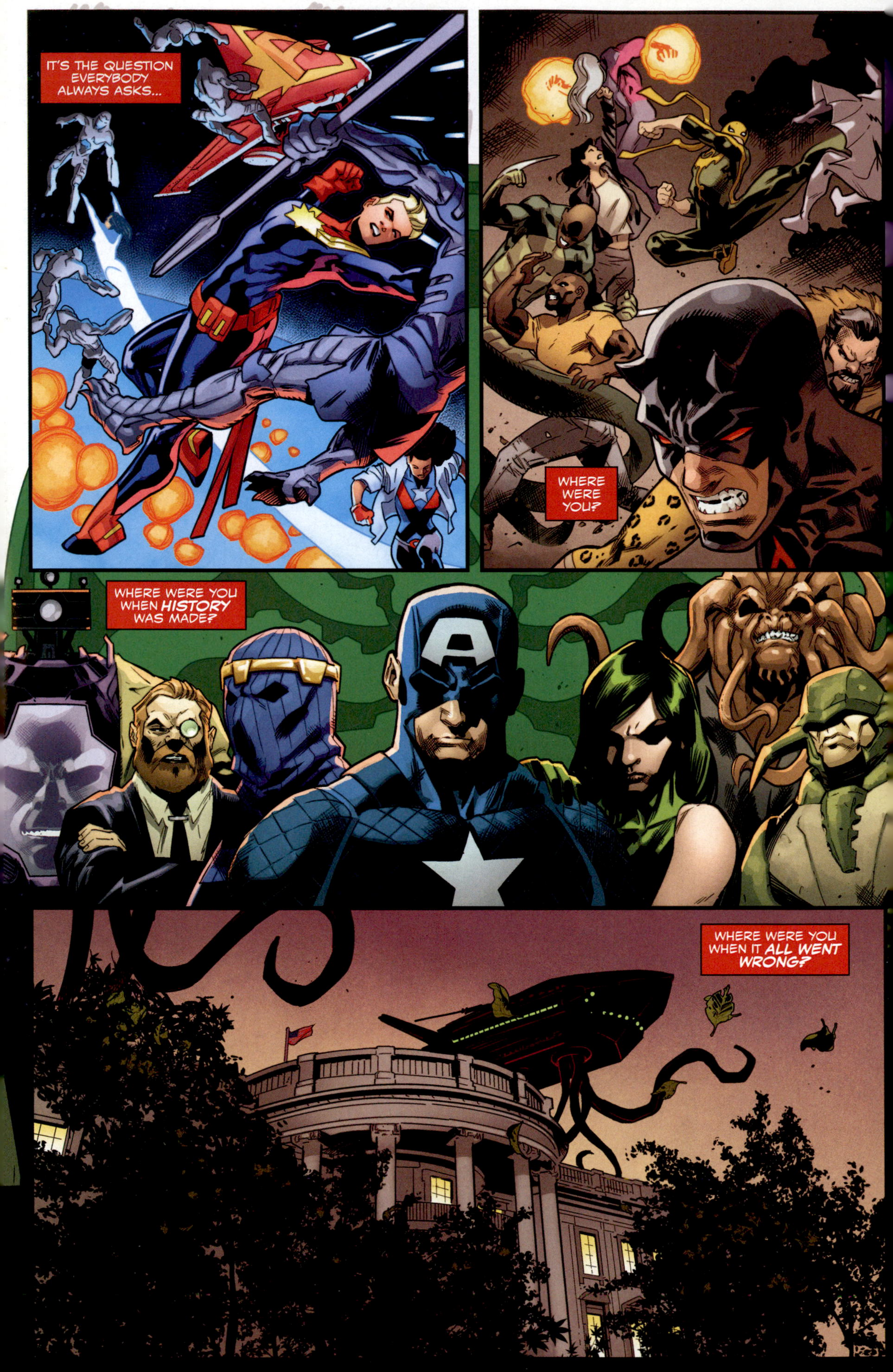
IT'S THE QUESTION EVERYBODY ALWAYS ASKS...
WHERE WERE YOU?
WHERE WERE YOU WHEN HISTORY WAS MADE?
WHERE WERE YOU WHEN IT ALL WENT WRONG?

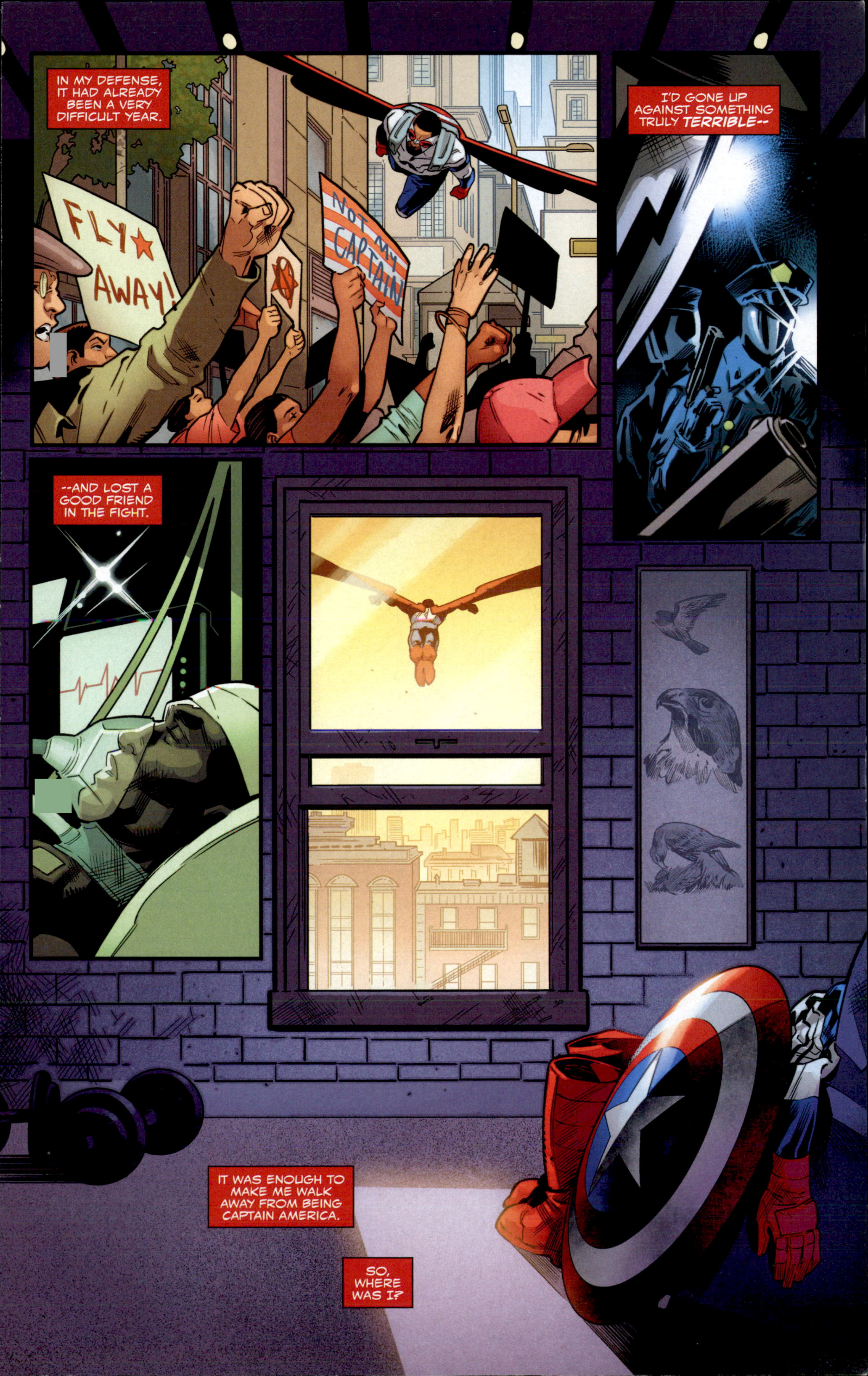
IN MY DEFENSE, IT HAD ALREADY BEEN A VERY DIFFICULT YEAR.
FLY★ AWAY!
NOT MY CAPTAIN
I'D GONE UP AGAINST SOMETHING TRULY *TERRIBLE*--
--AND LOST A GOOD FRIEND IN THE FIGHT.
IT WAS ENOUGH TO MAKE ME WALK AWAY FROM BEING CAPTAIN AMERICA.
SO, WHERE WAS I?

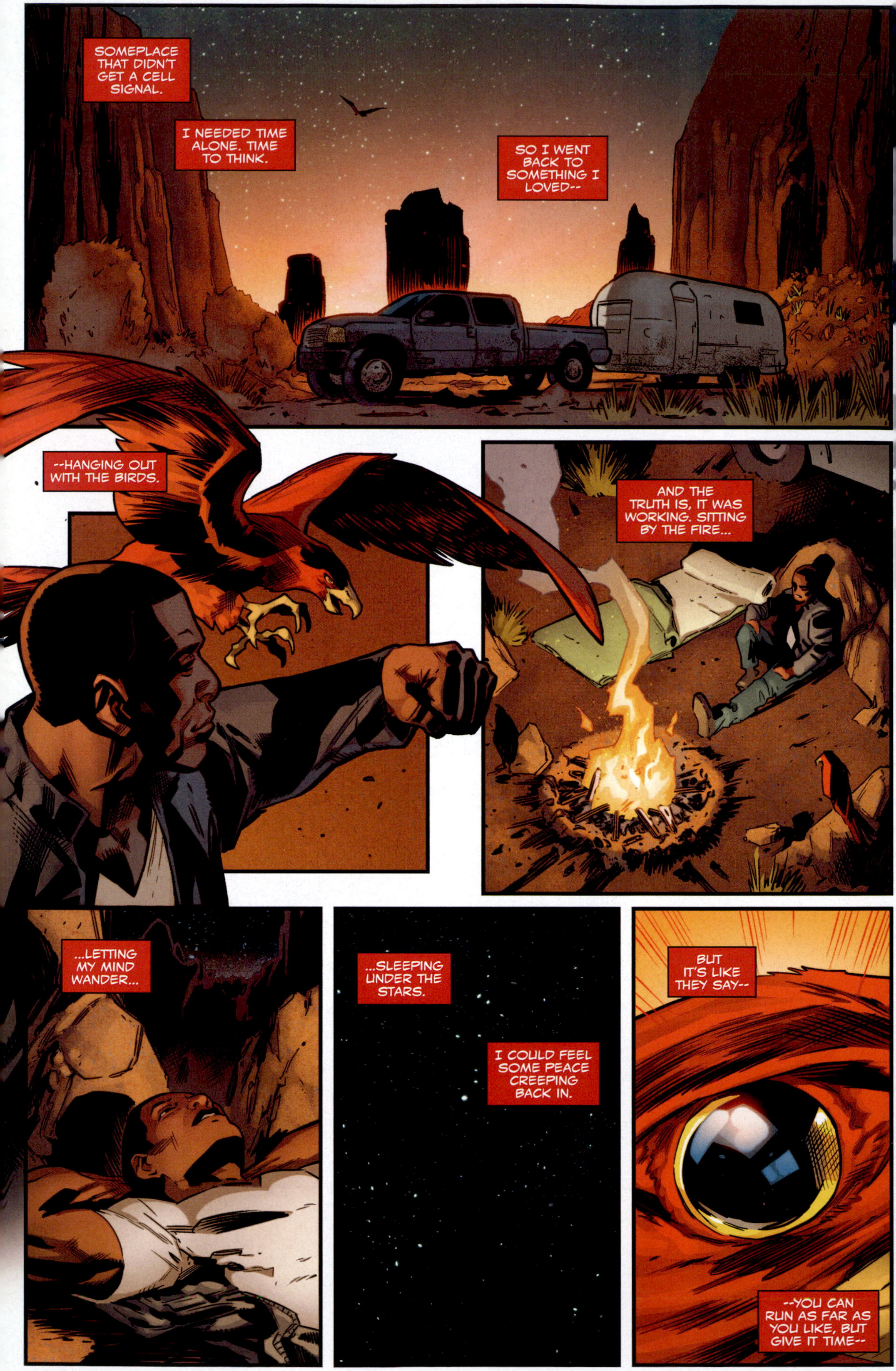
SOMEPLACE THAT DIDN'T GET A CELL SIGNAL.
I NEEDED TIME ALONE. TIME TO THINK.
SO I WENT BACK TO SOMETHING I LOVED--
--HANGING OUT WITH THE BIRDS.
AND THE TRUTH IS, IT WAS WORKING. SITTING BY THE FIRE...
...LETTING MY MIND WANDER...
...SLEEPING UNDER THE STARS.
I COULD FEEL SOME PEACE CREEPING BACK IN.
BUT IT'S LIKE THEY SAY--
--YOU CAN RUN AS FAR AS YOU LIKE, BUT GIVE IT TIME--

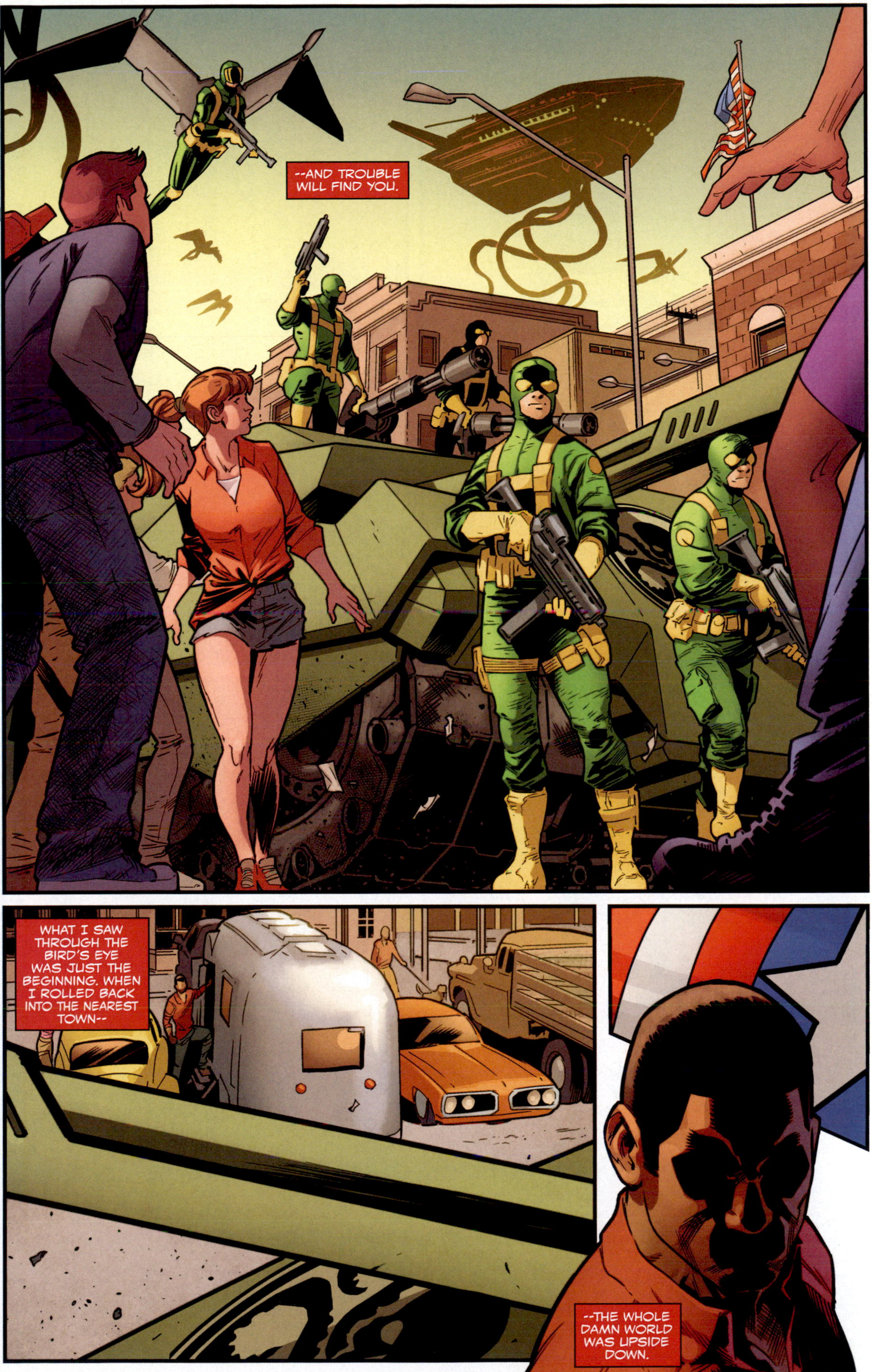
--AND TROUBLE WILL FIND YOU.
WHAT I SAW THROUGH THE BIRD'S EYE WAS JUST THE BEGINNING. WHEN I ROLLED BACK INTO THE NEAREST TOWN--
--THE WHOLE DAMN WORLD WAS UPSIDE DOWN.

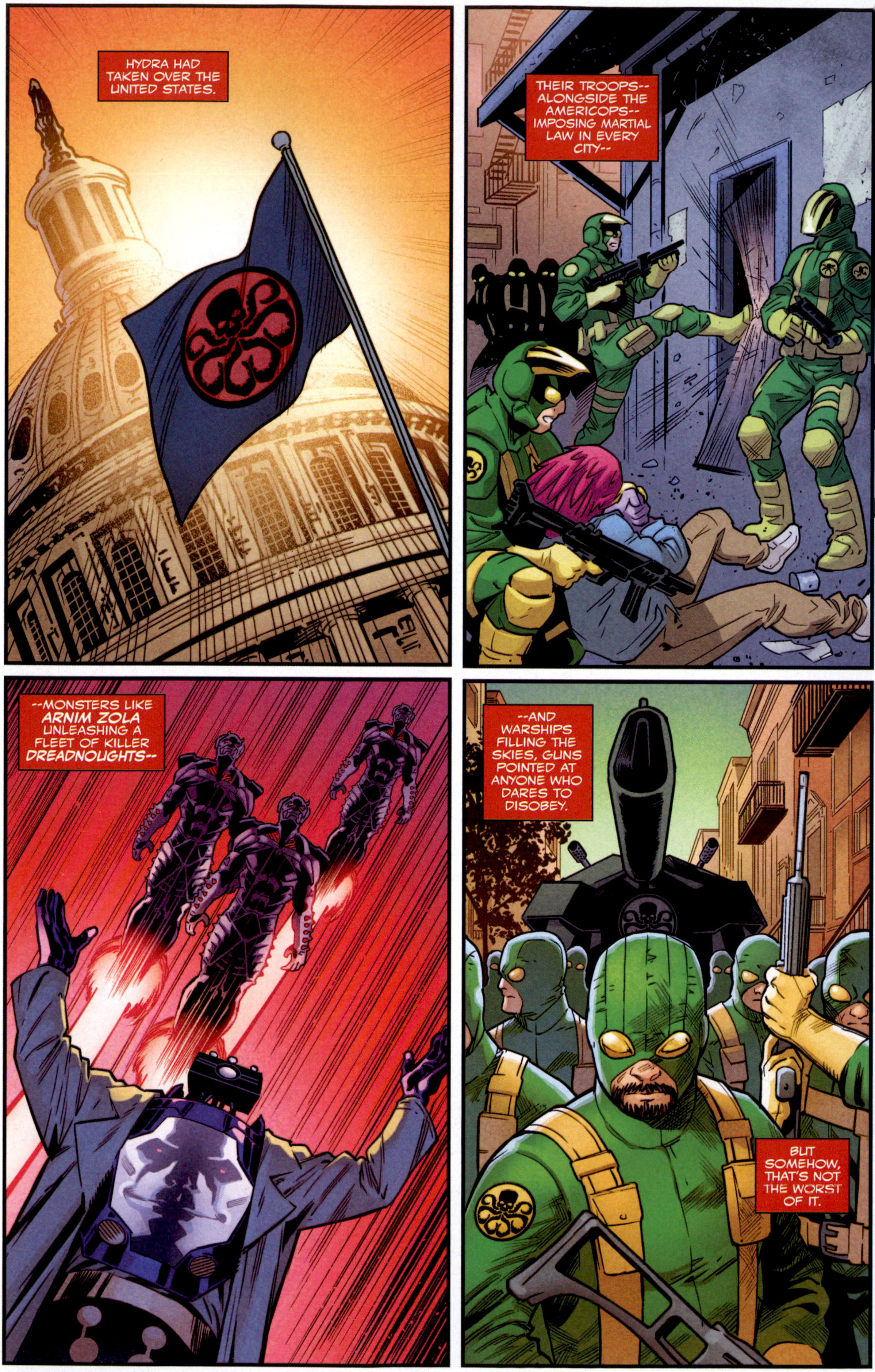
HYDRA HAD TAKEN OVER THE UNITED STATES.
THEIR TROOPS-- ALONGSIDE THE AMERICOPS-- IMPOSING MARTIAL LAW IN EVERY CITY--
--MONSTERS LIKE ARNIM ZOLA UNLEASHING A FLEET OF KILLER DREADNOUGHTS--
--AND WARSHIPS FILLING THE SKIES, GUNS POINTED AT ANYONE WHO DARES TO DISOBEY.
BUT SOMEHOW, THAT'S NOT THE WORST OF IT.

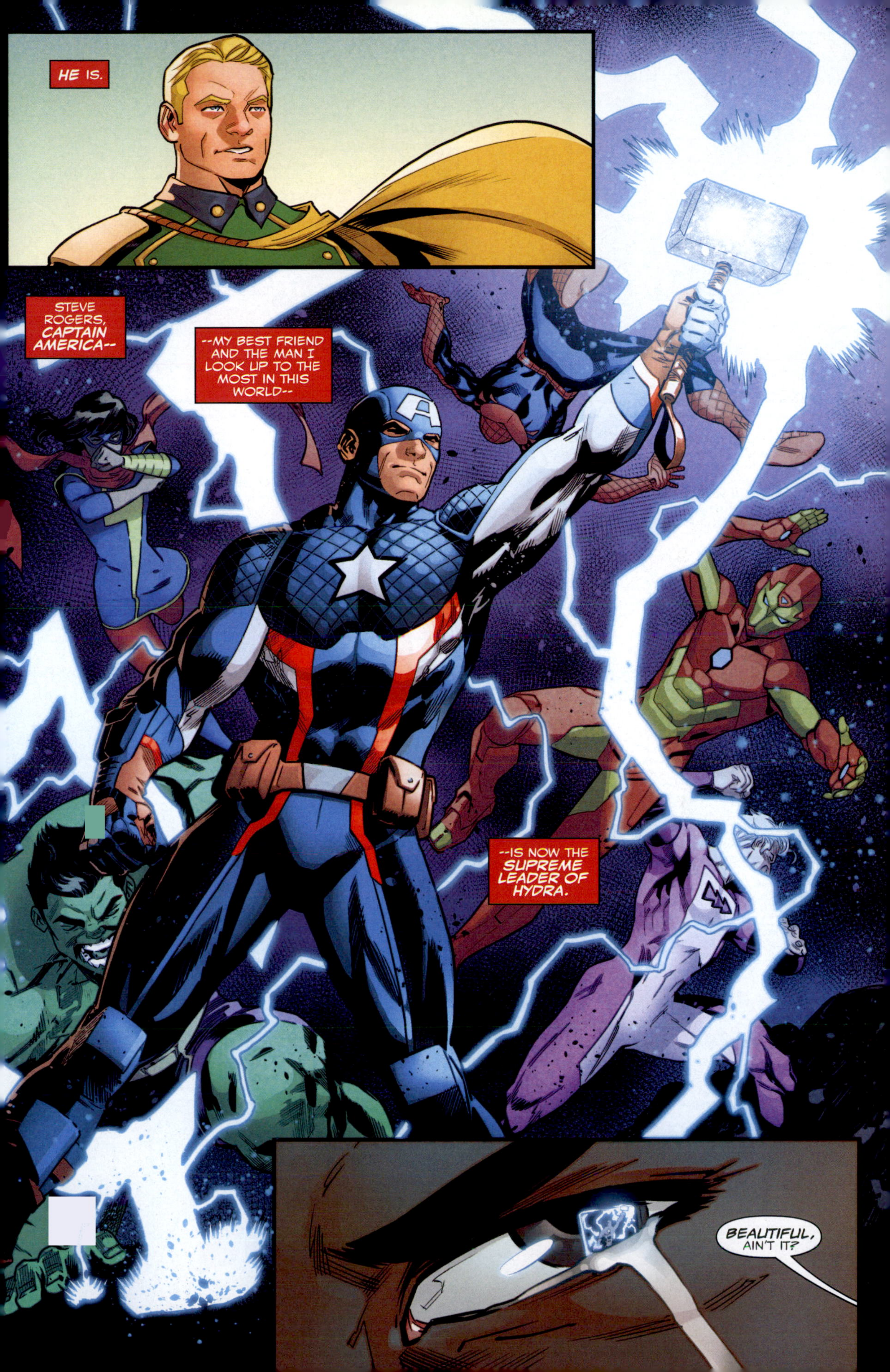
HE IS.
STEVE ROGERS, CAPTAIN AMERICA--
--MY BEST FRIEND AND THE MAN I LOOK UP TO THE MOST IN THIS WORLD--
--IS NOW THE SUPREME LEADER OF HYDRA.
BEAUTIFUL, AIN'T IT?

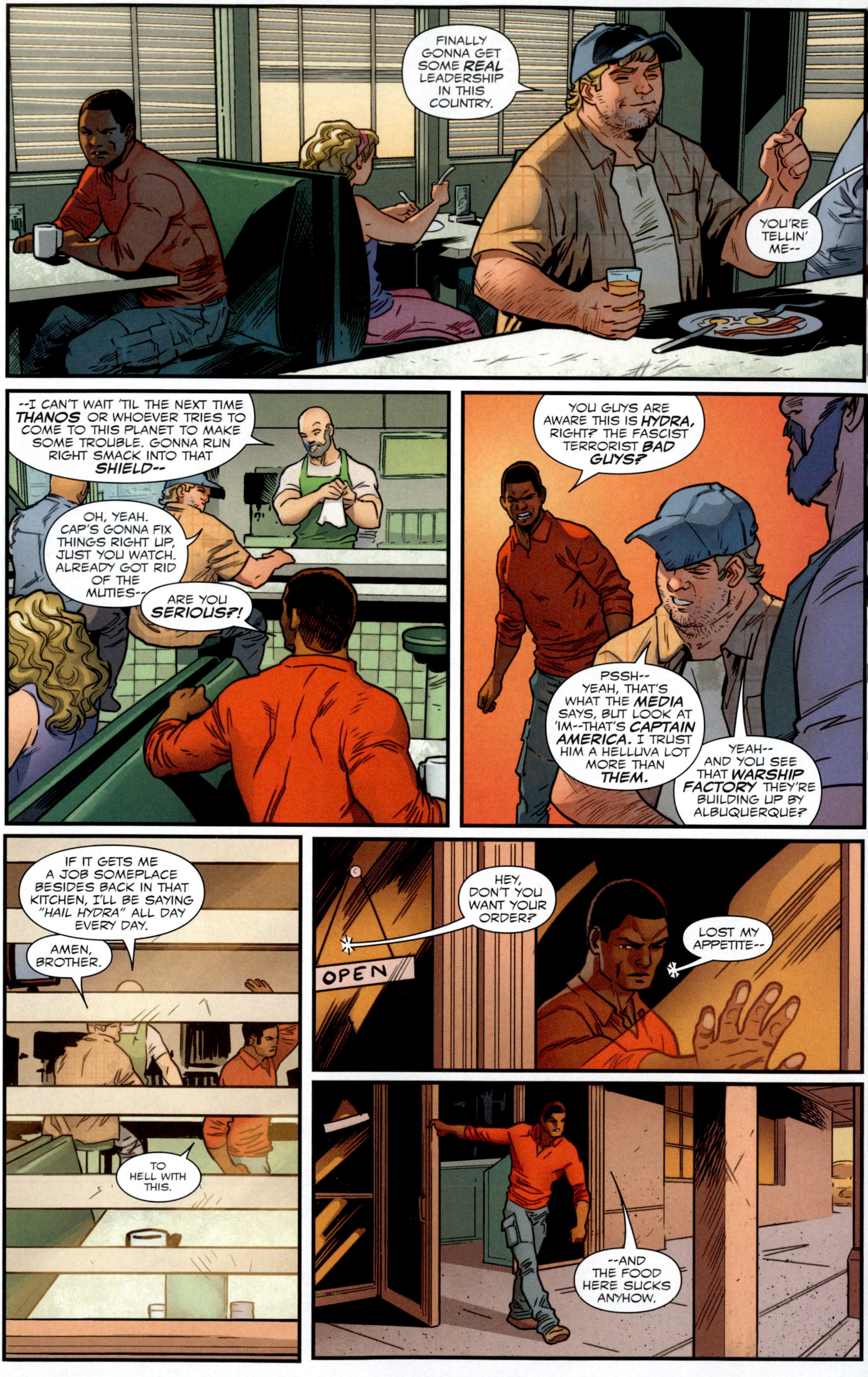
FINALLY GONNA GET SOME REAL LEADERSHIP IN THIS COUNTRY.
YOU'RE TELLIN' ME--
--I CAN'T WAIT 'TIL THE NEXT TIME THANOS OR WHOEVER TRIES TO COME TO THIS PLANET TO MAKE SOME TROUBLE. GONNA RUN RIGHT SMACK INTO THAT SHIELD--
OH, YEAH. CAP'S GONNA FIX THINGS RIGHT UP, JUST YOU WATCH. ALREADY GOT RID OF THE MUTIES--
ARE YOU SERIOUS?!
YOU GUYS ARE AWARE THIS IS HYDRA, RIGHT? THE FASCIST TERRORIST BAD GUYS?
PSSH-- YEAH, THAT'S WHAT THE MEDIA SAYS, BUT LOOK AT 'IM--THAT'S CAPTAIN AMERICA. I TRUST HIM A HELLUVA LOT MORE THAN THEM.
YEAH-- AND YOU SEE THAT WARSHIP FACTORY THEY'RE BUILDING UP BY ALBUQUERQUE?
IF IT GETS ME A JOB SOMEPLACE BESIDES BACK IN THAT KITCHEN, I'LL BE SAYING "HAIL HYDRA" ALL DAY EVERY DAY.
AMEN, BROTHER.
TO HELL WITH THIS.
HEY, DON'T YOU WANT YOUR ORDER?
OPEN
LOST MY APPETITE--
--AND THE FOOD HERE SUCKS ANYHOW.

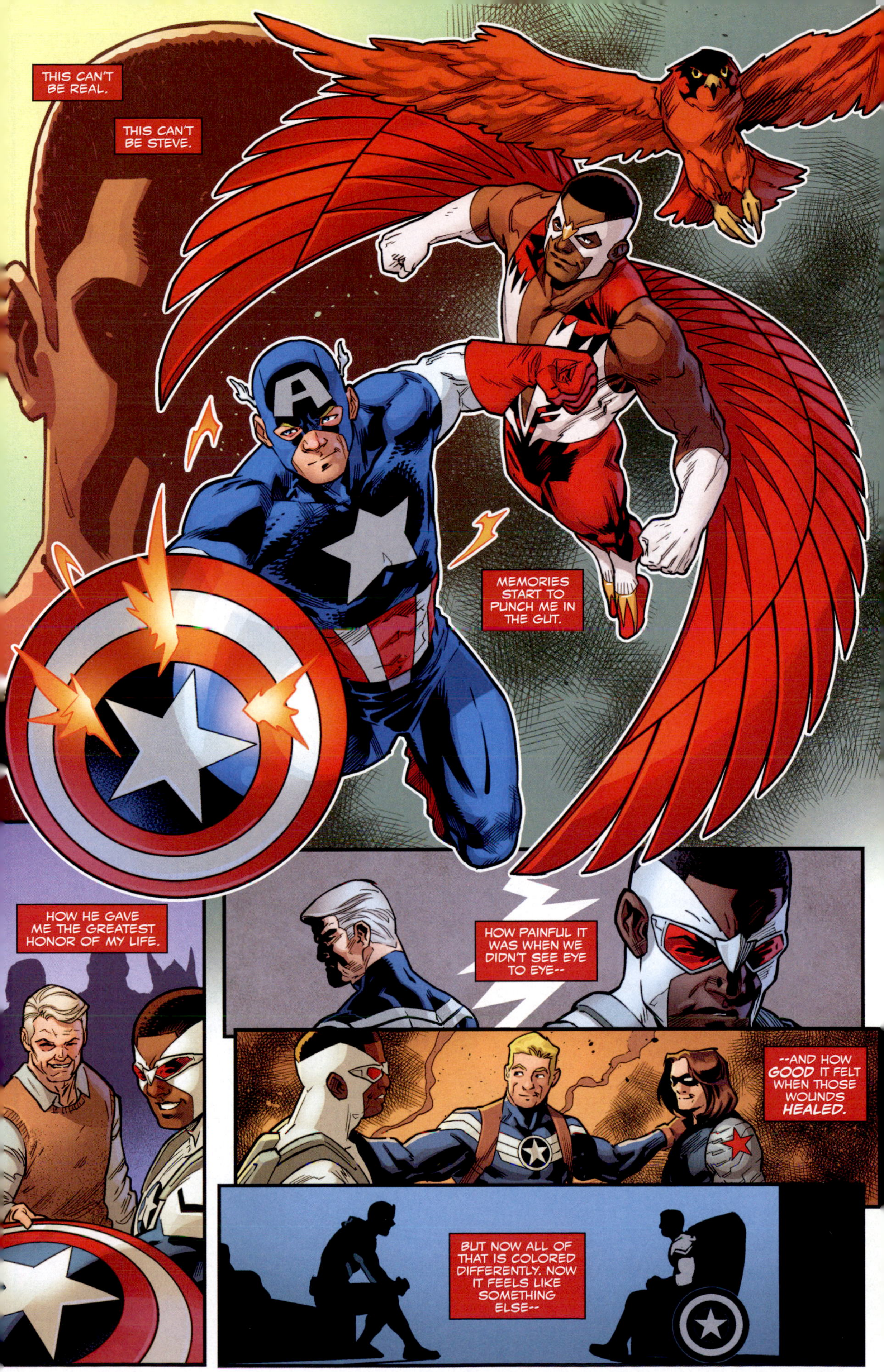
THIS CAN'T BE REAL.
THIS CAN'T BE STEVE.
MEMORIES START TO PUNCH ME IN THE GUT.
HOW HE GAVE ME THE GREATEST HONOR OF MY LIFE.
HOW PAINFUL IT WAS WHEN WE DIDN'T SEE EYE TO EYE--
--AND HOW GOOD IT FELT WHEN THOSE WOUNDS HEALED.
BUT NOW ALL OF THAT IS COLORED DIFFERENTLY. NOW IT FEELS LIKE SOMETHING ELSE--

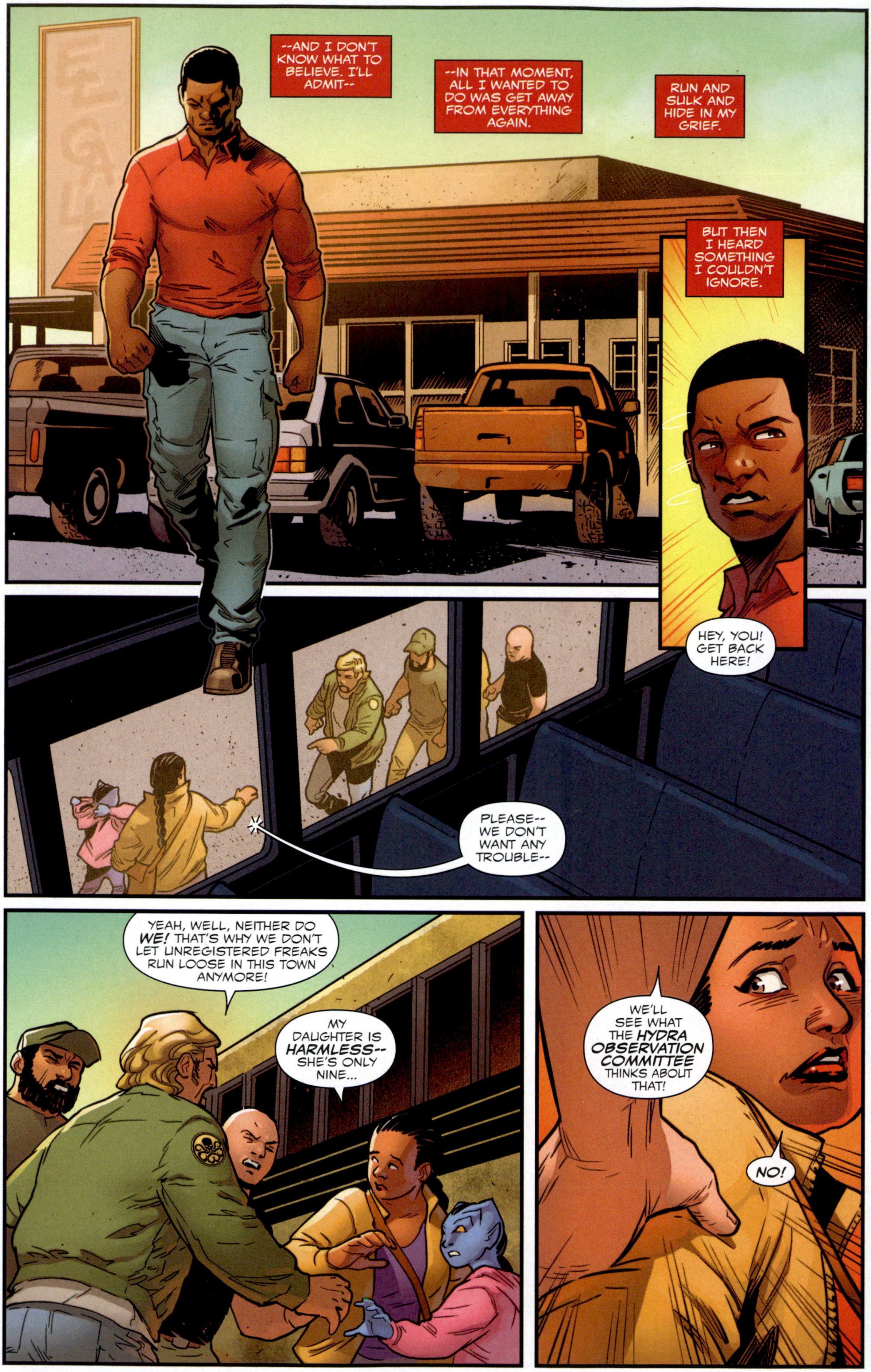
--AND I DON'T KNOW WHAT TO BELIEVE. I'LL ADMIT--
--IN THAT MOMENT, ALL I WANTED TO DO WAS GET AWAY FROM EVERYTHING AGAIN.
RUN AND SULK AND HIDE IN MY GRIEF.
BUT THEN I HEARD SOMETHING I COULDN'T IGNORE.
HEY, YOU! GET BACK HERE!
PLEASE-- WE DON'T WANT ANY TROUBLE--
YEAH, WELL, NEITHER DO **WE!** THAT'S WHY WE DON'T LET UNREGISTERED FREAKS RUN LOOSE IN THIS TOWN ANYMORE!
MY DAUGHTER IS **HARMLESS--** SHE'S ONLY NINE...
WE'LL SEE WHAT THE **HYDRA OBSERVATION COMMITTEE** THINKS ABOUT THAT!
NO!

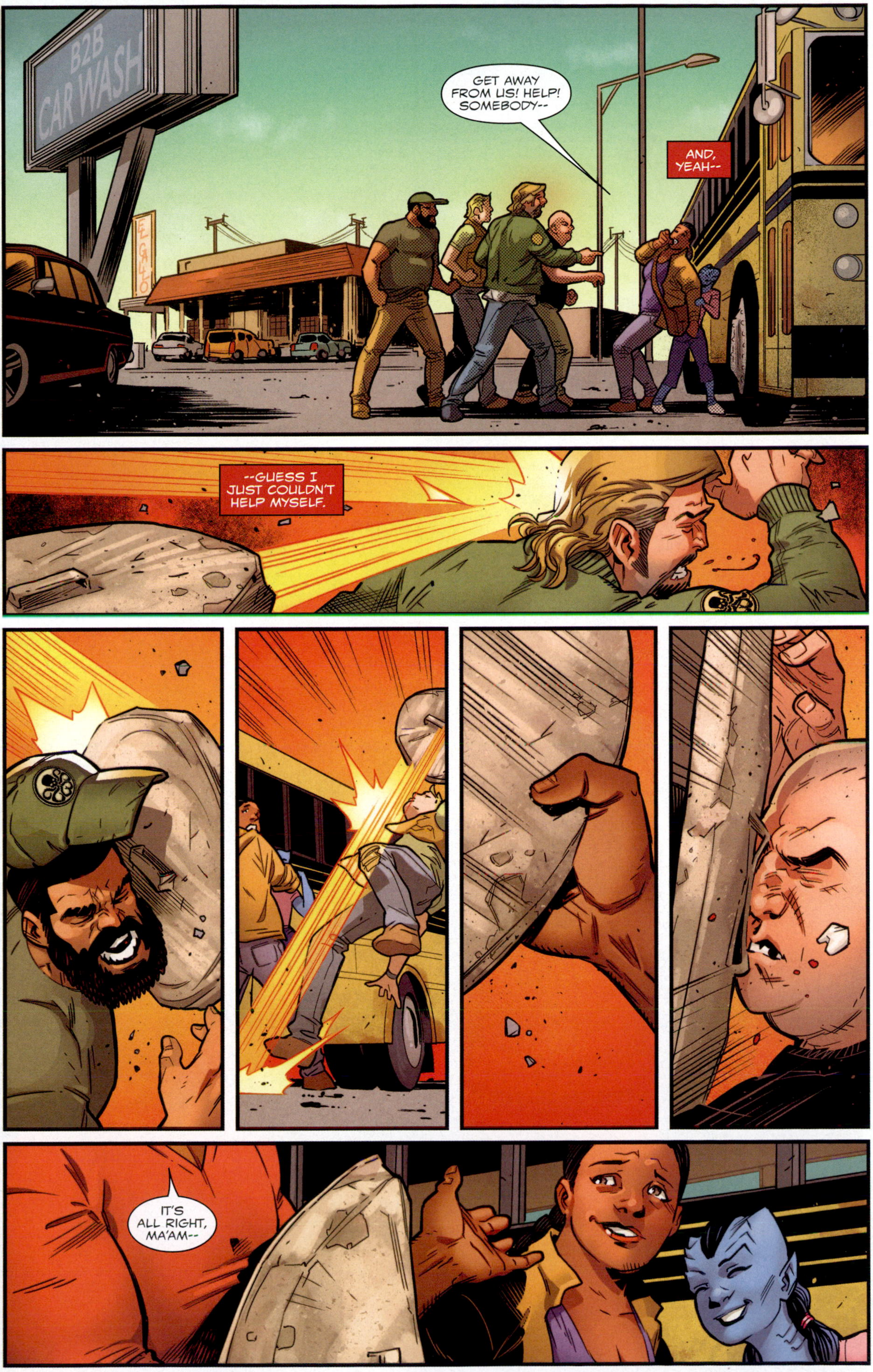
B2B CAR WASH
GET AWAY FROM US! HELP! SOMEBODY--
AND, YEAH--
--GUESS I JUST COULDN'T HELP MYSELF.
IT'S ALL RIGHT, MA'AM--

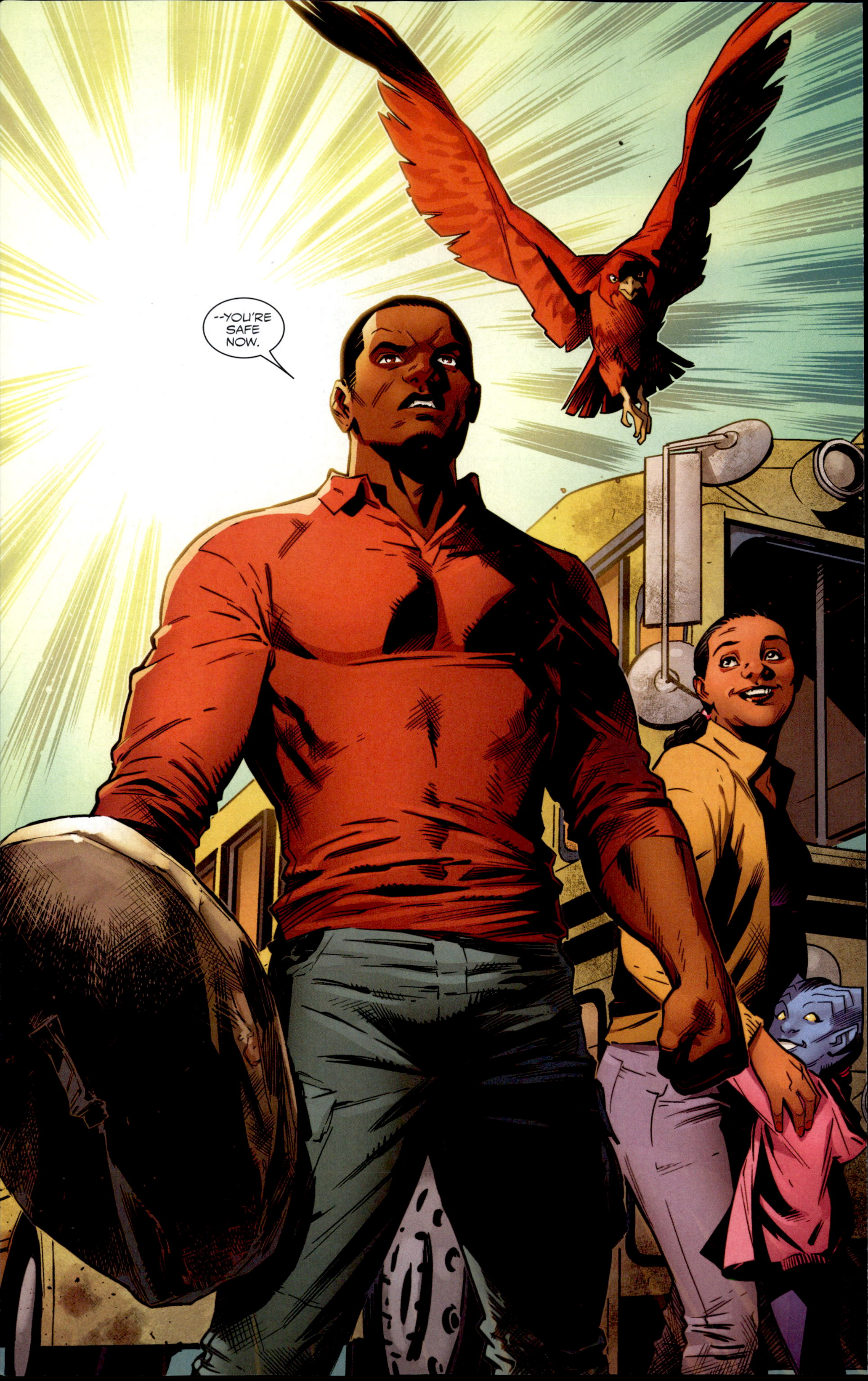
--YOU'RE SAFE NOW.

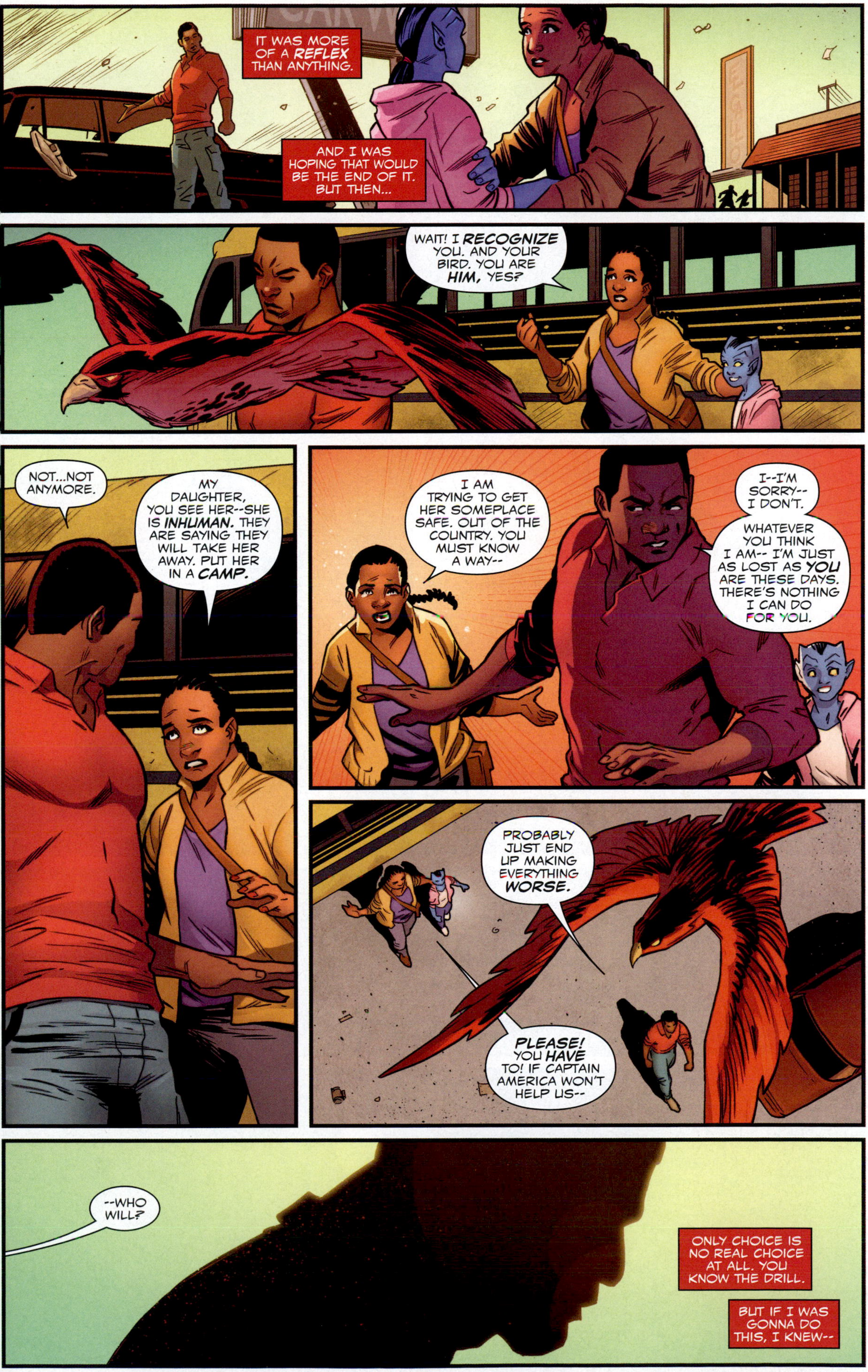
IT WAS MORE OF A REFLEX THAN ANYTHING.
AND I WAS HOPING THAT WOULD BE THE END OF IT. BUT THEN...
WAIT! I RECOGNIZE YOU. AND YOUR BIRD. YOU ARE HIM, YES?
NOT...NOT ANYMORE.
MY DAUGHTER, YOU SEE HER--SHE IS INHUMAN. THEY ARE SAYING THEY WILL TAKE HER AWAY. PUT HER IN A CAMP.
I AM TRYING TO GET HER SOMEPLACE SAFE. OUT OF THE COUNTRY. YOU MUST KNOW A WAY--
I--I'M SORRY-- I DON'T.
WHATEVER YOU THINK I AM-- I'M JUST AS LOST AS YOU ARE THESE DAYS. THERE'S NOTHING I CAN DO FOR YOU.
PROBABLY JUST END UP MAKING EVERYTHING WORSE.
PLEASE! YOU HAVE TO! IF CAPTAIN AMERICA WON'T HELP US--
--WHO WILL?
ONLY CHOICE IS NO REAL CHOICE AT ALL. YOU KNOW THE DRILL.
BUT IF I WAS GONNA DO THIS, I KNEW--

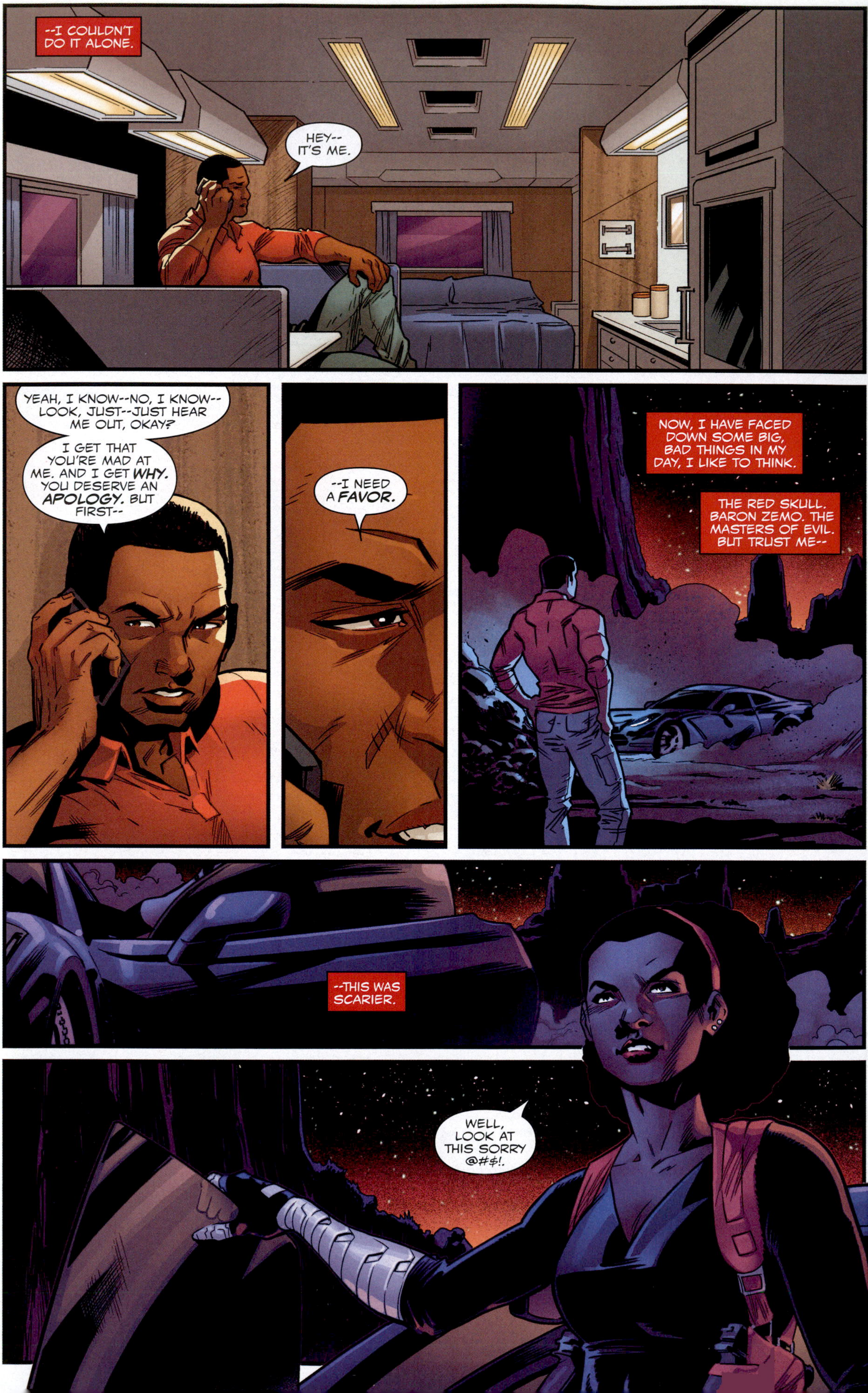
--I COULDN'T DO IT ALONE.
HEY-- IT'S ME.
YEAH, I KNOW--NO, I KNOW-- LOOK, JUST--JUST HEAR ME OUT, OKAY?
I GET THAT YOU'RE MAD AT ME. AND I GET WHY. YOU DESERVE AN APOLOGY. BUT FIRST--
--I NEED A FAVOR.
NOW, I HAVE FACED DOWN SOME BIG, BAD THINGS IN MY DAY, I LIKE TO THINK.
THE RED SKULL. BARON ZEMO. THE MASTERS OF EVIL. BUT TRUST ME--
--THIS WAS SCARIER.
WELL, LOOK AT THIS SORRY @#$!.

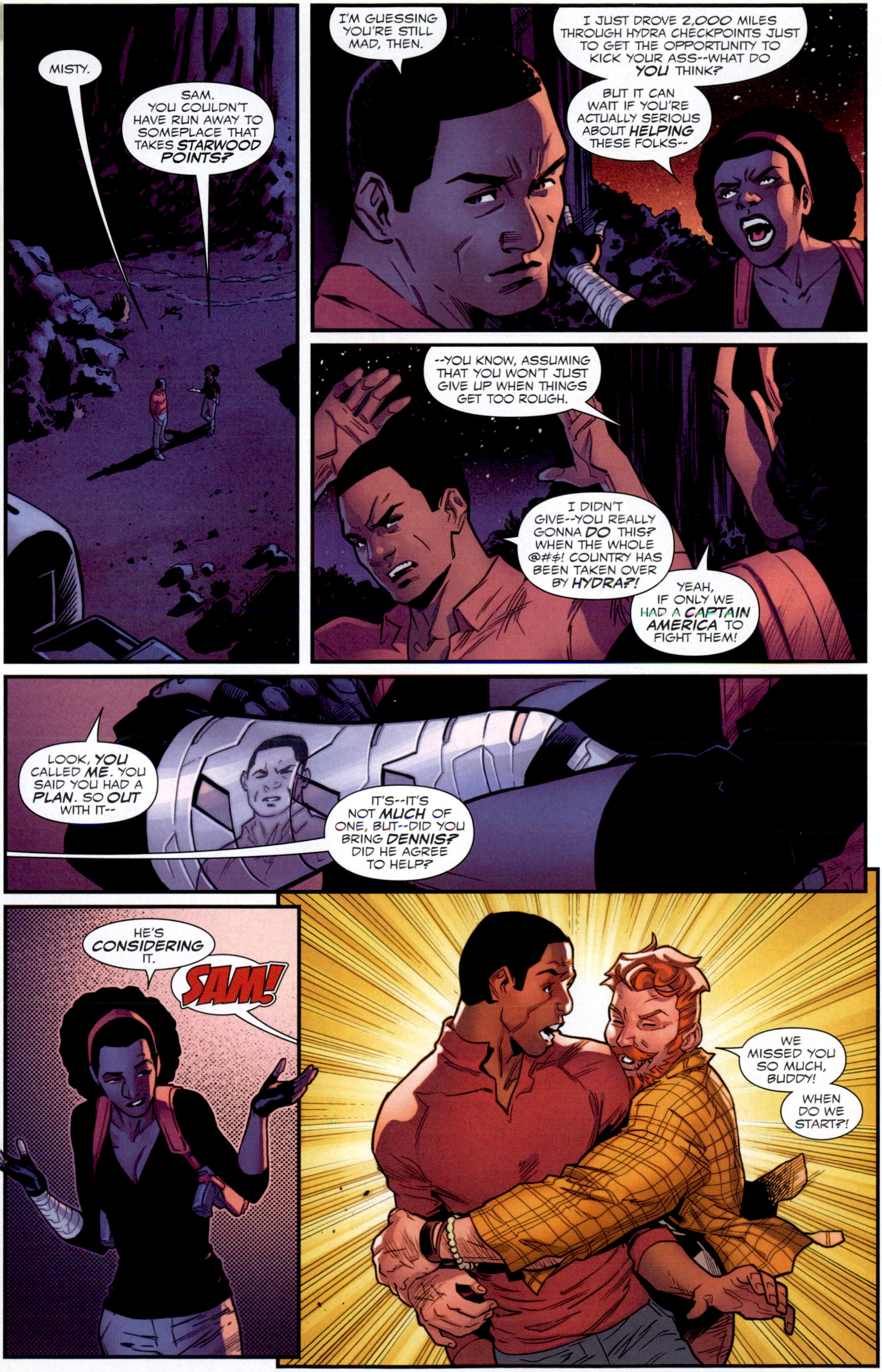
MISTY.
SAM. YOU COULDN'T HAVE RUN AWAY TO SOMEPLACE THAT TAKES STARWOOD POINTS?
I'M GUESSING YOU'RE STILL MAD, THEN.
I JUST DROVE 2,000 MILES THROUGH HYDRA CHECKPOINTS JUST TO GET THE OPPORTUNITY TO KICK YOUR ASS--WHAT DO YOU THINK?
BUT IT CAN WAIT IF YOU'RE ACTUALLY SERIOUS ABOUT HELPING THESE FOLKS--
--YOU KNOW, ASSUMING THAT YOU WON'T JUST GIVE UP WHEN THINGS GET TOO ROUGH.
I DIDN'T GIVE--YOU REALLY GONNA DO THIS? WHEN THE WHOLE @#$! COUNTRY HAS BEEN TAKEN OVER BY HYDRA?!
YEAH, IF ONLY WE HAD A CAPTAIN AMERICA TO FIGHT THEM!
LOOK, YOU CALLED ME. YOU SAID YOU HAD A PLAN. SO OUT WITH IT--
IT'S--IT'S NOT MUCH OF ONE, BUT--DID YOU BRING DENNIS? DID HE AGREE TO HELP?
HE'S CONSIDERING IT.
SAM!
WE MISSED YOU SO MUCH, BUDDY!
WHEN DO WE START?!

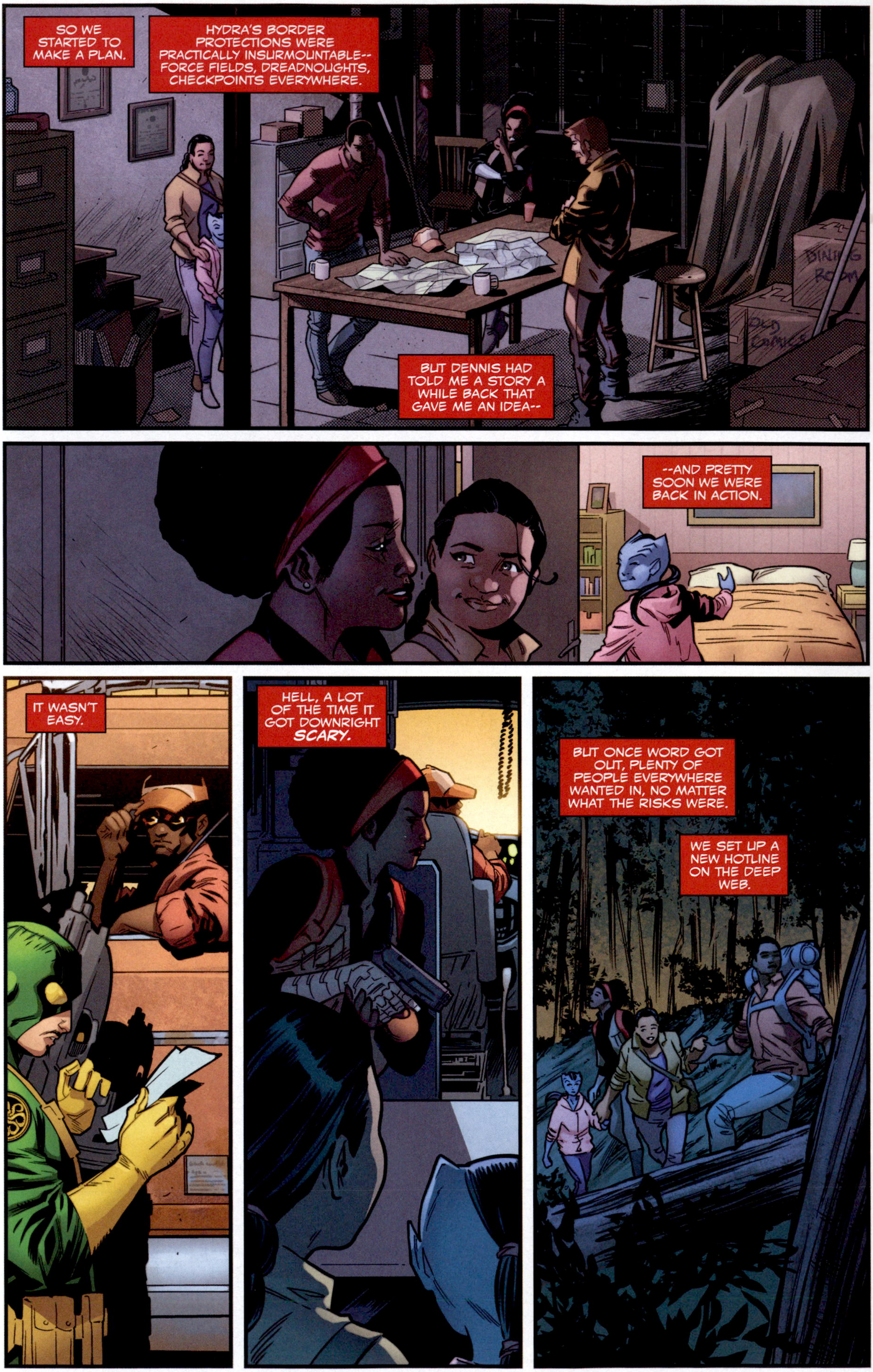
SO WE STARTED TO MAKE A PLAN.
HYDRA'S BORDER PROTECTIONS WERE PRACTICALLY INSURMOUNTABLE-- FORCE FIELDS, DREADNOUGHTS, CHECKPOINTS EVERYWHERE.
BUT DENNIS HAD TOLD ME A STORY A WHILE BACK THAT GAVE ME AN IDEA--
--AND PRETTY SOON WE WERE BACK IN ACTION.
IT WASN'T EASY.
HELL, A LOT OF THE TIME IT GOT DOWNRIGHT *SCARY.*
BUT ONCE WORD GOT OUT, PLENTY OF PEOPLE EVERYWHERE WANTED IN, NO MATTER WHAT THE RISKS WERE.
WE SET UP A NEW HOTLINE ON THE DEEP WEB.

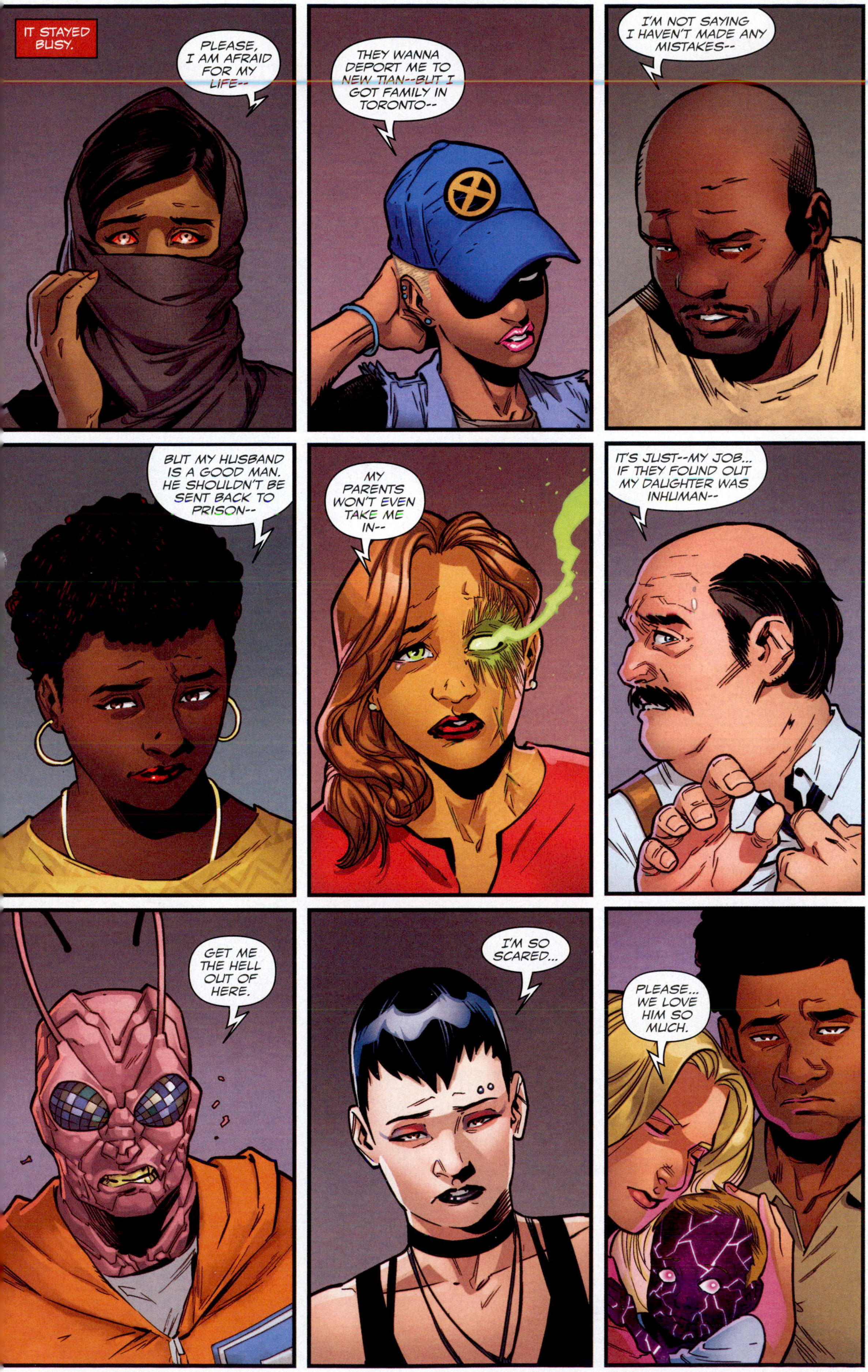
IT STAYED BUSY.
PLEASE, I AM AFRAID FOR MY LIFE--
THEY WANNA DEPORT ME TO NEW TIAN--BUT I GOT FAMILY IN TORONTO--
I'M NOT SAYING I HAVEN'T MADE ANY MISTAKES--
BUT MY HUSBAND IS A GOOD MAN. HE SHOULDN'T BE SENT BACK TO PRISON--
MY PARENTS WON'T EVEN TAKE ME IN--
IT'S JUST--MY JOB... IF THEY FOUND OUT MY DAUGHTER WAS INHUMAN--
GET ME THE HELL OUT OF HERE.
I'M SO SCARED...
PLEASE... WE LOVE HIM SO MUCH.

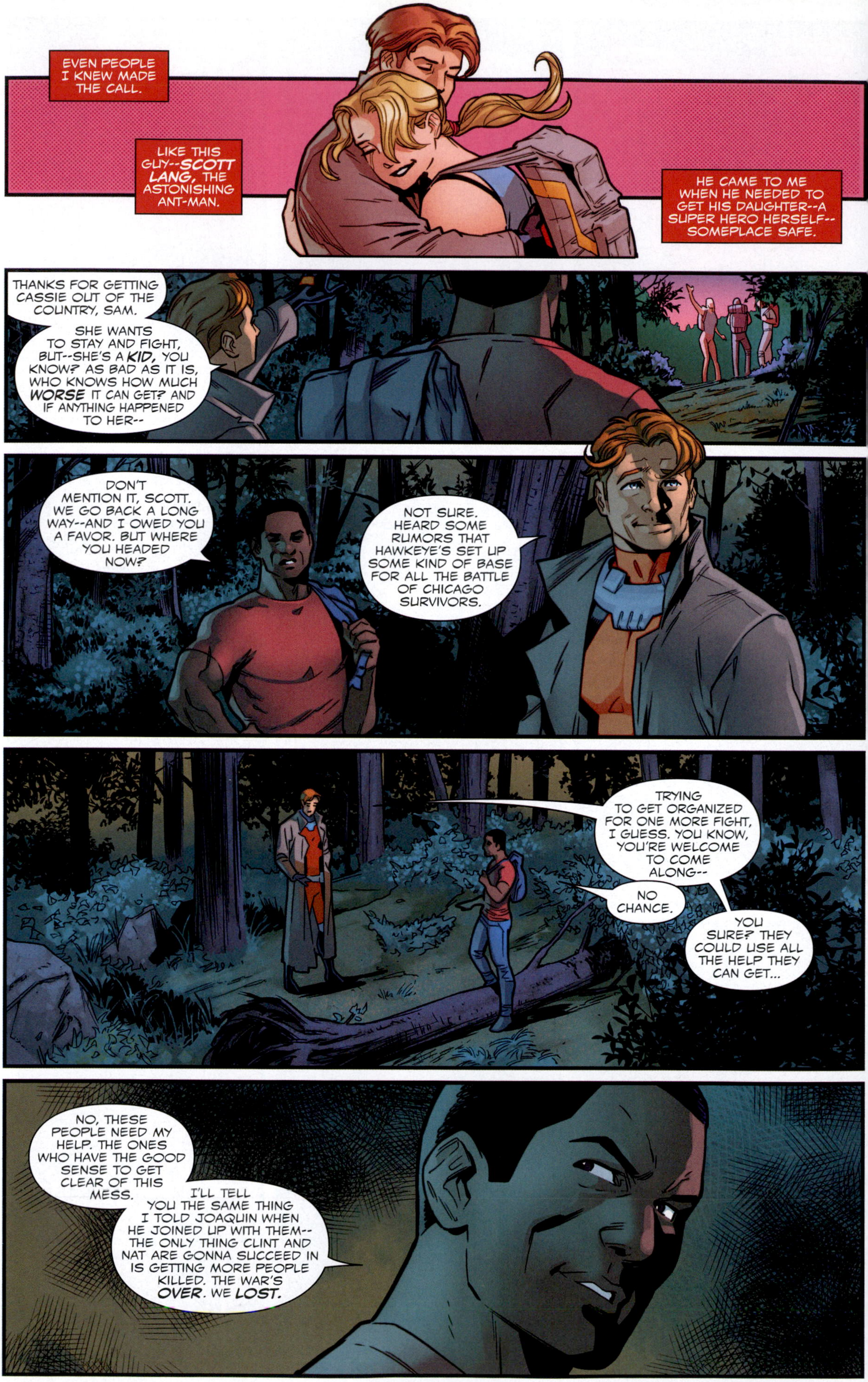
EVEN PEOPLE I KNEW MADE THE CALL.
LIKE THIS GUY--SCOTT LANG, THE ASTONISHING ANT-MAN.
HE CAME TO ME WHEN HE NEEDED TO GET HIS DAUGHTER--A SUPER HERO HERSELF--SOMEPLACE SAFE.
THANKS FOR GETTING CASSIE OUT OF THE COUNTRY, SAM.
SHE WANTS TO STAY AND FIGHT, BUT--SHE'S A KID, YOU KNOW? AS BAD AS IT IS, WHO KNOWS HOW MUCH WORSE IT CAN GET? AND IF ANYTHING HAPPENED TO HER--
DON'T MENTION IT, SCOTT. WE GO BACK A LONG WAY--AND I OWED YOU A FAVOR. BUT WHERE YOU HEADED NOW?
NOT SURE. HEARD SOME RUMORS THAT HAWKEYE'S SET UP SOME KIND OF BASE FOR ALL THE BATTLE OF CHICAGO SURVIVORS.
TRYING TO GET ORGANIZED FOR ONE MORE FIGHT, I GUESS. YOU KNOW, YOU'RE WELCOME TO COME ALONG--
NO CHANCE.
YOU SURE? THEY COULD USE ALL THE HELP THEY CAN GET...
NO, THESE PEOPLE NEED MY HELP. THE ONES WHO HAVE THE GOOD SENSE TO GET CLEAR OF THIS MESS.
I'LL TELL YOU THE SAME THING I TOLD JOAQUIN WHEN HE JOINED UP WITH THEM--THE ONLY THING CLINT AND NAT ARE GONNA SUCCEED IN IS GETTING MORE PEOPLE KILLED. THE WAR'S OVER. WE LOST.

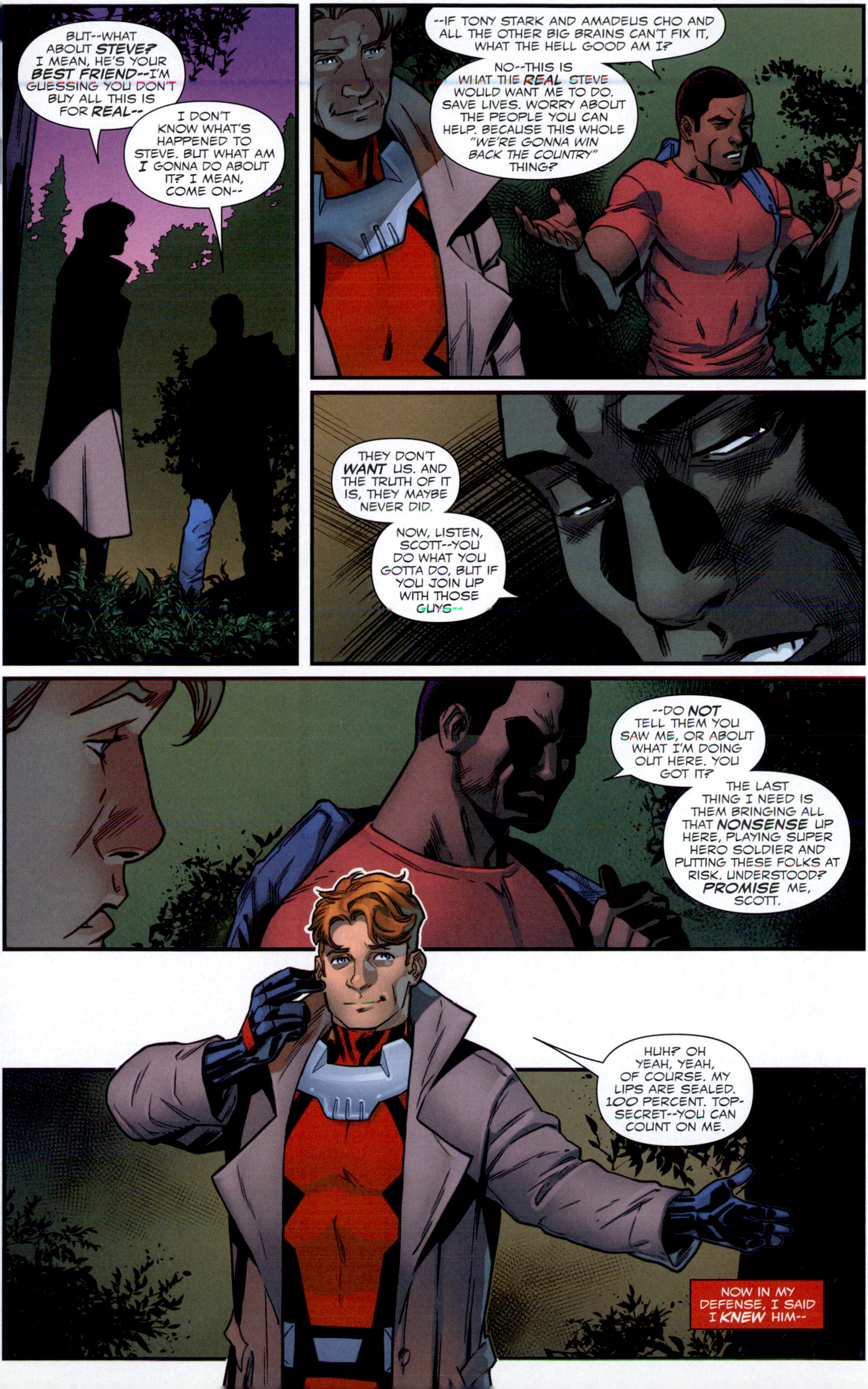
BUT--WHAT ABOUT STEVE? I MEAN, HE'S YOUR BEST FRIEND--I'M GUESSING YOU DON'T BUY ALL THIS IS FOR REAL--
I DON'T KNOW WHAT'S HAPPENED TO STEVE. BUT WHAT AM I GONNA DO ABOUT IT? I MEAN, COME ON--
--IF TONY STARK AND AMADEUS CHO AND ALL THE OTHER BIG BRAINS CAN'T FIX IT, WHAT THE HELL GOOD AM I?
NO--THIS IS WHAT THE REAL STEVE WOULD WANT ME TO DO. SAVE LIVES. WORRY ABOUT THE PEOPLE YOU CAN HELP. BECAUSE THIS WHOLE "WE'RE GONNA WIN BACK THE COUNTRY" THING?
THEY DON'T WANT US. AND THE TRUTH OF IT IS, THEY MAYBE NEVER DID.
NOW, LISTEN, SCOTT--YOU DO WHAT YOU GOTTA DO, BUT IF YOU JOIN UP WITH THOSE GUYS--
--DO NOT TELL THEM YOU SAW ME, OR ABOUT WHAT I'M DOING OUT HERE. YOU GOT IT?
THE LAST THING I NEED IS THEM BRINGING ALL THAT NONSENSE UP HERE, PLAYING SUPER HERO SOLDIER AND PUTTING THESE FOLKS AT RISK. UNDERSTOOD? PROMISE ME, SCOTT.
HUH? OH YEAH, YEAH, OF COURSE. MY LIPS ARE SEALED. 100 PERCENT. TOP-SECRET--YOU CAN COUNT ON ME.
NOW IN MY DEFENSE, I SAID I KNEW HIM--

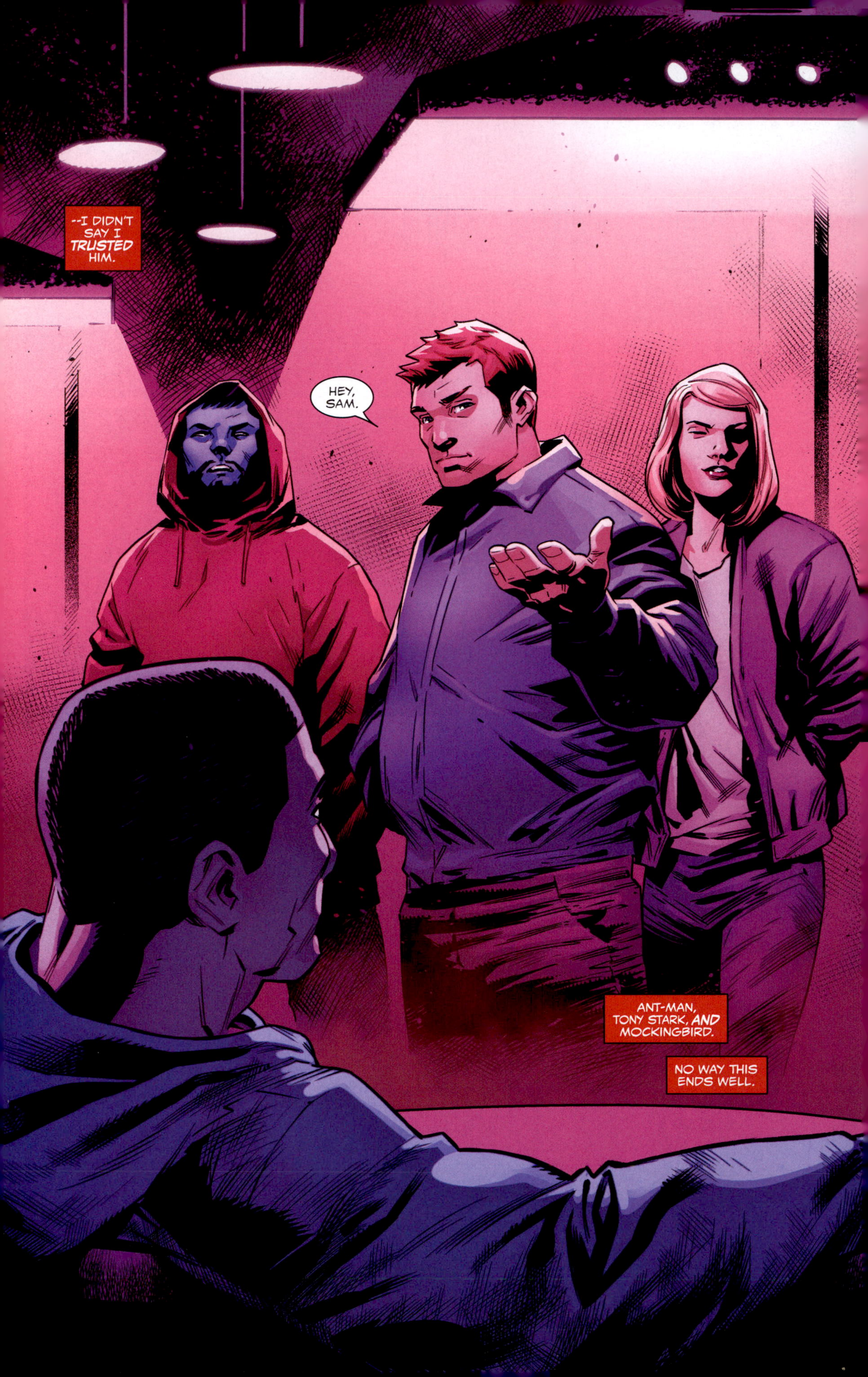
--I DIDN'T SAY I *TRUSTED* HIM.
HEY, SAM.
ANT-MAN, TONY STARK, *AND* MOCKINGBIRD.
NO WAY THIS ENDS WELL.

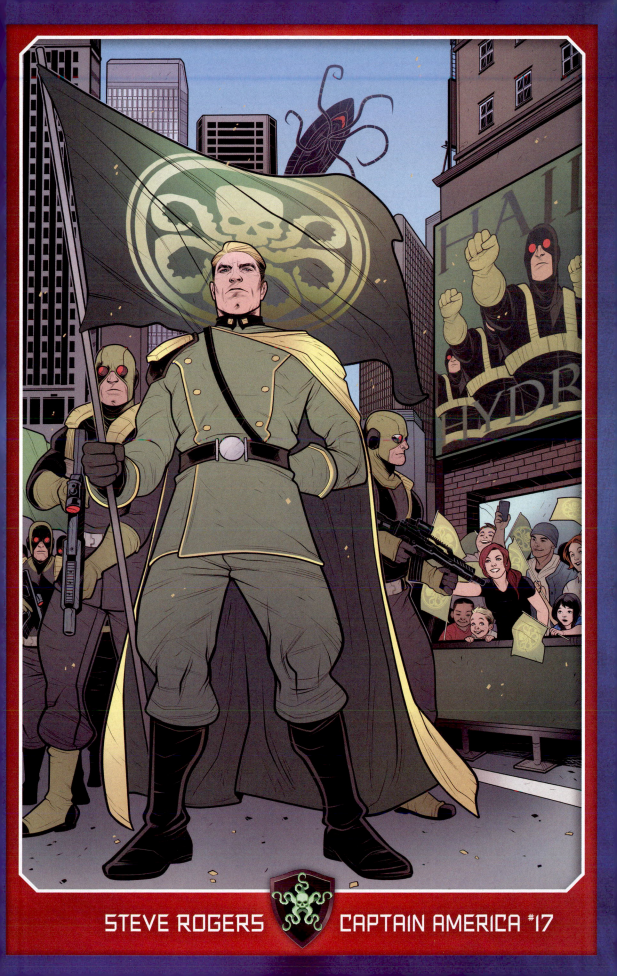

STEVE ROGERS   CAPTAIN AMERICA #17

Super-Soldier. Avenger. Agent of Hydra. He is...

Steve ★ Rogers
CAPTAIN AMERICA

A Cosmic Cube transformed Steve Rogers, Captain America, into the ultimate Hydra sleeper agent. After months of careful manipulation, Steve Rogers took control of S.H.I.E.L.D. and used a moment of international crisis to claim the country for Hydra.

Inhumans are closely monitored, and mutants have been relocated to a homeland in New Tian. Earth's most powerful heroes are stranded beyond Earth's Planetary Defense Shield, at the mercy of a Chitauri invasion--or trapped inside the Darkforce bubble that envelops New York City. The handful of heroes that remain plot against Captain America from a hidden base near Las Vegas--a fact that caused Hydra High Command to bomb the city into oblivion.

*This issue takes place after SECRET EMPIRE #2.

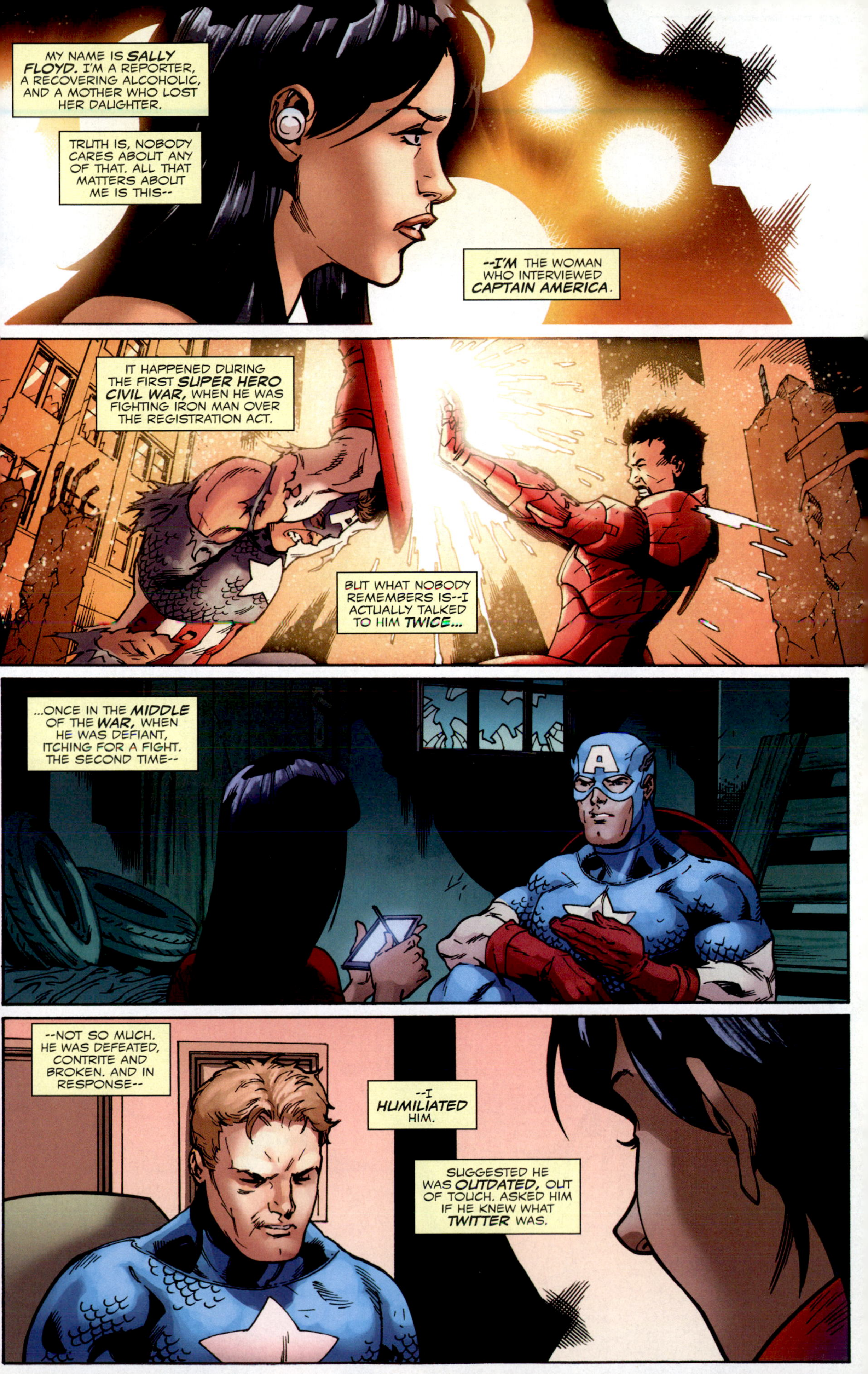

MY NAME IS SALLY FLOYD. I'M A REPORTER, A RECOVERING ALCOHOLIC, AND A MOTHER WHO LOST HER DAUGHTER.
TRUTH IS, NOBODY CARES ABOUT ANY OF THAT. ALL THAT MATTERS ABOUT ME IS THIS--
--I'M THE WOMAN WHO INTERVIEWED CAPTAIN AMERICA.
IT HAPPENED DURING THE FIRST SUPER HERO CIVIL WAR, WHEN HE WAS FIGHTING IRON MAN OVER THE REGISTRATION ACT.
BUT WHAT NOBODY REMEMBERS IS--I ACTUALLY TALKED TO HIM TWICE...
...ONCE IN THE MIDDLE OF THE WAR, WHEN HE WAS DEFIANT, ITCHING FOR A FIGHT. THE SECOND TIME--
--NOT SO MUCH. HE WAS DEFEATED, CONTRITE AND BROKEN. AND IN RESPONSE--
--I HUMILIATED HIM.
SUGGESTED HE WAS OUTDATED, OUT OF TOUCH. ASKED HIM IF HE KNEW WHAT TWITTER WAS.

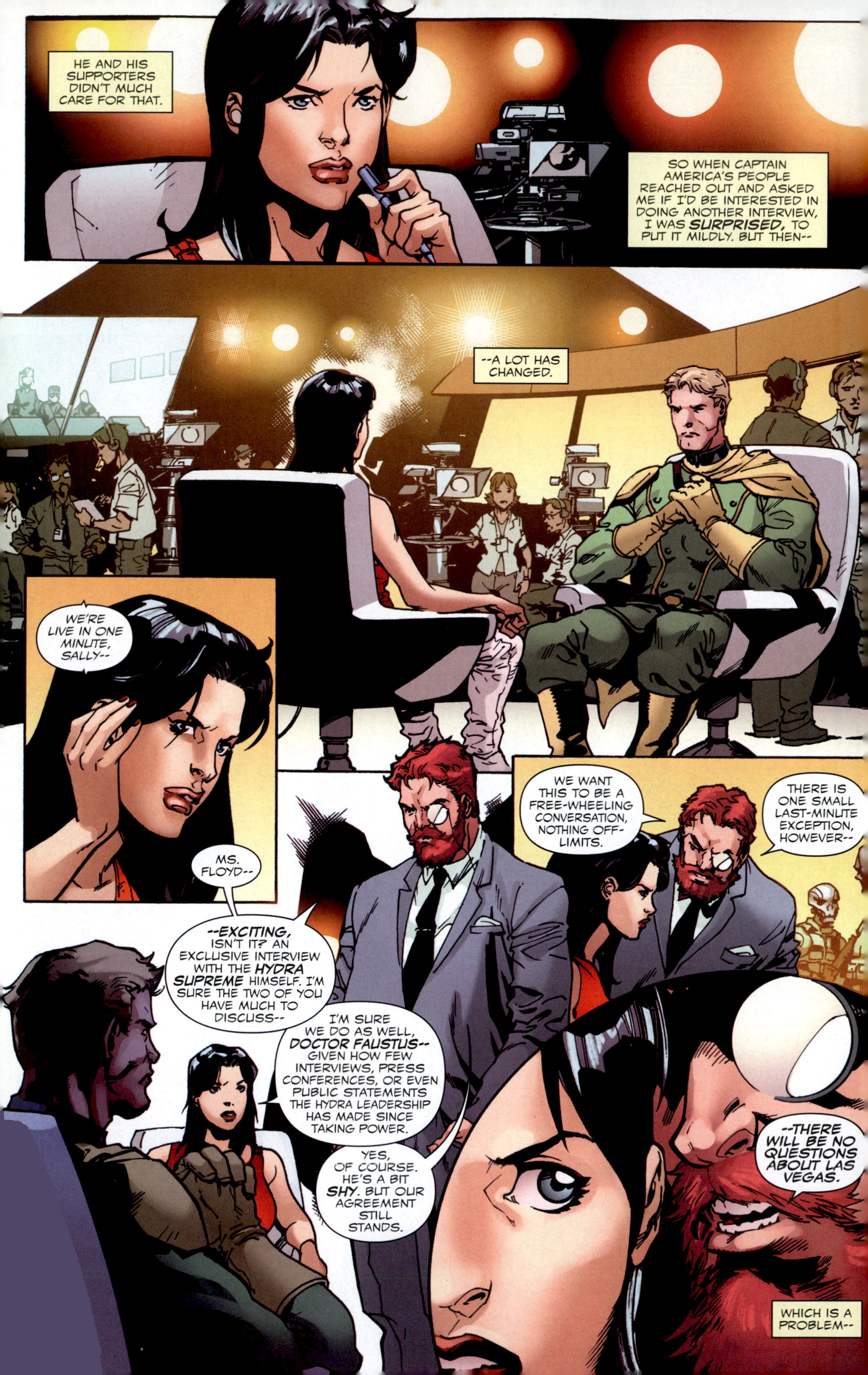
HE AND HIS SUPPORTERS DIDN'T MUCH CARE FOR THAT.
SO WHEN CAPTAIN AMERICA'S PEOPLE REACHED OUT AND ASKED ME IF I'D BE INTERESTED IN DOING ANOTHER INTERVIEW, I WAS SURPRISED, TO PUT IT MILDLY. BUT THEN--
--A LOT HAS CHANGED.
WE'RE LIVE IN ONE MINUTE, SALLY--
MS. FLOYD--
--EXCITING, ISN'T IT? AN EXCLUSIVE INTERVIEW WITH THE HYDRA SUPREME HIMSELF. I'M SURE THE TWO OF YOU HAVE MUCH TO DISCUSS--
I'M SURE WE DO AS WELL, DOCTOR FAUSTUS-- GIVEN HOW FEW INTERVIEWS, PRESS CONFERENCES, OR EVEN PUBLIC STATEMENTS THE HYDRA LEADERSHIP HAS MADE SINCE TAKING POWER.
YES, OF COURSE. HE'S A BIT SHY. BUT OUR AGREEMENT STILL STANDS.
WE WANT THIS TO BE A FREE-WHEELING CONVERSATION, NOTHING OFF-LIMITS.
THERE IS ONE SMALL LAST-MINUTE EXCEPTION, HOWEVER--
--THERE WILL BE NO QUESTIONS ABOUT LAS VEGAS.
WHICH IS A PROBLEM--

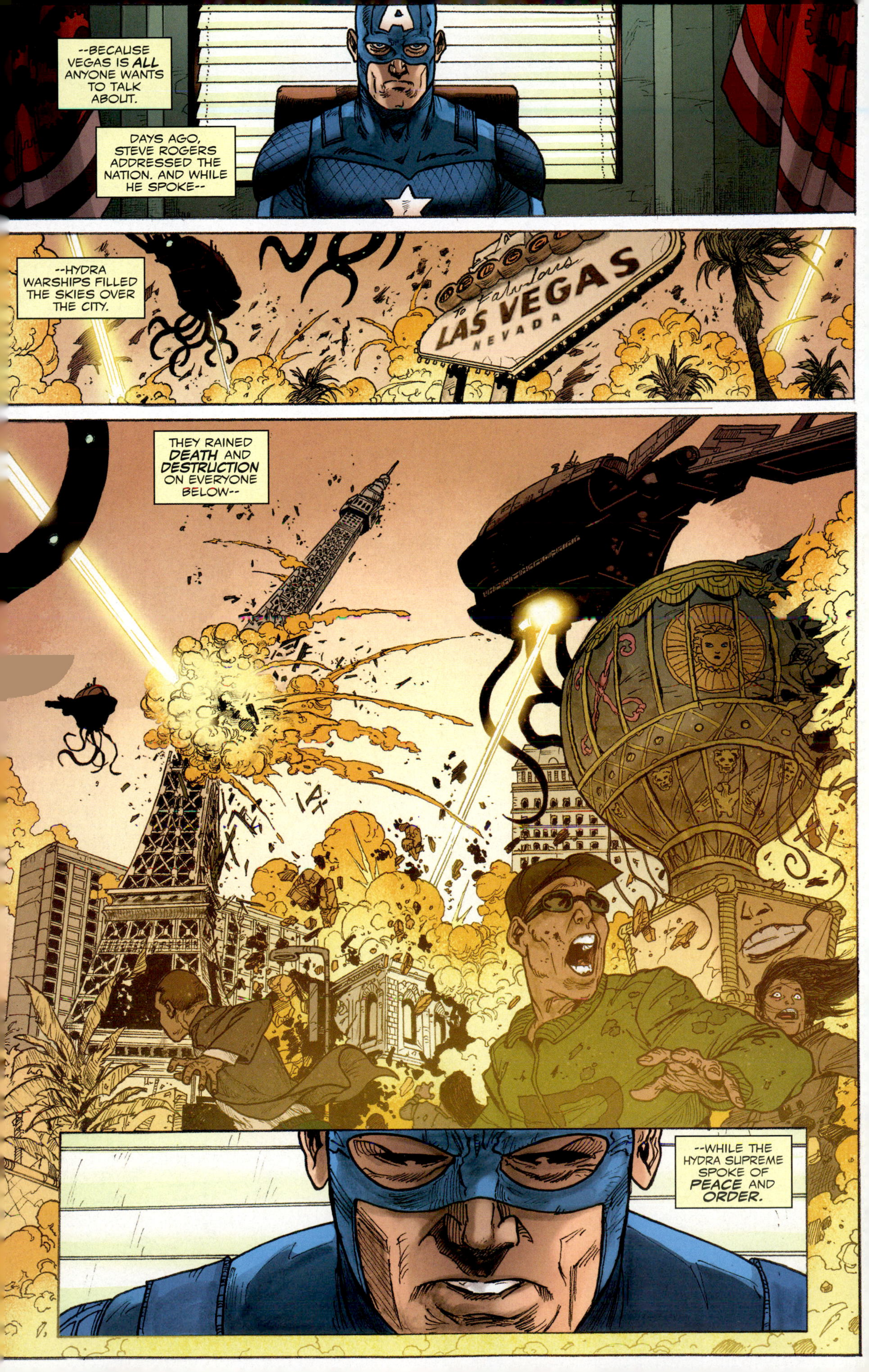
--BECAUSE VEGAS IS **ALL** ANYONE WANTS TO TALK ABOUT.
DAYS AGO, STEVE ROGERS ADDRESSED THE NATION. AND WHILE HE SPOKE--
--HYDRA WARSHIPS FILLED THE SKIES OVER THE CITY.
to Fabulous
LAS VEGAS
NEVADA
THEY RAINED **DEATH** AND **DESTRUCTION** ON EVERYONE BELOW--
--WHILE THE HYDRA SUPREME SPOKE OF **PEACE** AND **ORDER.**

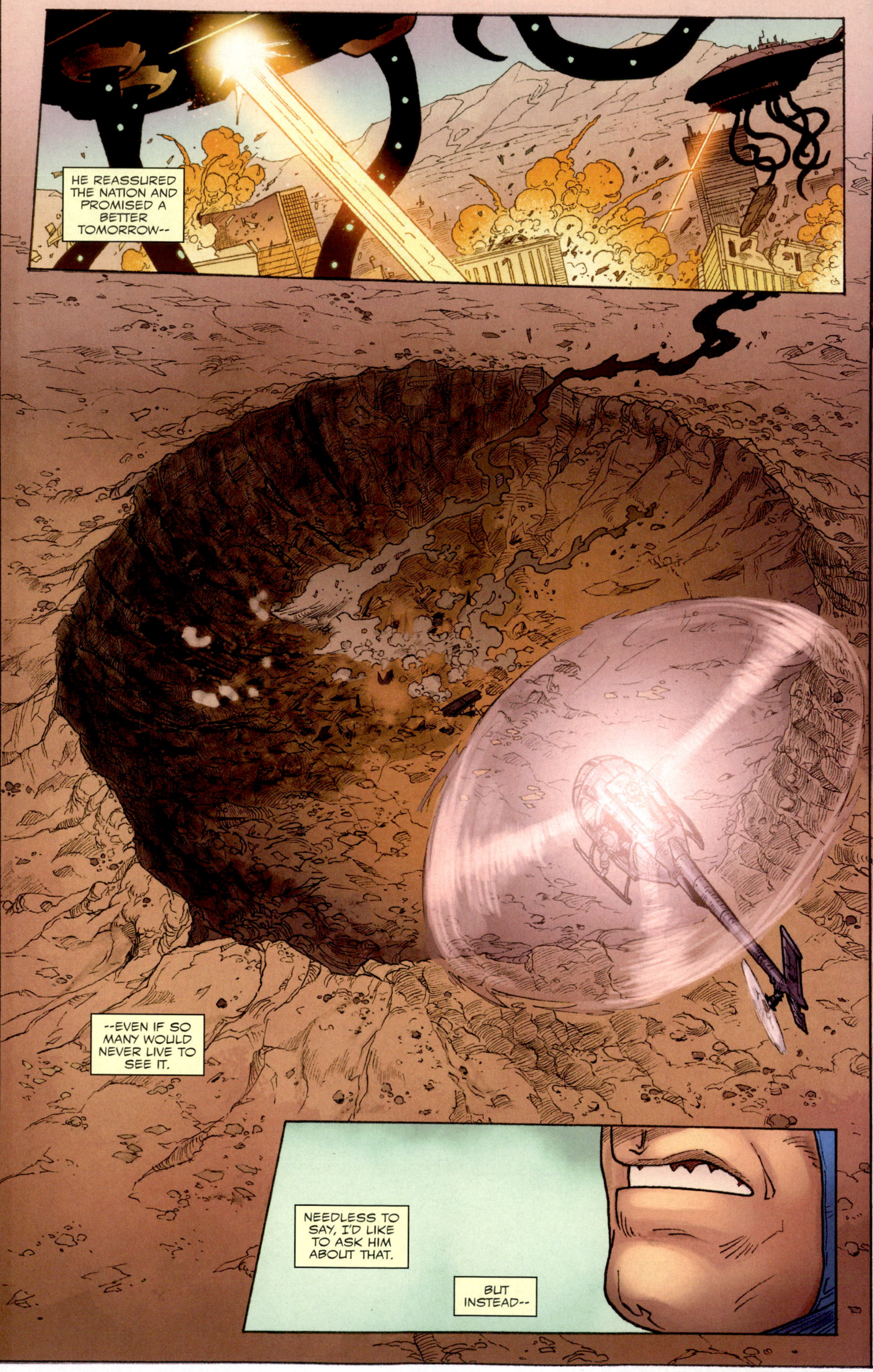
HE REASSURED THE NATION AND PROMISED A BETTER TOMORROW--
--EVEN IF SO MANY WOULD NEVER LIVE TO SEE IT.
NEEDLESS TO SAY, I'D LIKE TO ASK HIM ABOUT THAT.
BUT INSTEAD--

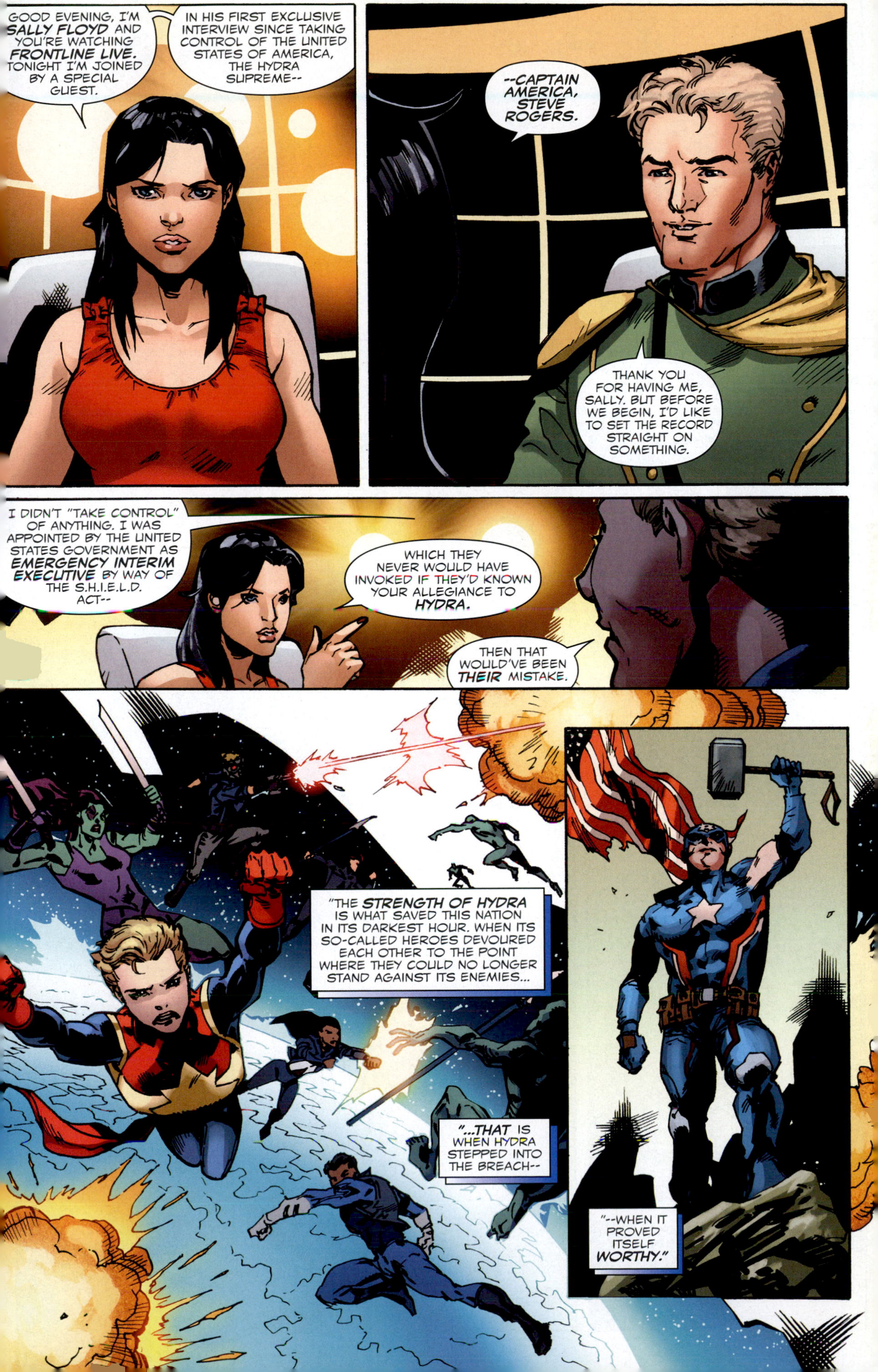
GOOD EVENING, I'M SALLY FLOYD AND YOU'RE WATCHING FRONTLINE LIVE. TONIGHT I'M JOINED BY A SPECIAL GUEST.
IN HIS FIRST EXCLUSIVE INTERVIEW SINCE TAKING CONTROL OF THE UNITED STATES OF AMERICA, THE HYDRA SUPREME--
--CAPTAIN AMERICA, STEVE ROGERS.
THANK YOU FOR HAVING ME, SALLY. BUT BEFORE WE BEGIN, I'D LIKE TO SET THE RECORD STRAIGHT ON SOMETHING.
I DIDN'T "TAKE CONTROL" OF ANYTHING. I WAS APPOINTED BY THE UNITED STATES GOVERNMENT AS EMERGENCY INTERIM EXECUTIVE BY WAY OF THE S.H.I.E.L.D. ACT--
WHICH THEY NEVER WOULD HAVE INVOKED IF THEY'D KNOWN YOUR ALLEGIANCE TO HYDRA.
THEN THAT WOULD'VE BEEN THEIR MISTAKE.
"THE STRENGTH OF HYDRA IS WHAT SAVED THIS NATION IN ITS DARKEST HOUR. WHEN ITS SO-CALLED HEROES DEVOURED EACH OTHER TO THE POINT WHERE THEY COULD NO LONGER STAND AGAINST ITS ENEMIES...
"...THAT IS WHEN HYDRA STEPPED INTO THE BREACH--
"--WHEN IT PROVED ITSELF WORTHY."

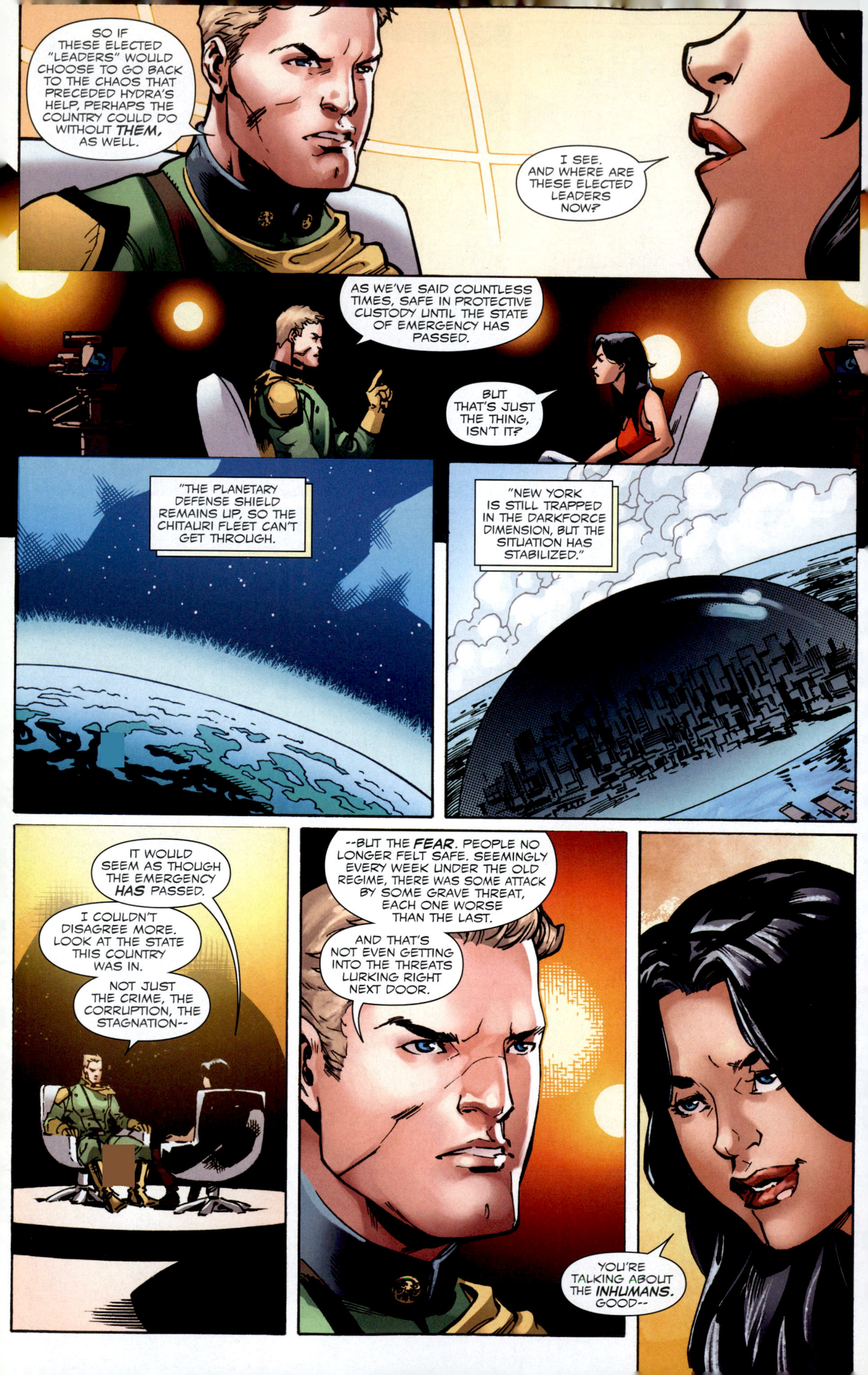
SO IF THESE ELECTED "LEADERS" WOULD CHOOSE TO GO BACK TO THE CHAOS THAT PRECEDED HYDRA'S HELP, PERHAPS THE COUNTRY COULD DO WITHOUT *THEM,* AS WELL.
I SEE. AND WHERE ARE THESE ELECTED LEADERS NOW?
AS WE'VE SAID COUNTLESS TIMES, SAFE IN PROTECTIVE CUSTODY UNTIL THE STATE OF EMERGENCY HAS PASSED.
BUT THAT'S JUST THE THING, ISN'T IT?
"THE PLANETARY DEFENSE SHIELD REMAINS UP, SO THE CHITAURI FLEET CAN'T GET THROUGH.
"NEW YORK IS STILL TRAPPED IN THE DARKFORCE DIMENSION, BUT THE SITUATION HAS STABILIZED."
IT WOULD SEEM AS THOUGH THE EMERGENCY *HAS* PASSED.
I COULDN'T DISAGREE MORE. LOOK AT THE STATE THIS COUNTRY WAS IN.
NOT JUST THE CRIME, THE CORRUPTION, THE STAGNATION--
--BUT THE *FEAR*. PEOPLE NO LONGER FELT SAFE. SEEMINGLY EVERY WEEK UNDER THE OLD REGIME, THERE WAS SOME ATTACK BY SOME GRAVE THREAT, EACH ONE WORSE THAN THE LAST.
AND THAT'S NOT EVEN GETTING INTO THE THREATS LURKING RIGHT NEXT DOOR.
YOU'RE TALKING ABOUT THE *INHUMANS.* GOOD--

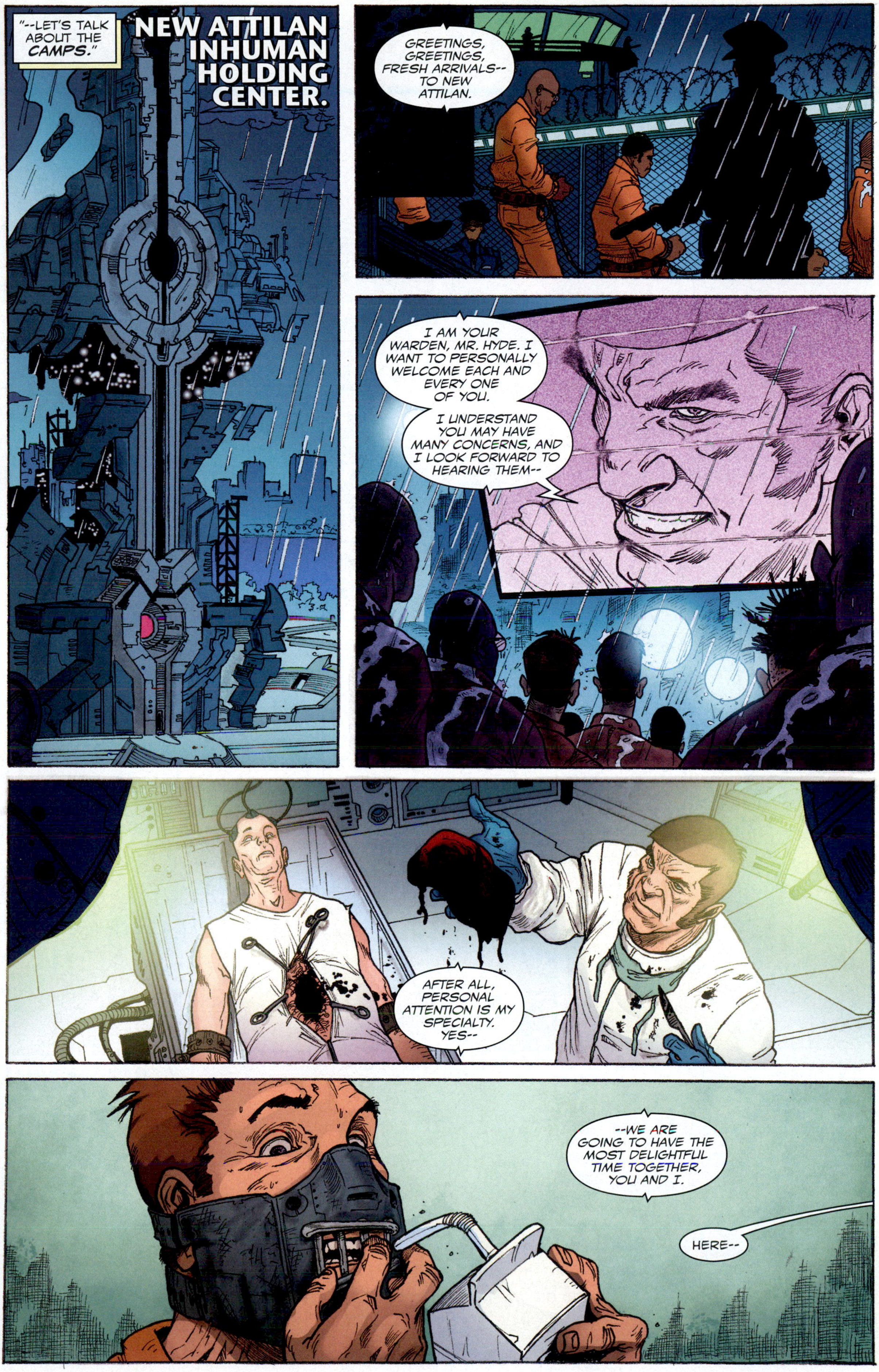
"--LET'S TALK ABOUT THE CAMPS."
NEW ATTILAN INHUMAN HOLDING CENTER.
GREETINGS, GREETINGS, FRESH ARRIVALS-- TO NEW ATTILAN.
I AM YOUR WARDEN, MR. HYDE. I WANT TO PERSONALLY WELCOME EACH AND EVERY ONE OF YOU.
I UNDERSTAND YOU MAY HAVE MANY CONCERNS, AND I LOOK FORWARD TO HEARING THEM--
AFTER ALL, PERSONAL ATTENTION IS MY SPECIALTY. YES--
--WE ARE GOING TO HAVE THE MOST DELIGHTFUL TIME TOGETHER, YOU AND I.
HERE--

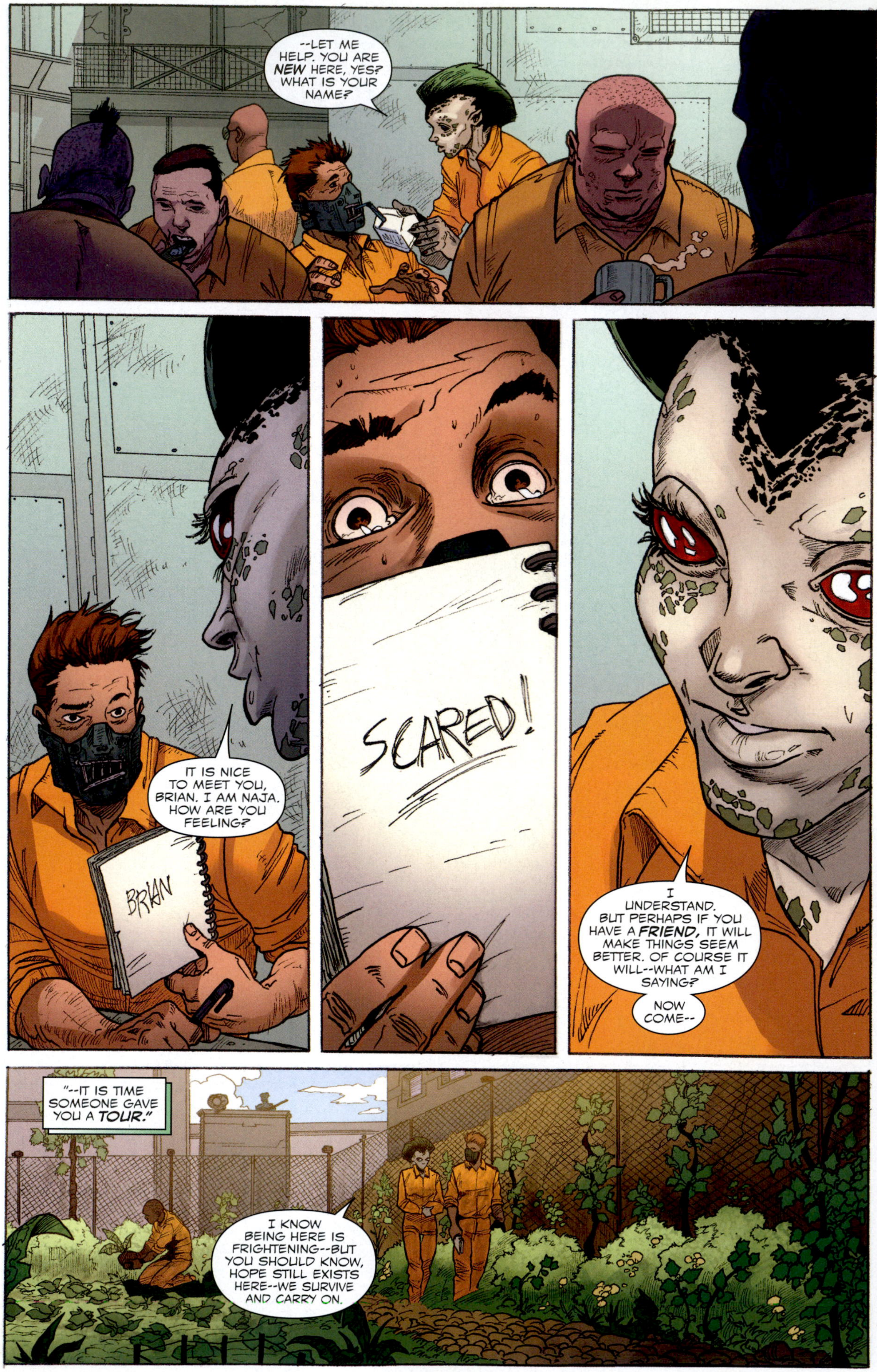
--LET ME HELP. YOU ARE NEW HERE, YES? WHAT IS YOUR NAME?
IT IS NICE TO MEET YOU, BRIAN. I AM NAJA. HOW ARE YOU FEELING?
BRIAN
SCARED!
I UNDERSTAND. BUT PERHAPS IF YOU HAVE A FRIEND, IT WILL MAKE THINGS SEEM BETTER. OF COURSE IT WILL--WHAT AM I SAYING?
NOW COME--
"--IT IS TIME SOMEONE GAVE YOU A TOUR."
I KNOW BEING HERE IS FRIGHTENING--BUT YOU SHOULD KNOW, HOPE STILL EXISTS HERE--WE SURVIVE AND CARRY ON.

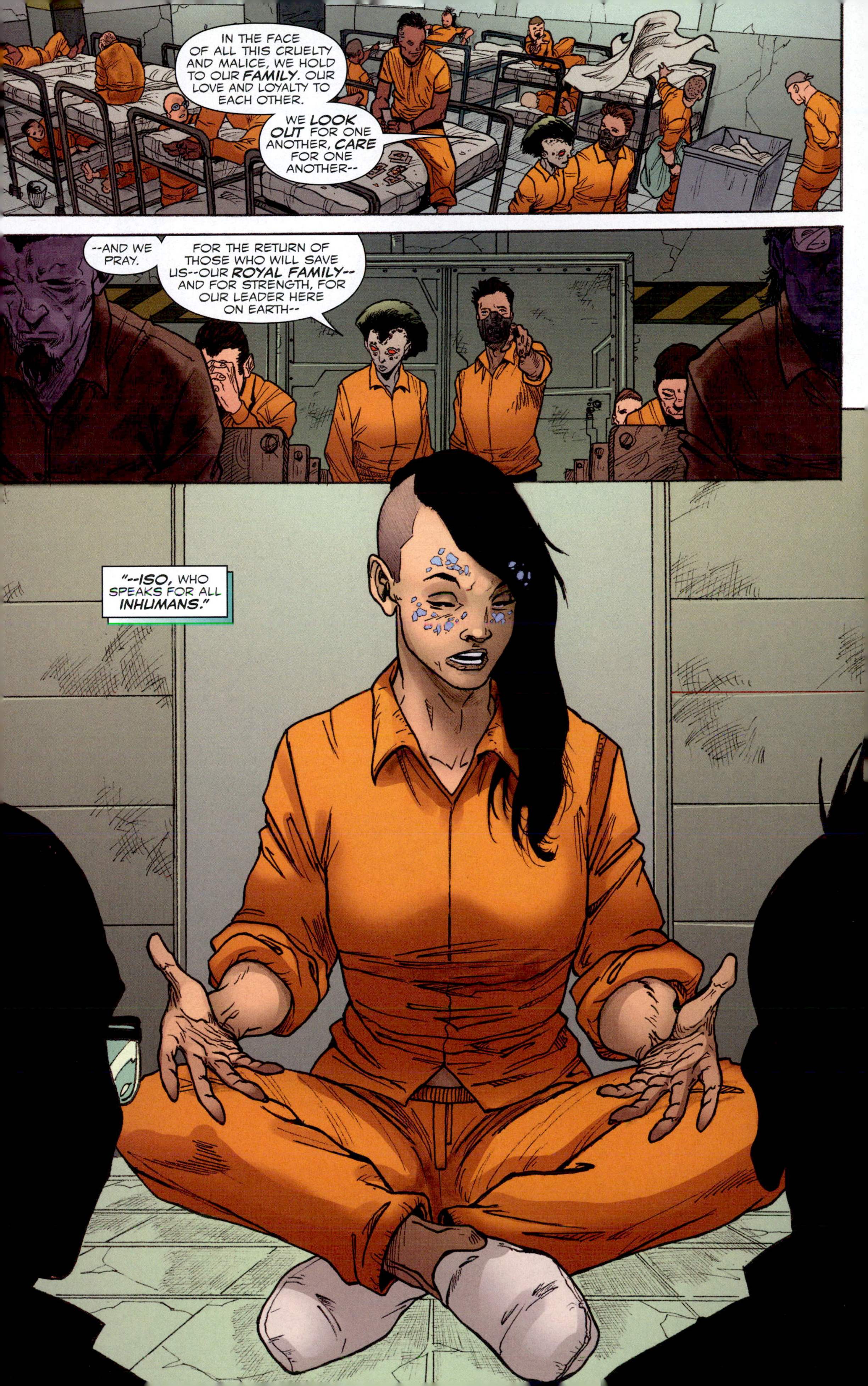
IN THE FACE OF ALL THIS CRUELTY AND MALICE, WE HOLD TO OUR FAMILY. OUR LOVE AND LOYALTY TO EACH OTHER.
WE LOOK OUT FOR ONE ANOTHER, CARE FOR ONE ANOTHER--
--AND WE PRAY.
FOR THE RETURN OF THOSE WHO WILL SAVE US--OUR ROYAL FAMILY--AND FOR STRENGTH, FOR OUR LEADER HERE ON EARTH--
"--ISO, WHO SPEAKS FOR ALL INHUMANS."

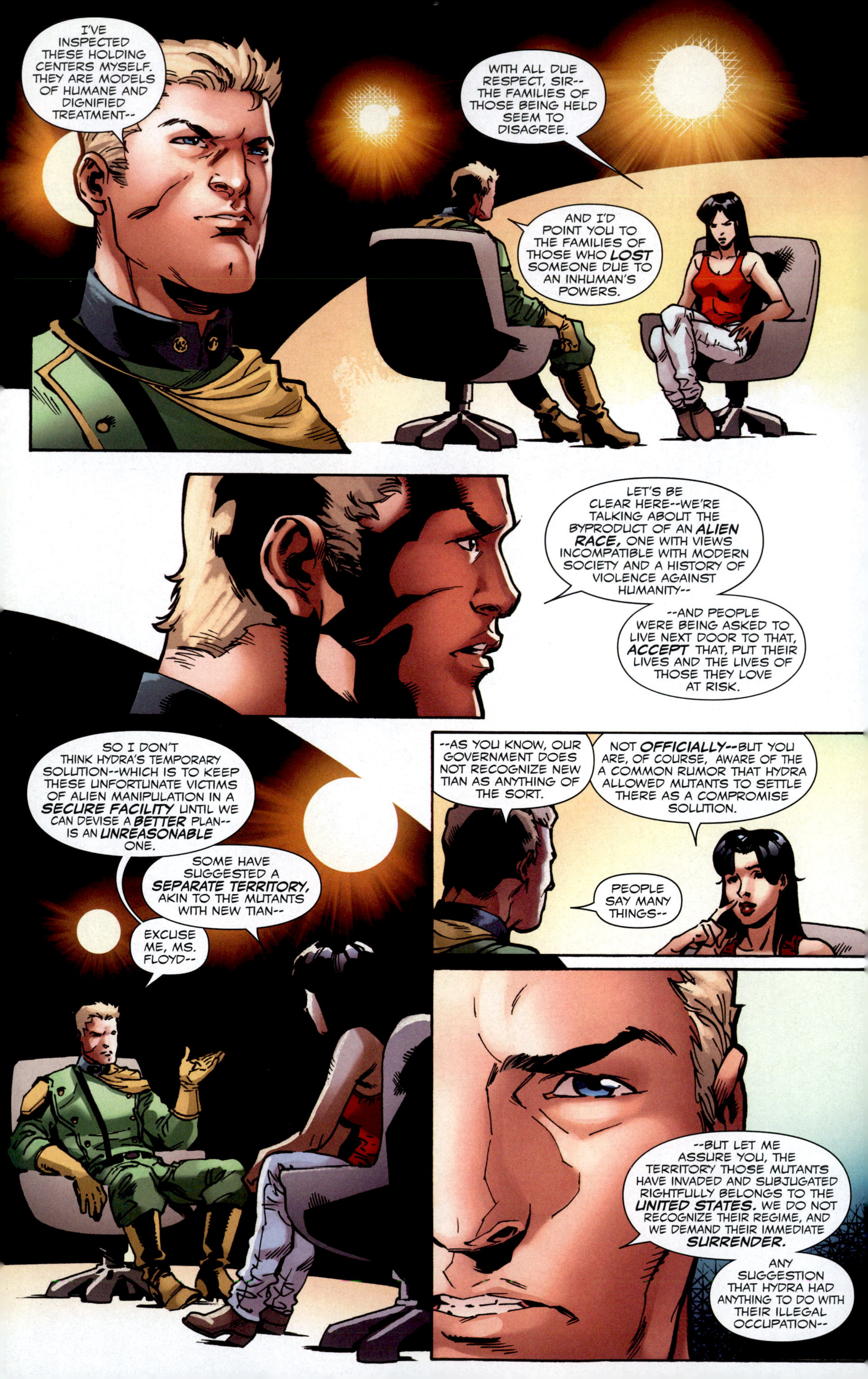
I'VE INSPECTED THESE HOLDING CENTERS MYSELF. THEY ARE MODELS OF HUMANE AND DIGNIFIED TREATMENT--
WITH ALL DUE RESPECT, SIR-- THE FAMILIES OF THOSE BEING HELD SEEM TO DISAGREE.
AND I'D POINT YOU TO THE FAMILIES OF THOSE WHO LOST SOMEONE DUE TO AN INHUMAN'S POWERS.
LET'S BE CLEAR HERE--WE'RE TALKING ABOUT THE BYPRODUCT OF AN ALIEN RACE, ONE WITH VIEWS INCOMPATIBLE WITH MODERN SOCIETY AND A HISTORY OF VIOLENCE AGAINST HUMANITY--
--AND PEOPLE WERE BEING ASKED TO LIVE NEXT DOOR TO THAT, ACCEPT THAT, PUT THEIR LIVES AND THE LIVES OF THOSE THEY LOVE AT RISK.
SO I DON'T THINK HYDRA'S TEMPORARY SOLUTION--WHICH IS TO KEEP THESE UNFORTUNATE VICTIMS OF ALIEN MANIPULATION IN A SECURE FACILITY UNTIL WE CAN DEVISE A BETTER PLAN--IS AN UNREASONABLE ONE.
SOME HAVE SUGGESTED A SEPARATE TERRITORY, AKIN TO THE MUTANTS WITH NEW TIAN--
EXCUSE ME, MS. FLOYD--
--AS YOU KNOW, OUR GOVERNMENT DOES NOT RECOGNIZE NEW TIAN AS ANYTHING OF THE SORT.
NOT OFFICIALLY--BUT YOU ARE, OF COURSE, AWARE OF THE A COMMON RUMOR THAT HYDRA ALLOWED MUTANTS TO SETTLE THERE AS A COMPROMISE SOLUTION.
PEOPLE SAY MANY THINGS--
--BUT LET ME ASSURE YOU, THE TERRITORY THOSE MUTANTS HAVE INVADED AND SUBJUGATED RIGHTFULLY BELONGS TO THE UNITED STATES. WE DO NOT RECOGNIZE THEIR REGIME, AND WE DEMAND THEIR IMMEDIATE SURRENDER.
ANY SUGGESTION THAT HYDRA HAD ANYTHING TO DO WITH THEIR ILLEGAL OCCUPATION--

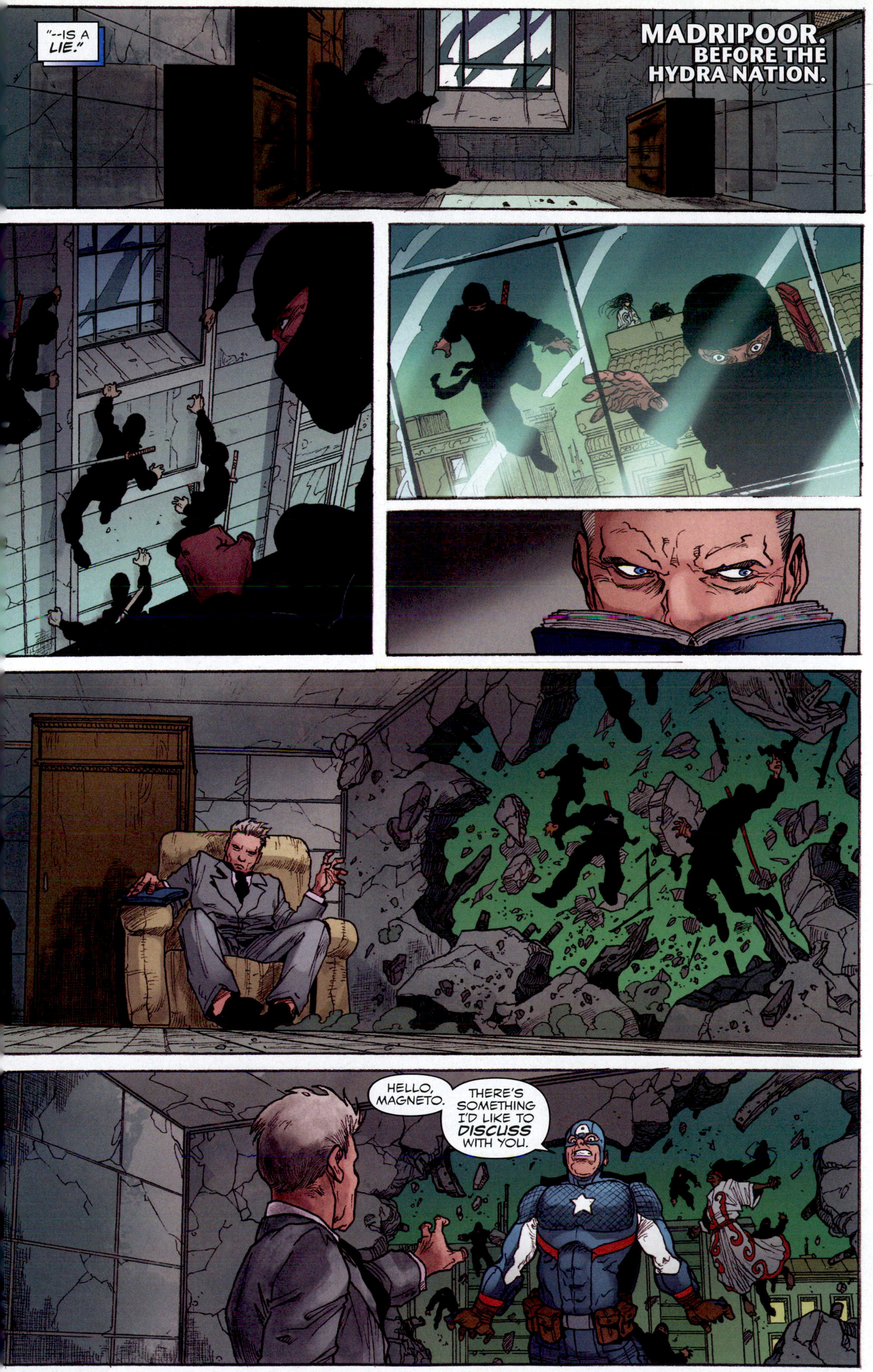
"--IS A LIE."
MADRIPOOR. BEFORE THE HYDRA NATION.
HELLO, MAGNETO.
THERE'S SOMETHING I'D LIKE TO DISCUSS WITH YOU.

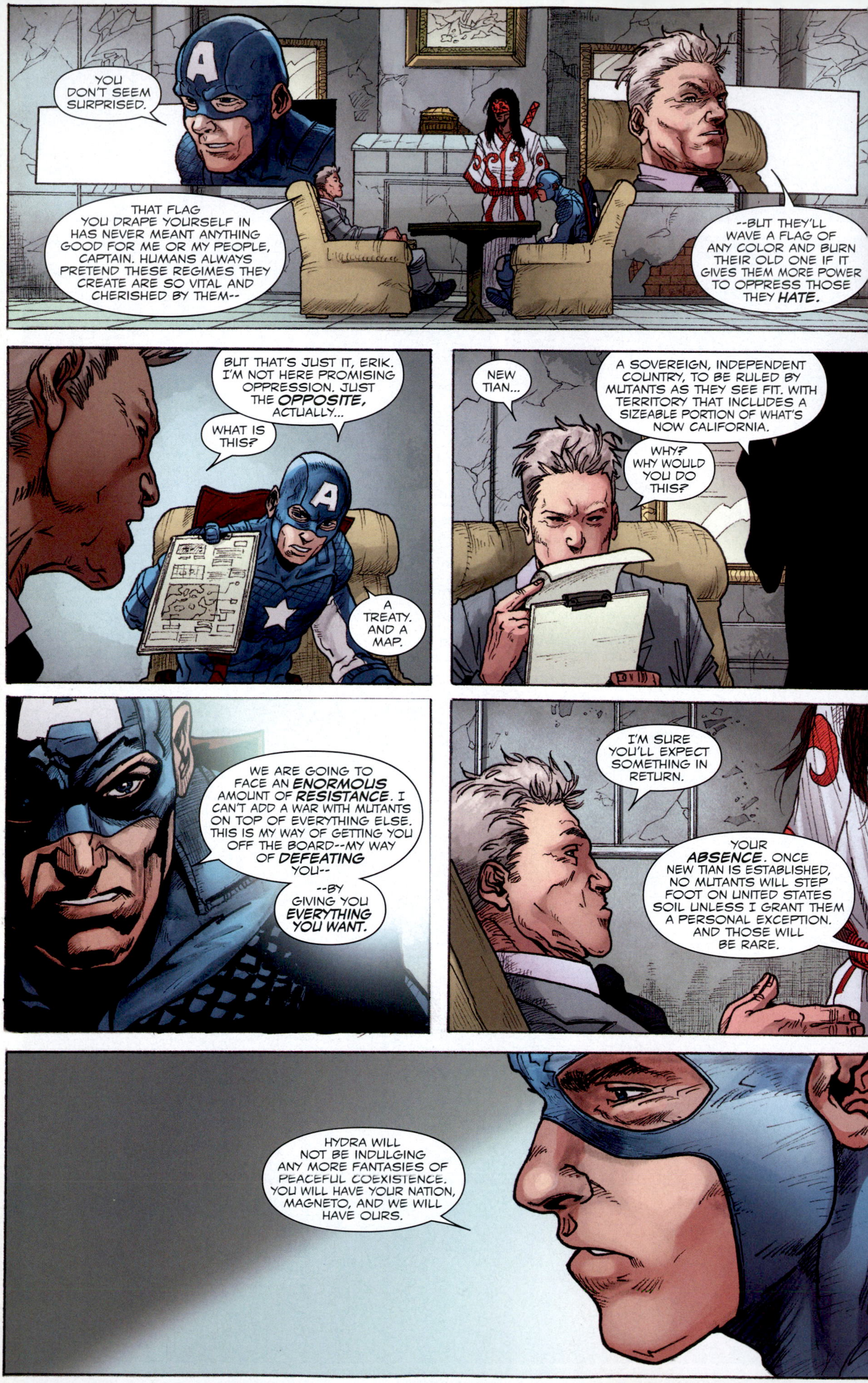

YOU DON'T SEEM SURPRISED.
THAT FLAG YOU DRAPE YOURSELF IN HAS NEVER MEANT ANYTHING GOOD FOR ME OR MY PEOPLE, CAPTAIN. HUMANS ALWAYS PRETEND THESE REGIMES THEY CREATE ARE SO VITAL AND CHERISHED BY THEM--
--BUT THEY'LL WAVE A FLAG OF ANY COLOR AND BURN THEIR OLD ONE IF IT GIVES THEM MORE POWER TO OPPRESS THOSE THEY **HATE.**
BUT THAT'S JUST IT, ERIK. I'M NOT HERE PROMISING OPPRESSION. JUST THE **OPPOSITE,** ACTUALLY...
WHAT IS THIS?
A TREATY. AND A MAP.
NEW TIAN...
A SOVEREIGN, INDEPENDENT COUNTRY, TO BE RULED BY MUTANTS AS THEY SEE FIT. WITH TERRITORY THAT INCLUDES A SIZEABLE PORTION OF WHAT'S NOW CALIFORNIA.
WHY? WHY WOULD YOU DO THIS?
WE ARE GOING TO FACE AN **ENORMOUS** AMOUNT OF **RESISTANCE**. I CAN'T ADD A WAR WITH MUTANTS ON TOP OF EVERYTHING ELSE. THIS IS MY WAY OF GETTING YOU OFF THE BOARD--MY WAY OF **DEFEATING** YOU--
--BY GIVING YOU **EVERYTHING YOU WANT.**
I'M SURE YOU'LL EXPECT SOMETHING IN RETURN.
YOUR **ABSENCE**. ONCE NEW TIAN IS ESTABLISHED, NO MUTANTS WILL STEP FOOT ON UNITED STATES SOIL UNLESS I GRANT THEM A PERSONAL EXCEPTION. AND THOSE WILL BE RARE.
HYDRA WILL NOT BE INDULGING ANY MORE FANTASIES OF PEACEFUL COEXISTENCE. YOU WILL HAVE YOUR NATION, MAGNETO, AND WE WILL HAVE OURS.

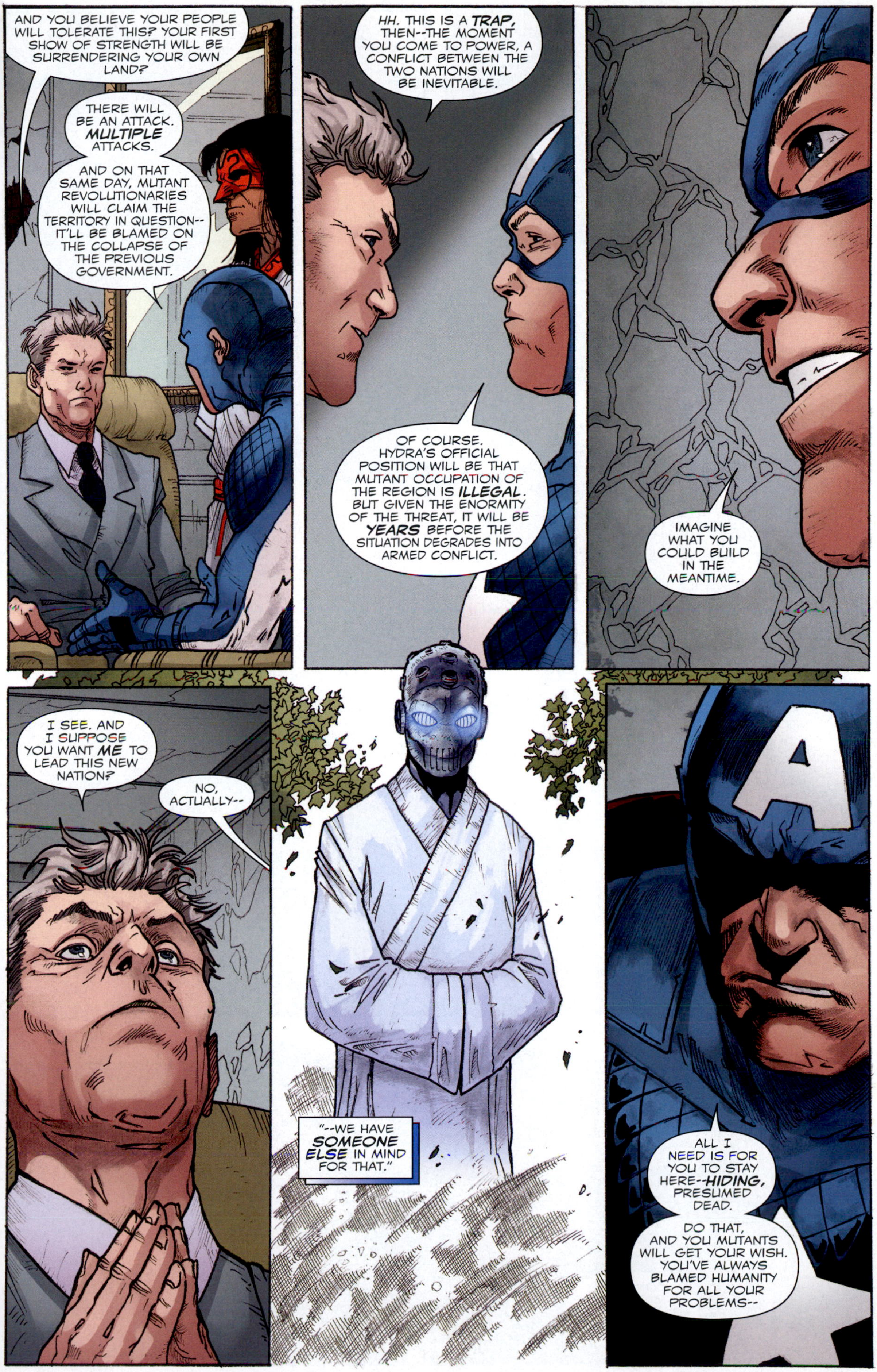
AND YOU BELIEVE YOUR PEOPLE WILL TOLERATE THIS? YOUR FIRST SHOW OF STRENGTH WILL BE SURRENDERING YOUR OWN LAND?
THERE WILL BE AN ATTACK. MULTIPLE ATTACKS.
AND ON THAT SAME DAY, MUTANT REVOLUTIONARIES WILL CLAIM THE TERRITORY IN QUESTION-- IT'LL BE BLAMED ON THE COLLAPSE OF THE PREVIOUS GOVERNMENT.
HH. THIS IS A TRAP, THEN--THE MOMENT YOU COME TO POWER, A CONFLICT BETWEEN THE TWO NATIONS WILL BE INEVITABLE.
OF COURSE. HYDRA'S OFFICIAL POSITION WILL BE THAT MUTANT OCCUPATION OF THE REGION IS ILLEGAL. BUT GIVEN THE ENORMITY OF THE THREAT, IT WILL BE YEARS BEFORE THE SITUATION DEGRADES INTO ARMED CONFLICT.
IMAGINE WHAT YOU COULD BUILD IN THE MEANTIME.
I SEE. AND I SUPPOSE YOU WANT ME TO LEAD THIS NEW NATION?
NO, ACTUALLY--
"--WE HAVE SOMEONE ELSE IN MIND FOR THAT."
ALL I NEED IS FOR YOU TO STAY HERE--HIDING, PRESUMED DEAD.
DO THAT, AND YOU MUTANTS WILL GET YOUR WISH. YOU'VE ALWAYS BLAMED HUMANITY FOR ALL YOUR PROBLEMS--

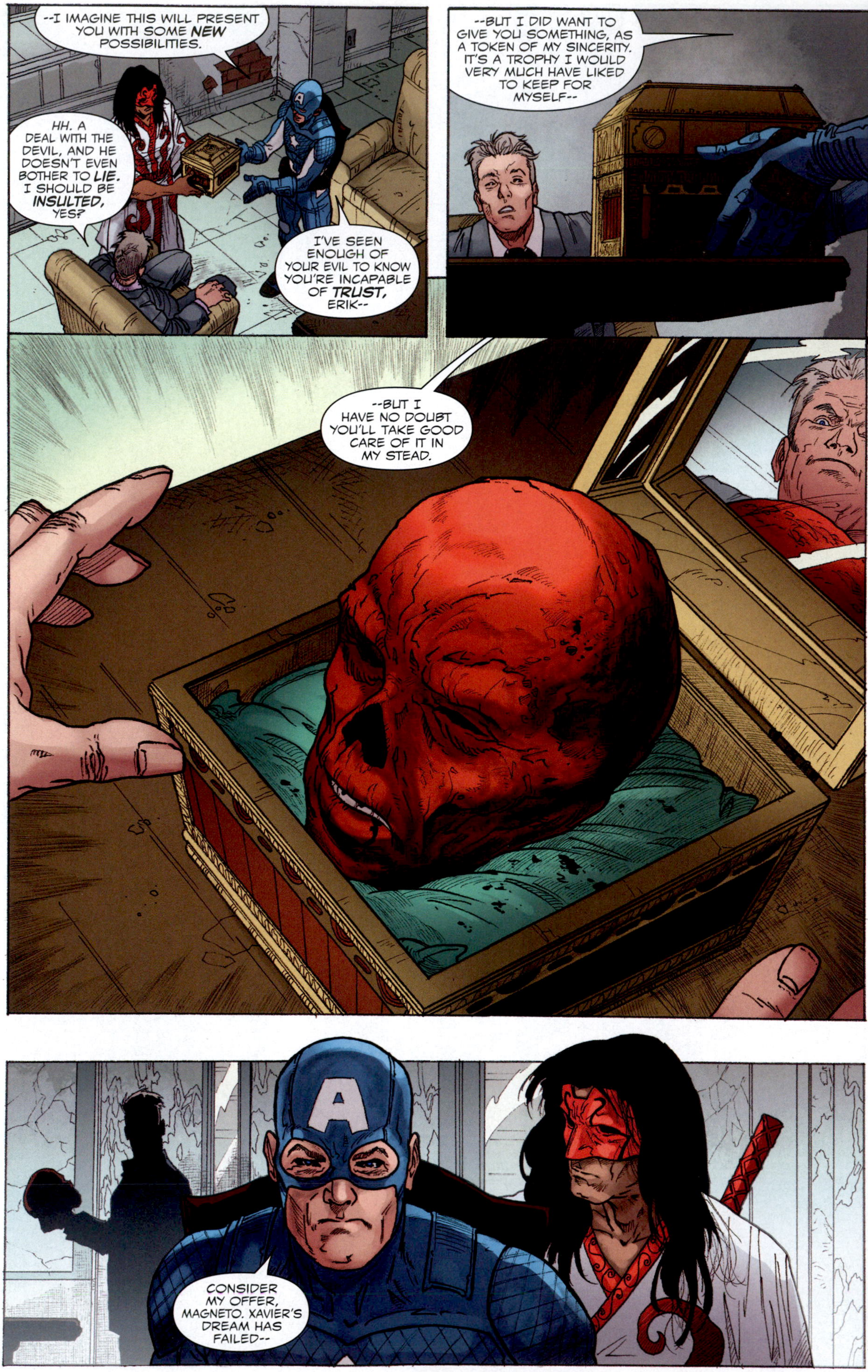
--I IMAGINE THIS WILL PRESENT YOU WITH SOME NEW POSSIBILITIES.
HH. A DEAL WITH THE DEVIL, AND HE DOESN'T EVEN BOTHER TO LIE. I SHOULD BE INSULTED, YES?
I'VE SEEN ENOUGH OF YOUR EVIL TO KNOW YOU'RE INCAPABLE OF TRUST, ERIK--
--BUT I DID WANT TO GIVE YOU SOMETHING, AS A TOKEN OF MY SINCERITY. IT'S A TROPHY I WOULD VERY MUCH HAVE LIKED TO KEEP FOR MYSELF--
--BUT I HAVE NO DOUBT YOU'LL TAKE GOOD CARE OF IT IN MY STEAD.
CONSIDER MY OFFER, MAGNETO. XAVIER'S DREAM HAS FAILED--

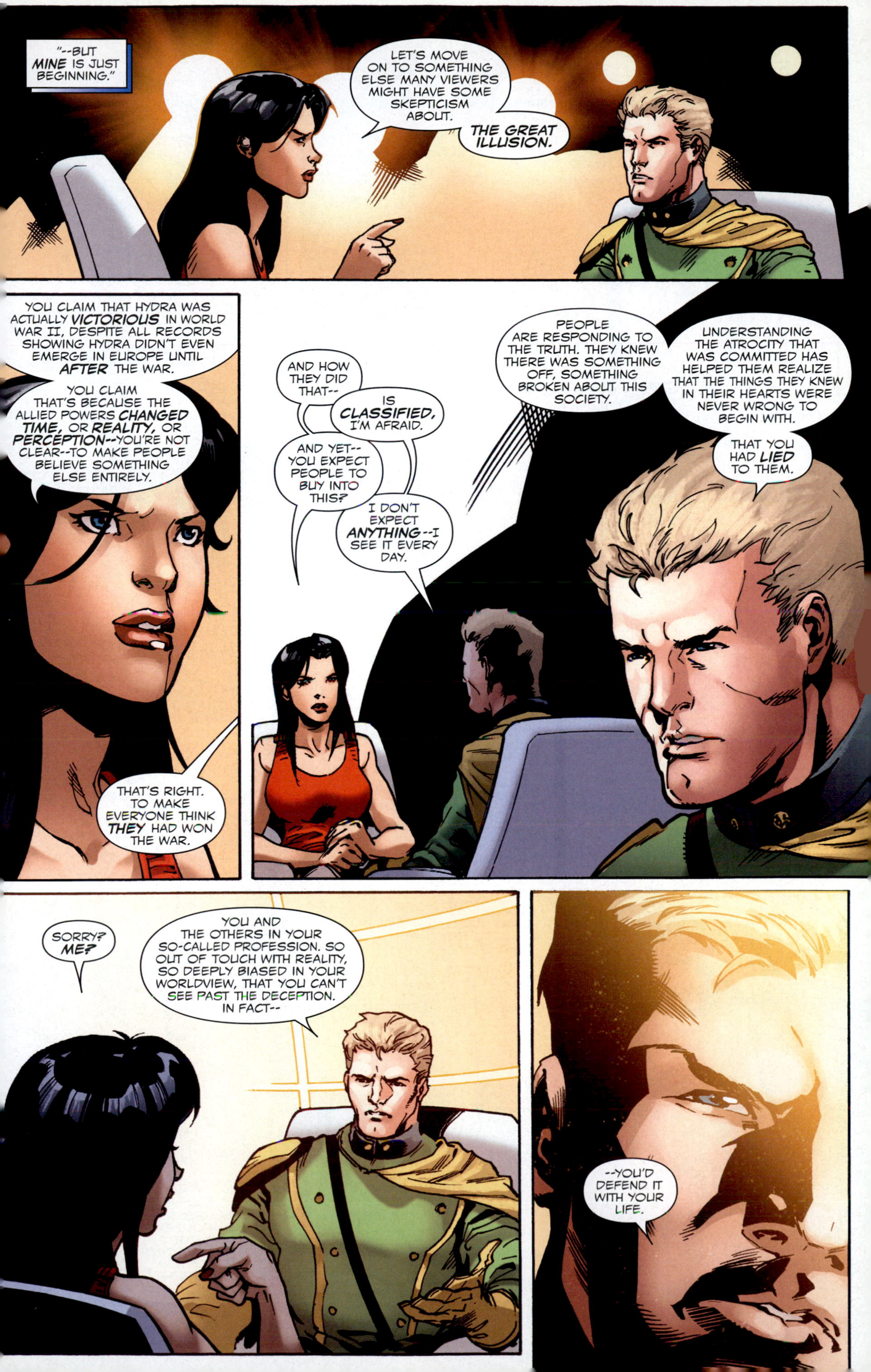
"--BUT MINE IS JUST BEGINNING."
LET'S MOVE ON TO SOMETHING ELSE MANY VIEWERS MIGHT HAVE SOME SKEPTICISM ABOUT.
THE GREAT ILLUSION.
YOU CLAIM THAT HYDRA WAS ACTUALLY VICTORIOUS IN WORLD WAR II, DESPITE ALL RECORDS SHOWING HYDRA DIDN'T EVEN EMERGE IN EUROPE UNTIL AFTER THE WAR.
YOU CLAIM THAT'S BECAUSE THE ALLIED POWERS CHANGED TIME, OR REALITY, OR PERCEPTION--YOU'RE NOT CLEAR--TO MAKE PEOPLE BELIEVE SOMETHING ELSE ENTIRELY.
THAT'S RIGHT. TO MAKE EVERYONE THINK THEY HAD WON THE WAR.
AND HOW THEY DID THAT--
IS CLASSIFIED, I'M AFRAID.
AND YET--YOU EXPECT PEOPLE TO BUY INTO THIS?
I DON'T EXPECT ANYTHING--I SEE IT EVERY DAY.
PEOPLE ARE RESPONDING TO THE TRUTH. THEY KNEW THERE WAS SOMETHING OFF, SOMETHING BROKEN ABOUT THIS SOCIETY.
UNDERSTANDING THE ATROCITY THAT WAS COMMITTED HAS HELPED THEM REALIZE THAT THE THINGS THEY KNEW IN THEIR HEARTS WERE NEVER WRONG TO BEGIN WITH.
THAT YOU HAD LIED TO THEM.
SORRY? ME?
YOU AND THE OTHERS IN YOUR SO-CALLED PROFESSION. SO OUT OF TOUCH WITH REALITY, SO DEEPLY BIASED IN YOUR WORLDVIEW, THAT YOU CAN'T SEE PAST THE DECEPTION. IN FACT--
--YOU'D DEFEND IT WITH YOUR LIFE.

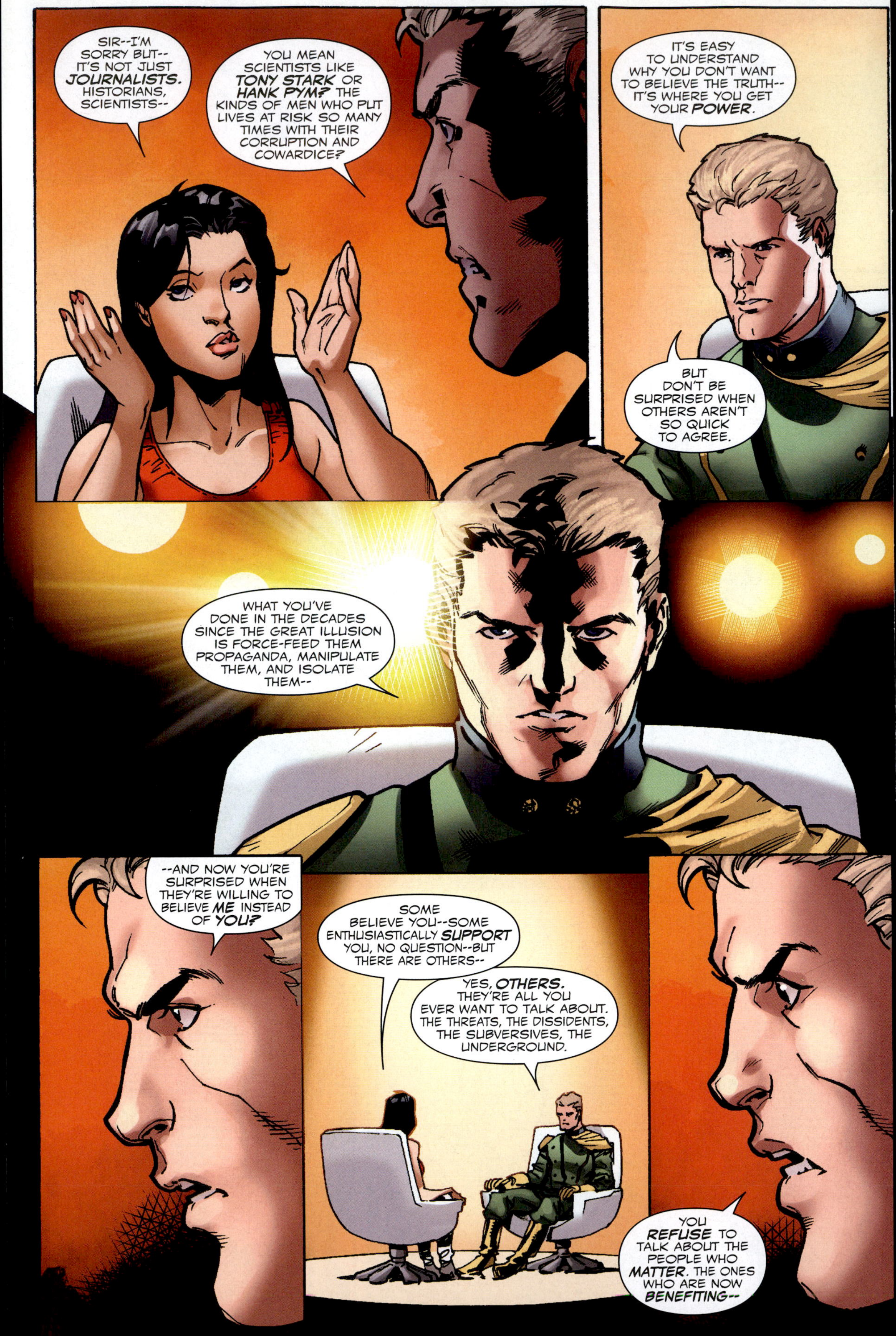
SIR--I'M SORRY BUT-- IT'S NOT JUST JOURNALISTS. HISTORIANS, SCIENTISTS--
YOU MEAN SCIENTISTS LIKE TONY STARK OR HANK PYM? THE KINDS OF MEN WHO PUT LIVES AT RISK SO MANY TIMES WITH THEIR CORRUPTION AND COWARDICE?
IT'S EASY TO UNDERSTAND WHY YOU DON'T WANT TO BELIEVE THE TRUTH-- IT'S WHERE YOU GET YOUR POWER.
BUT DON'T BE SURPRISED WHEN OTHERS AREN'T SO QUICK TO AGREE.
WHAT YOU'VE DONE IN THE DECADES SINCE THE GREAT ILLUSION IS FORCE-FEED THEM PROPAGANDA, MANIPULATE THEM, AND ISOLATE THEM--
--AND NOW YOU'RE SURPRISED WHEN THEY'RE WILLING TO BELIEVE ME INSTEAD OF YOU?
SOME BELIEVE YOU--SOME ENTHUSIASTICALLY SUPPORT YOU, NO QUESTION--BUT THERE ARE OTHERS--
YES, OTHERS. THEY'RE ALL YOU EVER WANT TO TALK ABOUT. THE THREATS, THE DISSIDENTS, THE SUBVERSIVES, THE UNDERGROUND.
YOU REFUSE TO TALK ABOUT THE PEOPLE WHO MATTER. THE ONES WHO ARE NOW BENEFITING--

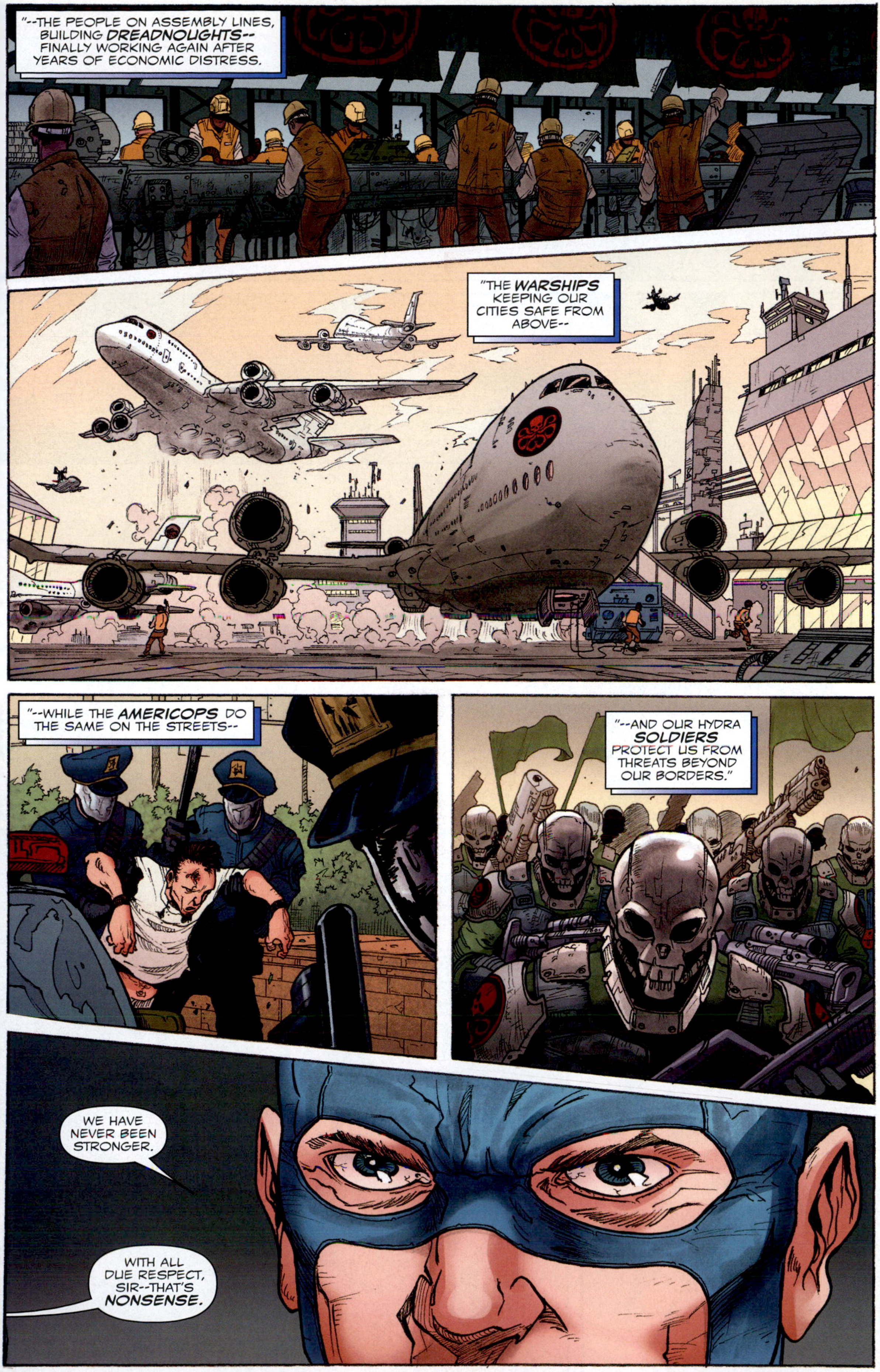
"--THE PEOPLE ON ASSEMBLY LINES, BUILDING DREADNOUGHTS-- FINALLY WORKING AGAIN AFTER YEARS OF ECONOMIC DISTRESS.
"THE WARSHIPS KEEPING OUR CITIES SAFE FROM ABOVE--
"--WHILE THE AMERICOPS DO THE SAME ON THE STREETS--
"--AND OUR HYDRA SOLDIERS PROTECT US FROM THREATS BEYOND OUR BORDERS."
WE HAVE NEVER BEEN STRONGER.
WITH ALL DUE RESPECT, SIR--THAT'S NONSENSE.

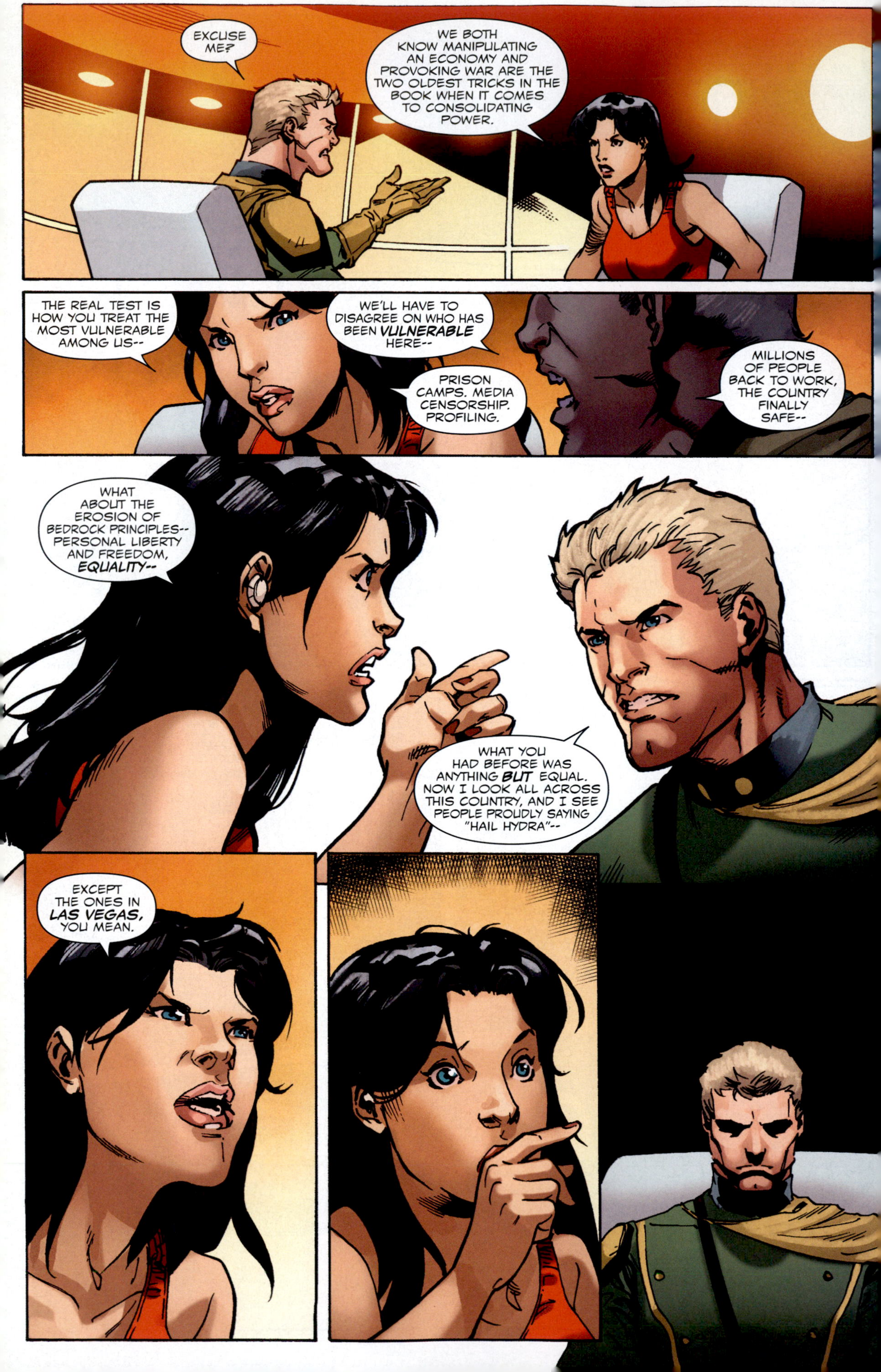
EXCUSE ME?
WE BOTH KNOW MANIPULATING AN ECONOMY AND PROVOKING WAR ARE THE TWO OLDEST TRICKS IN THE BOOK WHEN IT COMES TO CONSOLIDATING POWER.
THE REAL TEST IS HOW YOU TREAT THE MOST VULNERABLE AMONG US--
WE'LL HAVE TO DISAGREE ON WHO HAS BEEN VULNERABLE HERE--
MILLIONS OF PEOPLE BACK TO WORK, THE COUNTRY FINALLY SAFE--
PRISON CAMPS. MEDIA CENSORSHIP. PROFILING.
WHAT ABOUT THE EROSION OF BEDROCK PRINCIPLES--PERSONAL LIBERTY AND FREEDOM, EQUALITY--
WHAT YOU HAD BEFORE WAS ANYTHING BUT EQUAL. NOW I LOOK ALL ACROSS THIS COUNTRY, AND I SEE PEOPLE PROUDLY SAYING "HAIL HYDRA"--
EXCEPT THE ONES IN LAS VEGAS, YOU MEAN.

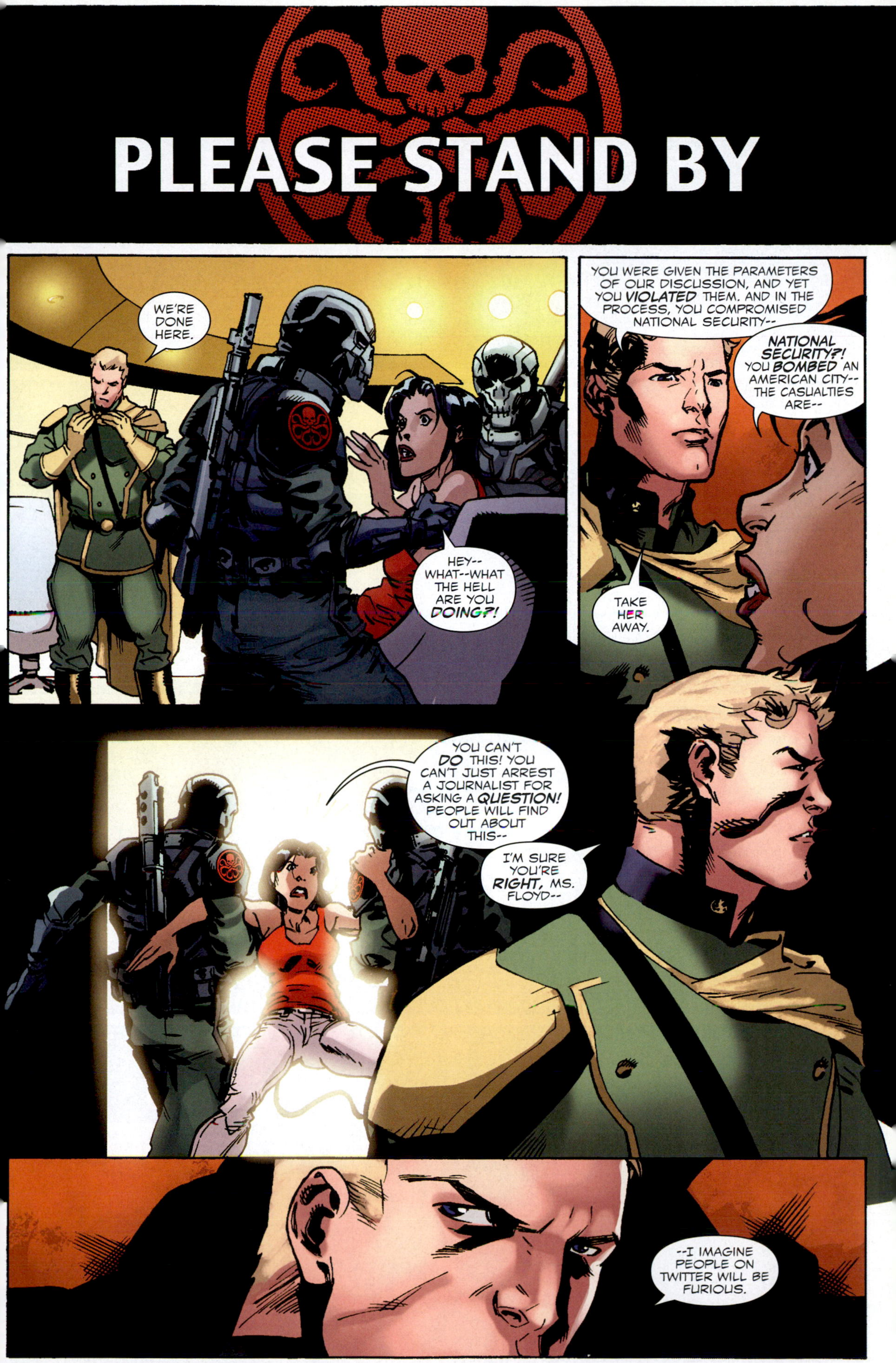
PLEASE STAND BY
WE'RE DONE HERE.
HEY--WHAT--WHAT THE HELL ARE YOU DOING?!
YOU WERE GIVEN THE PARAMETERS OF OUR DISCUSSION, AND YET YOU VIOLATED THEM. AND IN THE PROCESS, YOU COMPROMISED NATIONAL SECURITY--
NATIONAL SECURITY?! YOU BOMBED AN AMERICAN CITY--THE CASUALTIES ARE--
TAKE HER AWAY.
YOU CAN'T DO THIS! YOU CAN'T JUST ARREST A JOURNALIST FOR ASKING A QUESTION! PEOPLE WILL FIND OUT ABOUT THIS--
I'M SURE YOU'RE RIGHT, MS. FLOYD--
--I IMAGINE PEOPLE ON TWITTER WILL BE FURIOUS.

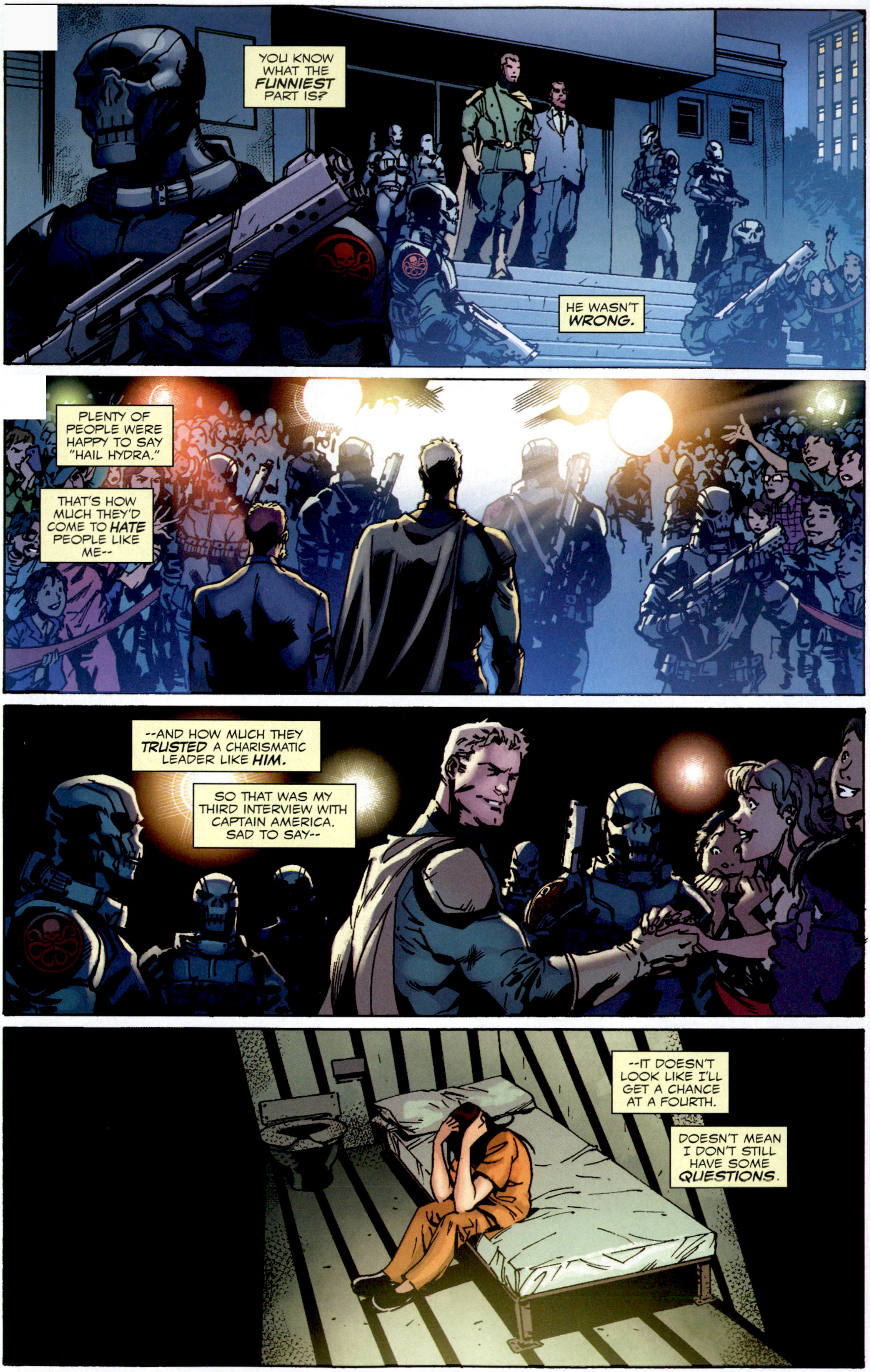
YOU KNOW WHAT THE FUNNIEST PART IS?
HE WASN'T WRONG.
PLENTY OF PEOPLE WERE HAPPY TO SAY "HAIL HYDRA."
THAT'S HOW MUCH THEY'D COME TO HATE PEOPLE LIKE ME--
--AND HOW MUCH THEY TRUSTED A CHARISMATIC LEADER LIKE HIM.
SO THAT WAS MY THIRD INTERVIEW WITH CAPTAIN AMERICA. SAD TO SAY--
--IT DOESN'T LOOK LIKE I'LL GET A CHANCE AT A FOURTH.
DOESN'T MEAN I DON'T STILL HAVE SOME QUESTIONS.

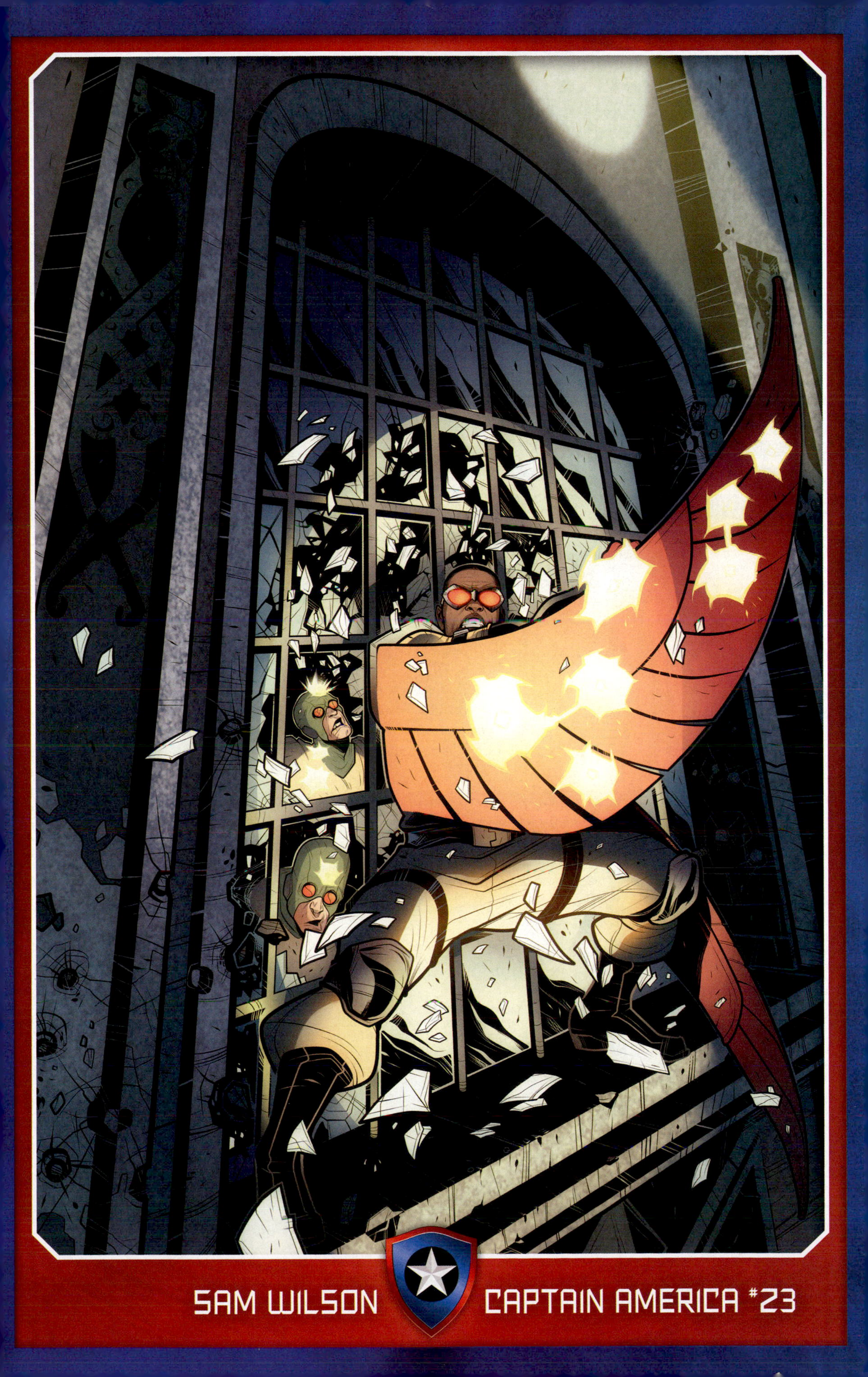
SAM WILSON
CAPTAIN AMERICA #23

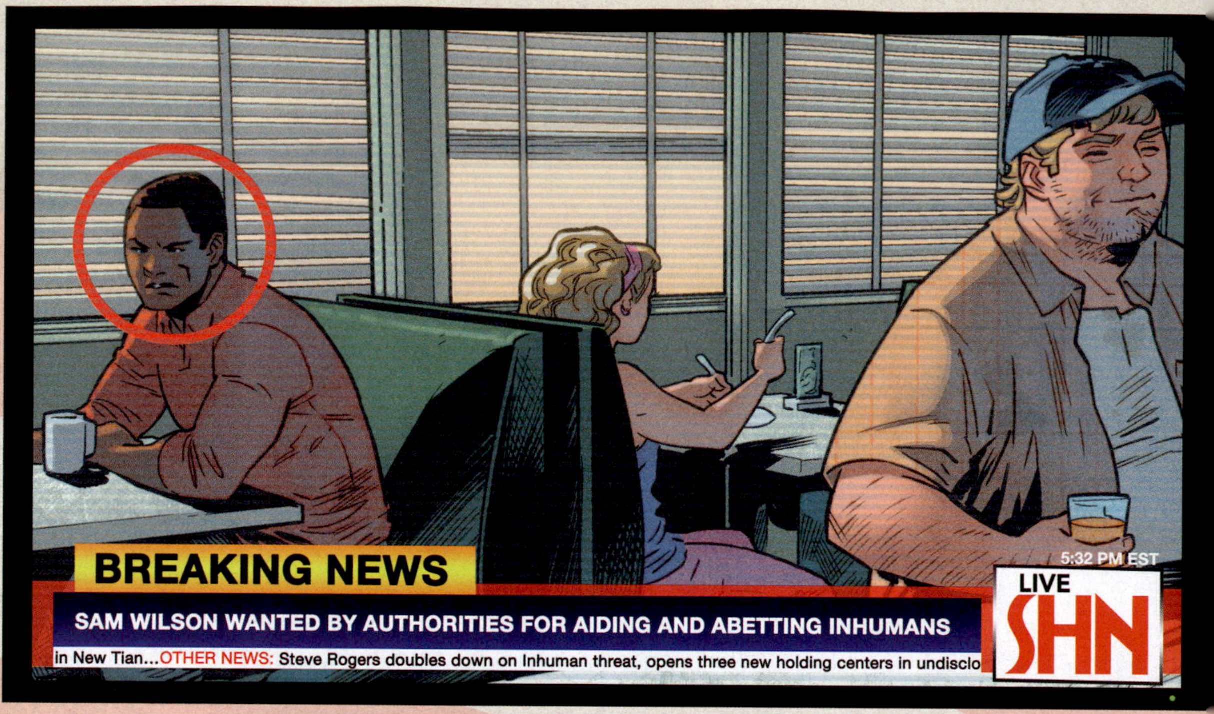
BREAKING NEWS
SAM WILSON WANTED BY AUTHORITIES FOR AIDING AND ABETTING INHUMANS
in New Tian...OTHER NEWS: Steve Rogers doubles down on Inhuman threat, opens three new holding centers in undisclo
5:32 PM EST
LIVE
SHN

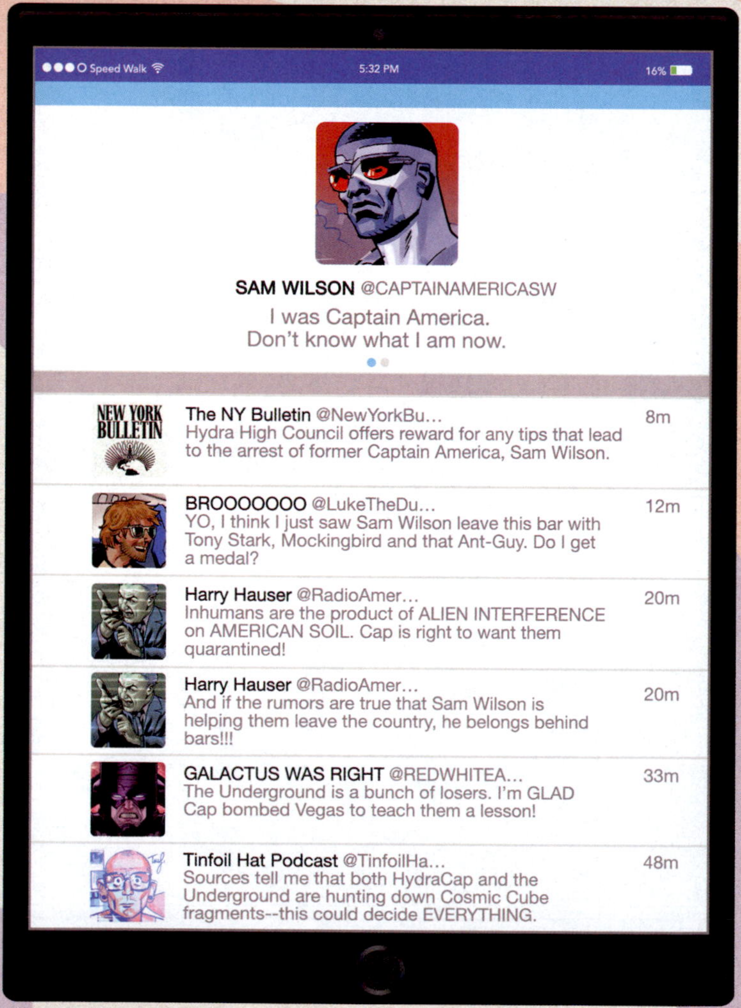
Speed Walk
5:32 PM
16%
SAM WILSON @CAPTAINAMERICASW
I was Captain America.
Don't know what I am now.
NEW YORK BULLETIN
The NY Bulletin @NewYorkBu...
Hydra High Council offers reward for any tips that lead to the arrest of former Captain America, Sam Wilson.
8m
BROOOOOOO @LukeTheDu...
YO, I think I just saw Sam Wilson leave this bar with Tony Stark, Mockingbird and that Ant-Guy. Do I get a medal?
12m
Harry Hauser @RadioAmer...
Inhumans are the product of ALIEN INTERFERENCE on AMERICAN SOIL. Cap is right to want them quarantined!
20m
Harry Hauser @RadioAmer...
And if the rumors are true that Sam Wilson is helping them leave the country, he belongs behind bars!!!
20m
GALACTUS WAS RIGHT @REDWHITEA...
The Underground is a bunch of losers. I'm GLAD Cap bombed Vegas to teach them a lesson!
33m
Tinfoil Hat Podcast @TinfoilHa...
Sources tell me that both HydraCap and the Underground are hunting down Cosmic Cube fragments--this could decide EVERYTHING.
48m

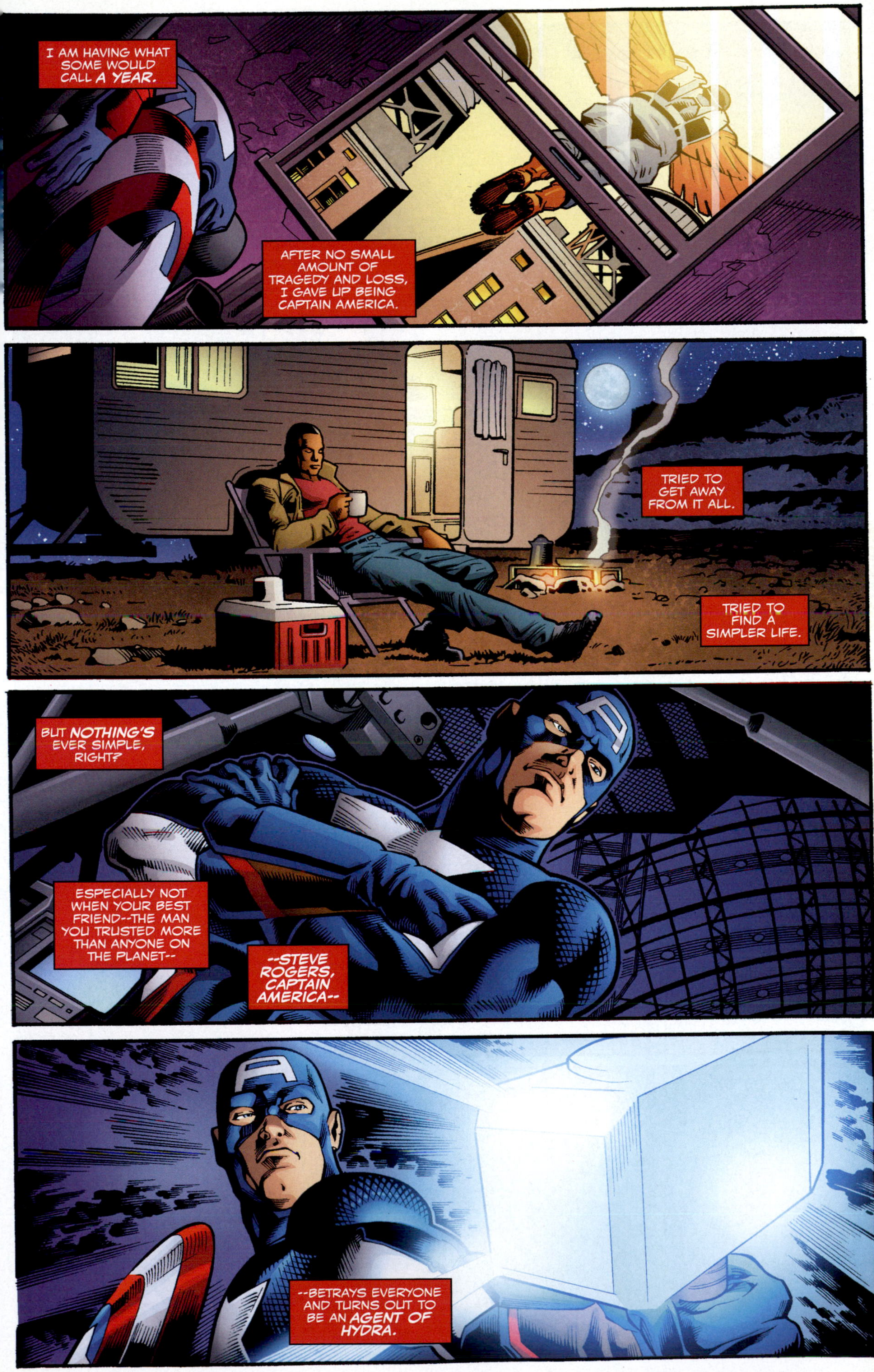
I AM HAVING WHAT SOME WOULD CALL A YEAR.
AFTER NO SMALL AMOUNT OF TRAGEDY AND LOSS, I GAVE UP BEING CAPTAIN AMERICA.
TRIED TO GET AWAY FROM IT ALL.
TRIED TO FIND A SIMPLER LIFE.
BUT NOTHING'S EVER SIMPLE, RIGHT?
ESPECIALLY NOT WHEN YOUR BEST FRIEND--THE MAN YOU TRUSTED MORE THAN ANYONE ON THE PLANET--
--STEVE ROGERS, CAPTAIN AMERICA--
--BETRAYS EVERYONE AND TURNS OUT TO BE AN AGENT OF HYDRA.

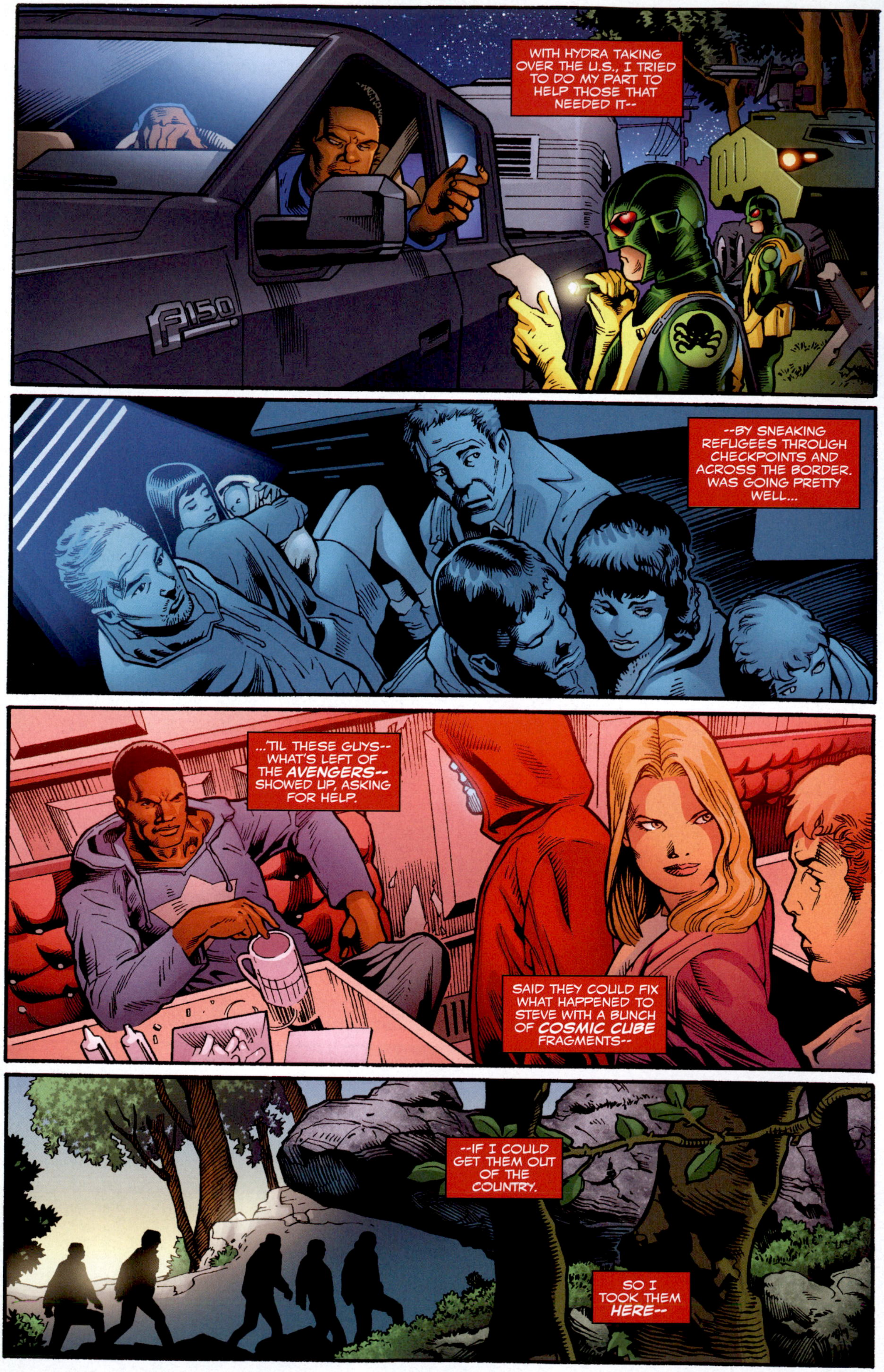

WITH HYDRA TAKING OVER THE U.S., I TRIED TO DO MY PART TO HELP THOSE THAT NEEDED IT--
F150
--BY SNEAKING REFUGEES THROUGH CHECKPOINTS AND ACROSS THE BORDER. WAS GOING PRETTY WELL...
...'TIL THESE GUYS-- WHAT'S LEFT OF THE **AVENGERS--** SHOWED UP, ASKING FOR HELP.
SAID THEY COULD FIX WHAT HAPPENED TO STEVE WITH A BUNCH OF ***COSMIC CUBE*** FRAGMENTS--
--IF I COULD GET THEM OUT OF THE COUNTRY.
SO I TOOK THEM ***HERE--***

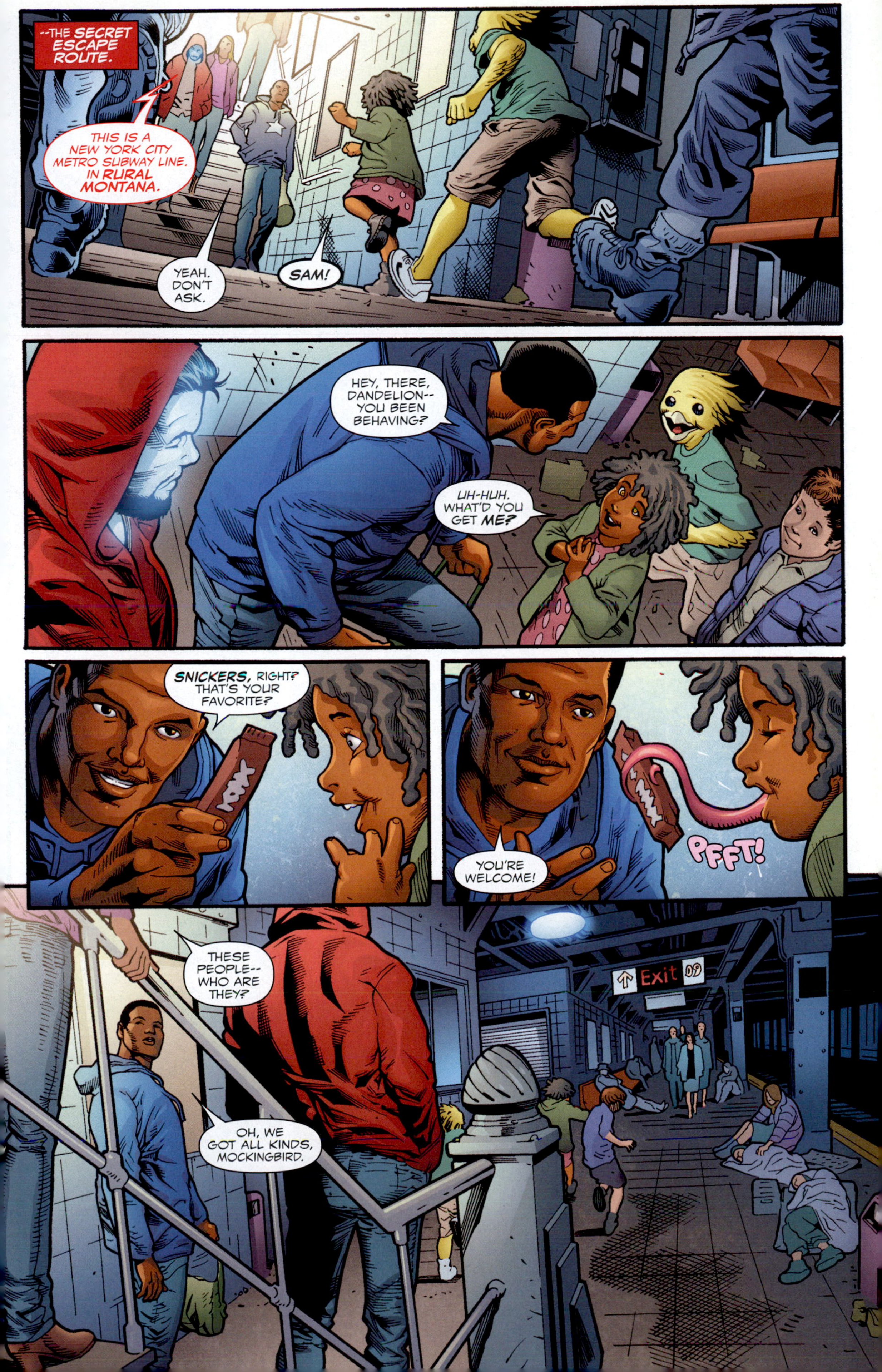
--THE SECRET ESCAPE ROUTE.
THIS IS A NEW YORK CITY METRO SUBWAY LINE. IN RURAL MONTANA.
YEAH. DON'T ASK.
SAM!
HEY, THERE, DANDELION-- YOU BEEN BEHAVING?
UH-HUH. WHAT'D YOU GET ME?
SNICKERS, RIGHT? THAT'S YOUR FAVORITE?
YOU'RE WELCOME!
PFFT!
THESE PEOPLE-- WHO ARE THEY?
OH, WE GOT ALL KINDS, MOCKINGBIRD.
Exit
09

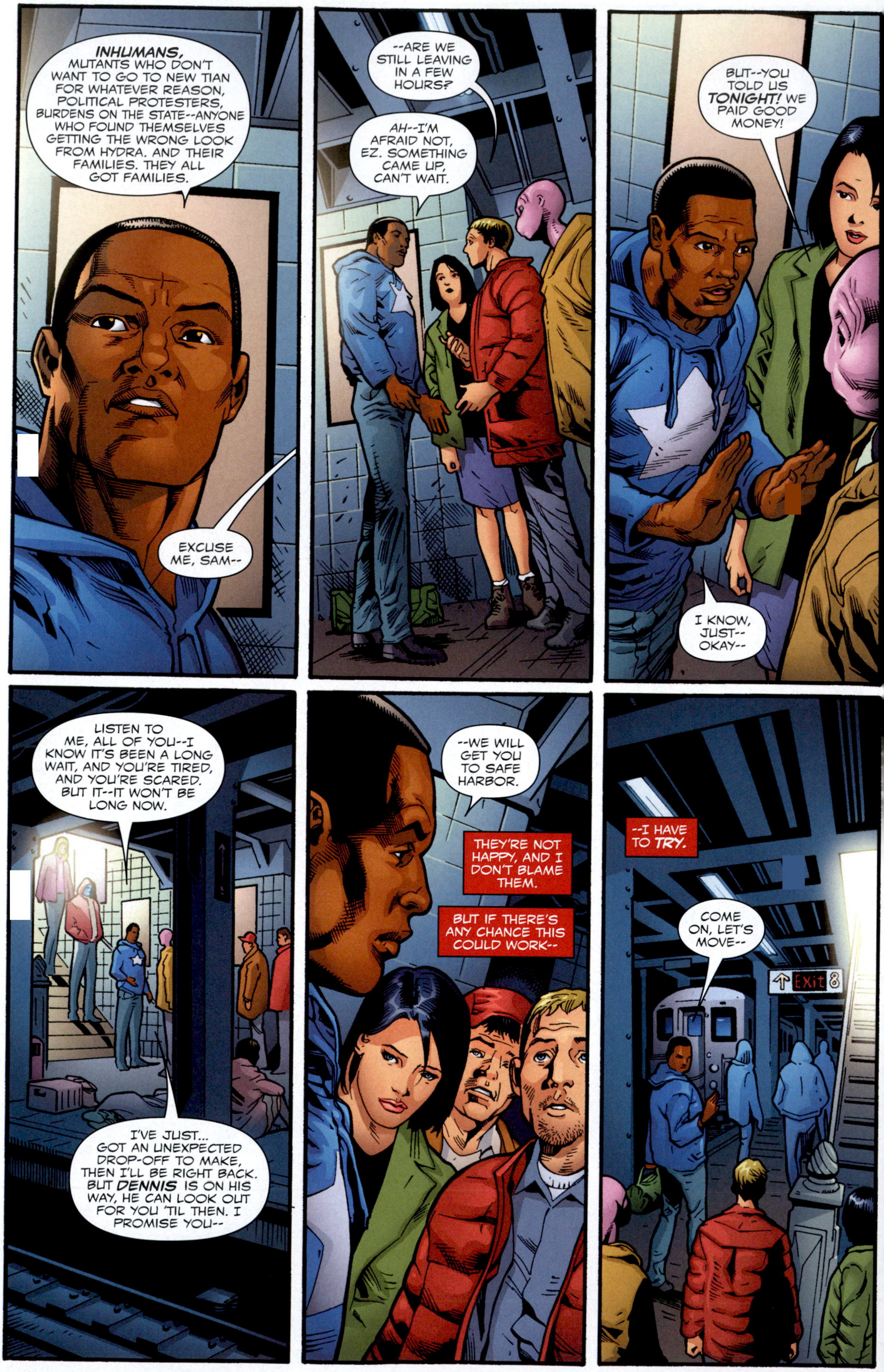
INHUMANS, MUTANTS WHO DON'T WANT TO GO TO NEW TIAN FOR WHATEVER REASON, POLITICAL PROTESTERS, BURDENS ON THE STATE--ANYONE WHO FOUND THEMSELVES GETTING THE WRONG LOOK FROM HYDRA. AND THEIR FAMILIES. THEY ALL GOT FAMILIES.
EXCUSE ME, SAM--
--ARE WE STILL LEAVING IN A FEW HOURS?
AH--I'M AFRAID NOT, EZ. SOMETHING CAME UP, CAN'T WAIT.
BUT--YOU TOLD US TONIGHT! WE PAID GOOD MONEY!
I KNOW, JUST-- OKAY--
LISTEN TO ME, ALL OF YOU--I KNOW IT'S BEEN A LONG WAIT, AND YOU'RE TIRED, AND YOU'RE SCARED. BUT IT--IT WON'T BE LONG NOW.
I'VE JUST... GOT AN UNEXPECTED DROP-OFF TO MAKE, THEN I'LL BE RIGHT BACK. BUT DENNIS IS ON HIS WAY, HE CAN LOOK OUT FOR YOU 'TIL THEN. I PROMISE YOU--
--WE WILL GET YOU TO SAFE HARBOR.
THEY'RE NOT HAPPY, AND I DON'T BLAME THEM.
BUT IF THERE'S ANY CHANCE THIS COULD WORK--
--I HAVE TO TRY.
COME ON, LET'S MOVE--
EXIT 8

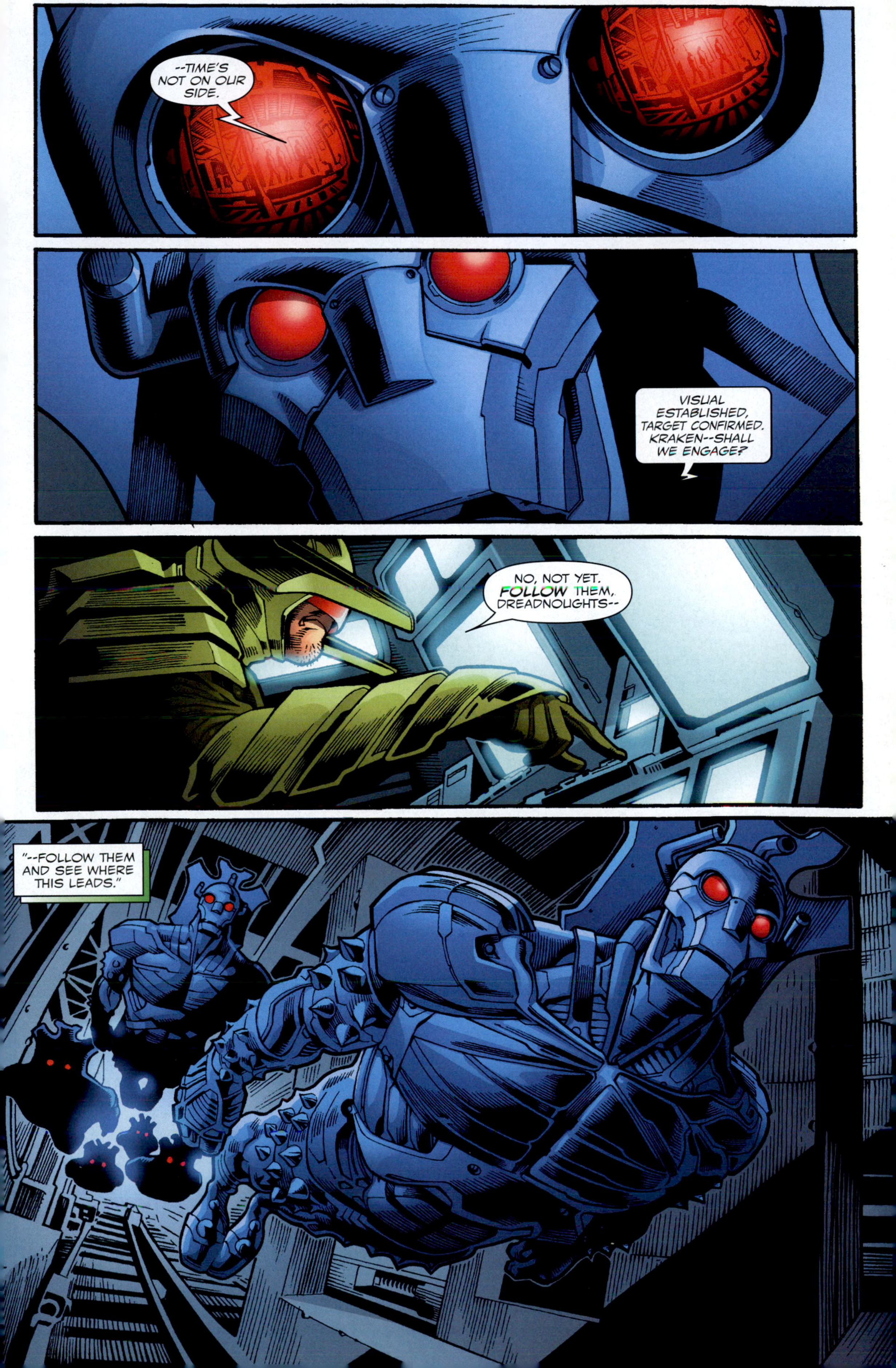
--TIME'S NOT ON OUR SIDE.
VISUAL ESTABLISHED, TARGET CONFIRMED. KRAKEN--SHALL WE ENGAGE?
NO, NOT YET. FOLLOW THEM, DREADNOUGHTS--
"--FOLLOW THEM AND SEE WHERE THIS LEADS."

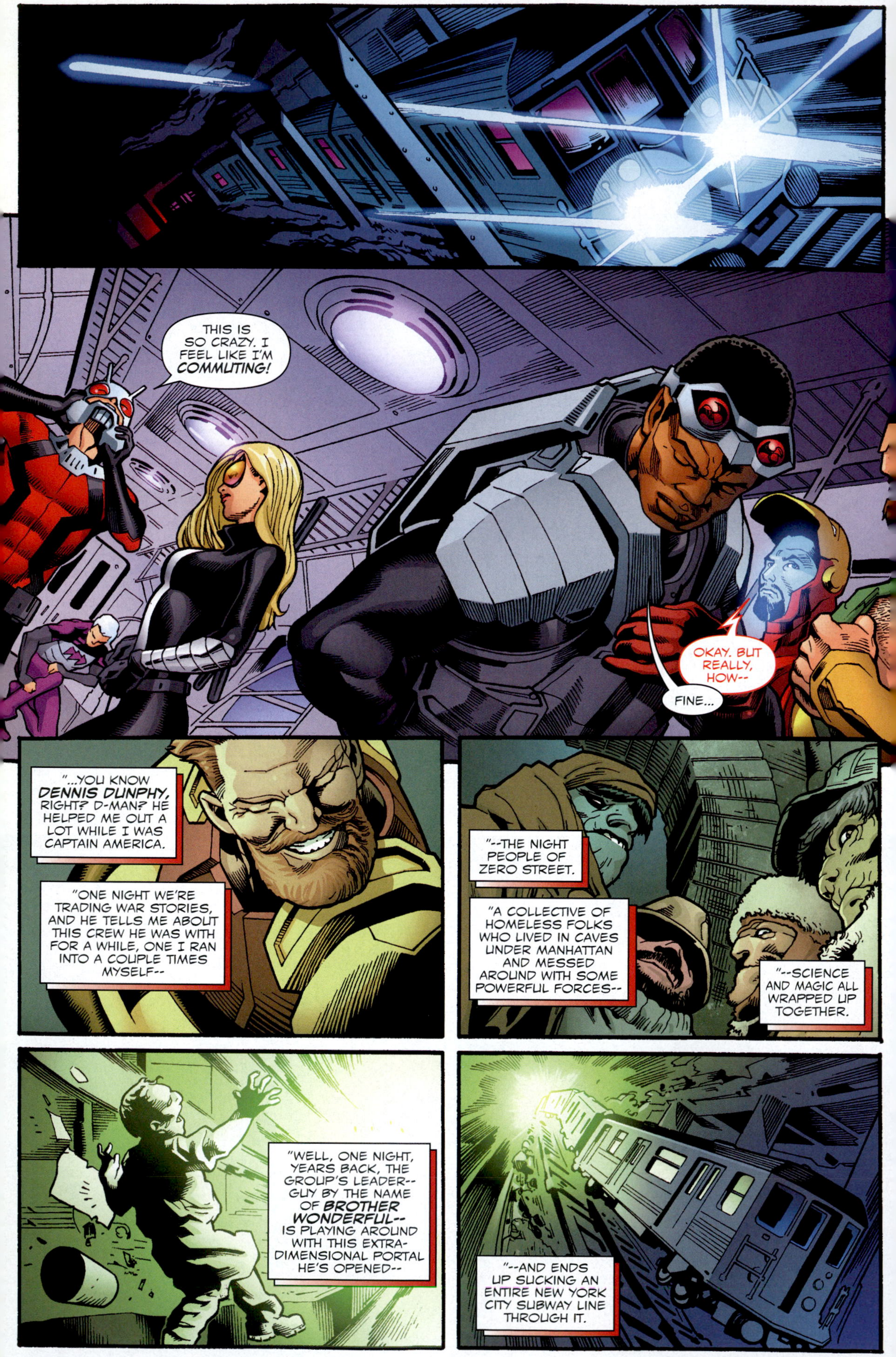

THIS IS SO CRAZY. I FEEL LIKE I'M COMMUTING!
OKAY. BUT REALLY, HOW--
FINE...
"...YOU KNOW DENNIS DUNPHY, RIGHT? D-MAN? HE HELPED ME OUT A LOT WHILE I WAS CAPTAIN AMERICA.
"ONE NIGHT WE'RE TRADING WAR STORIES, AND HE TELLS ME ABOUT THIS CREW HE WAS WITH FOR A WHILE, ONE I RAN INTO A COUPLE TIMES MYSELF--
"--THE NIGHT PEOPLE OF ZERO STREET.
"A COLLECTIVE OF HOMELESS FOLKS WHO LIVED IN CAVES UNDER MANHATTAN AND MESSED AROUND WITH SOME POWERFUL FORCES--
"--SCIENCE AND MAGIC ALL WRAPPED UP TOGETHER.
"WELL, ONE NIGHT, YEARS BACK, THE GROUP'S LEADER--GUY BY THE NAME OF BROTHER WONDERFUL--IS PLAYING AROUND WITH THIS EXTRA-DIMENSIONAL PORTAL HE'S OPENED--
"--AND ENDS UP SUCKING AN ENTIRE NEW YORK CITY SUBWAY LINE THROUGH IT.

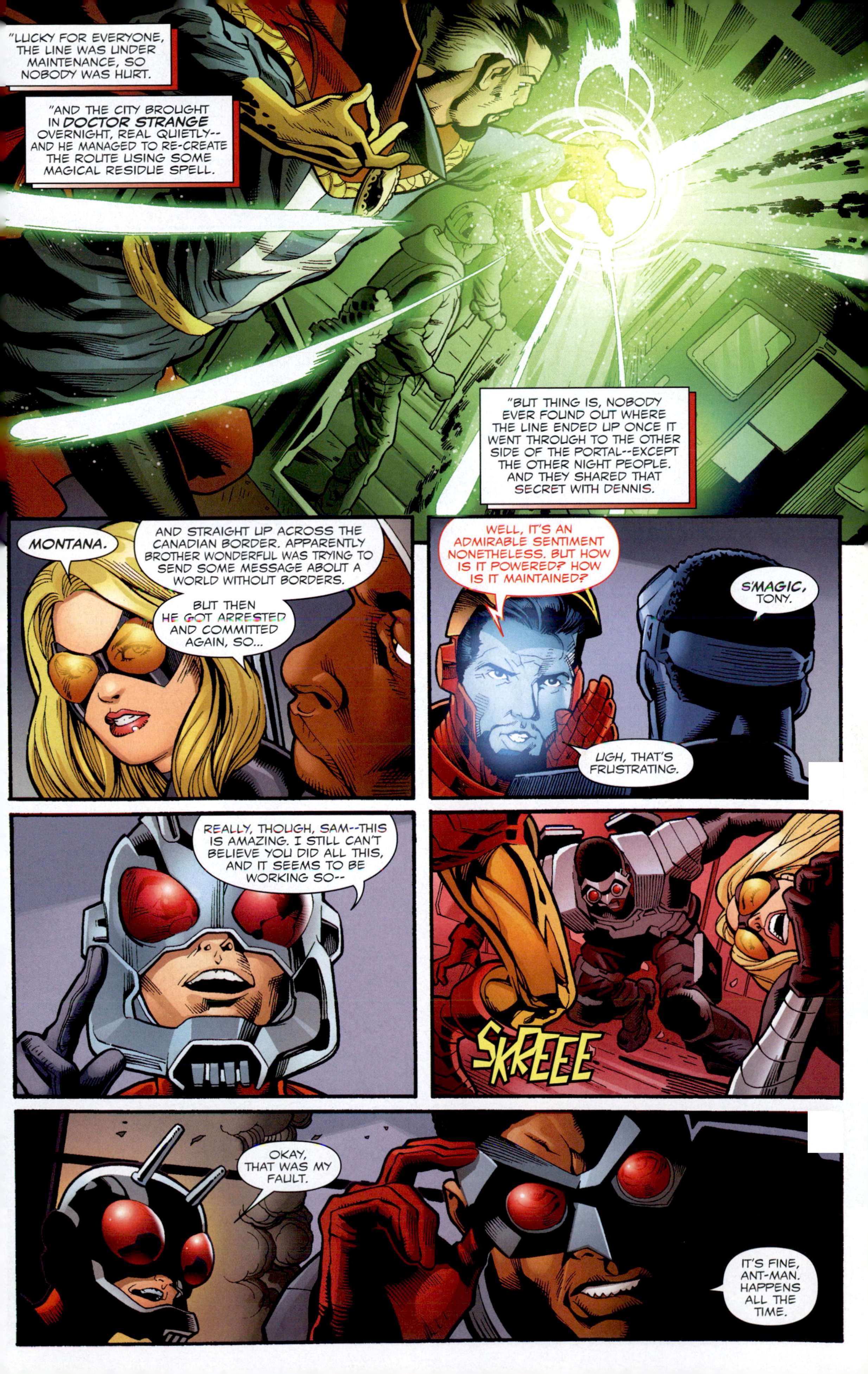

"LUCKY FOR EVERYONE, THE LINE WAS UNDER MAINTENANCE, SO NOBODY WAS HURT.
"AND THE CITY BROUGHT IN DOCTOR STRANGE OVERNIGHT, REAL QUIETLY--AND HE MANAGED TO RE-CREATE THE ROUTE USING SOME MAGICAL RESIDUE SPELL.
"BUT THING IS, NOBODY EVER FOUND OUT WHERE THE LINE ENDED UP ONCE IT WENT THROUGH TO THE OTHER SIDE OF THE PORTAL--EXCEPT THE OTHER NIGHT PEOPLE. AND THEY SHARED THAT SECRET WITH DENNIS.
MONTANA.
AND STRAIGHT UP ACROSS THE CANADIAN BORDER. APPARENTLY BROTHER WONDERFUL WAS TRYING TO SEND SOME MESSAGE ABOUT A WORLD WITHOUT BORDERS.
BUT THEN HE GOT ARRESTED AND COMMITTED AGAIN, SO...
WELL, IT'S AN ADMIRABLE SENTIMENT NONETHELESS. BUT HOW IS IT POWERED? HOW IS IT MAINTAINED?
S'MAGIC, TONY.
UGH, THAT'S FRUSTRATING.
REALLY, THOUGH, SAM--THIS IS AMAZING. I STILL CAN'T BELIEVE YOU DID ALL THIS, AND IT SEEMS TO BE WORKING SO--
SKREEE
OKAY, THAT WAS MY FAULT.
IT'S FINE, ANT-MAN. HAPPENS ALL THE TIME.

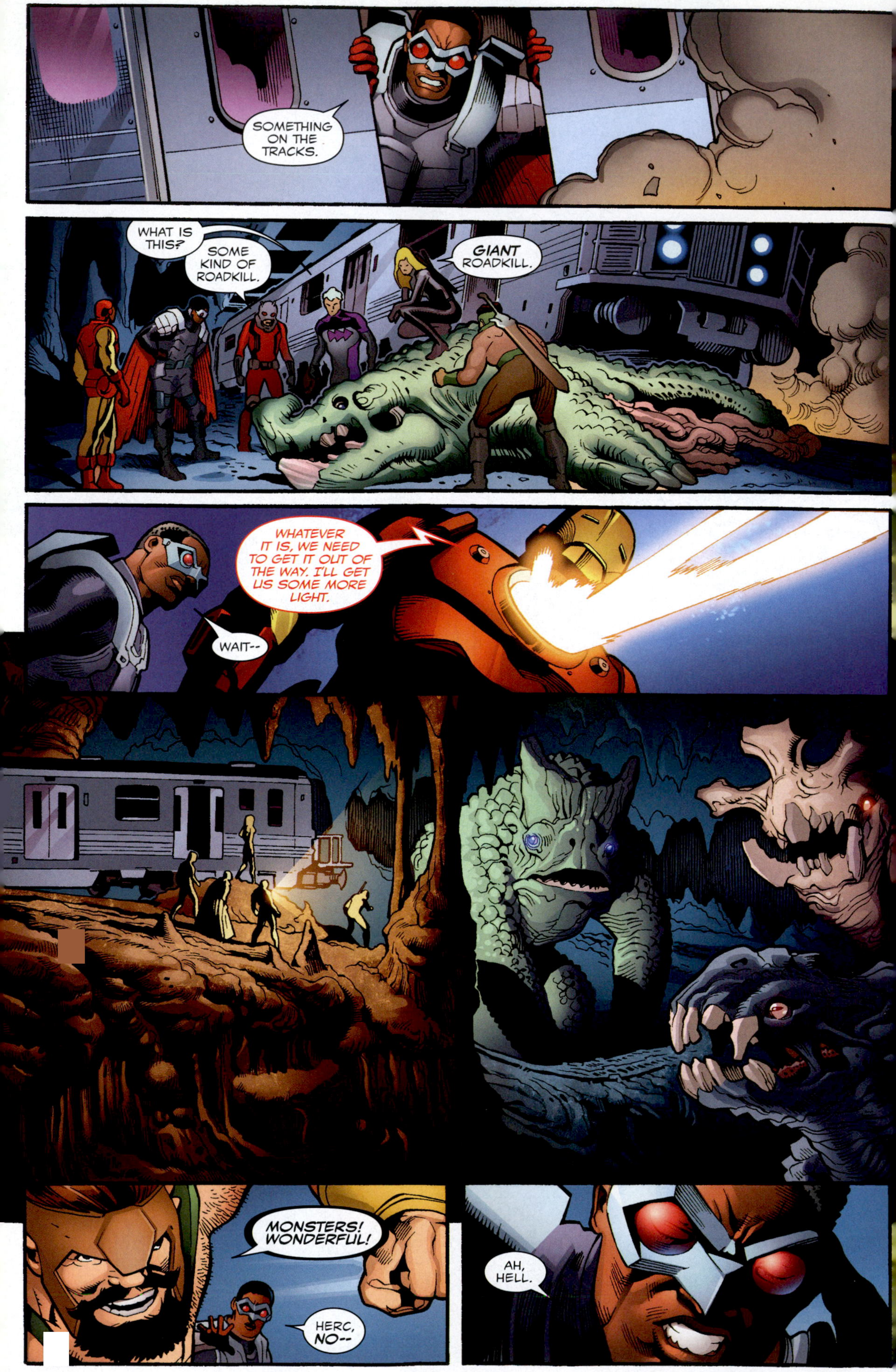
SOMETHING ON THE TRACKS.
WHAT IS THIS?
SOME KIND OF ROADKILL.
GIANT ROADKILL.
WHATEVER IT IS, WE NEED TO GET IT OUT OF THE WAY. I'LL GET US SOME MORE LIGHT.
WAIT--
MONSTERS! WONDERFUL!
HERC, NO--
AH, HELL.

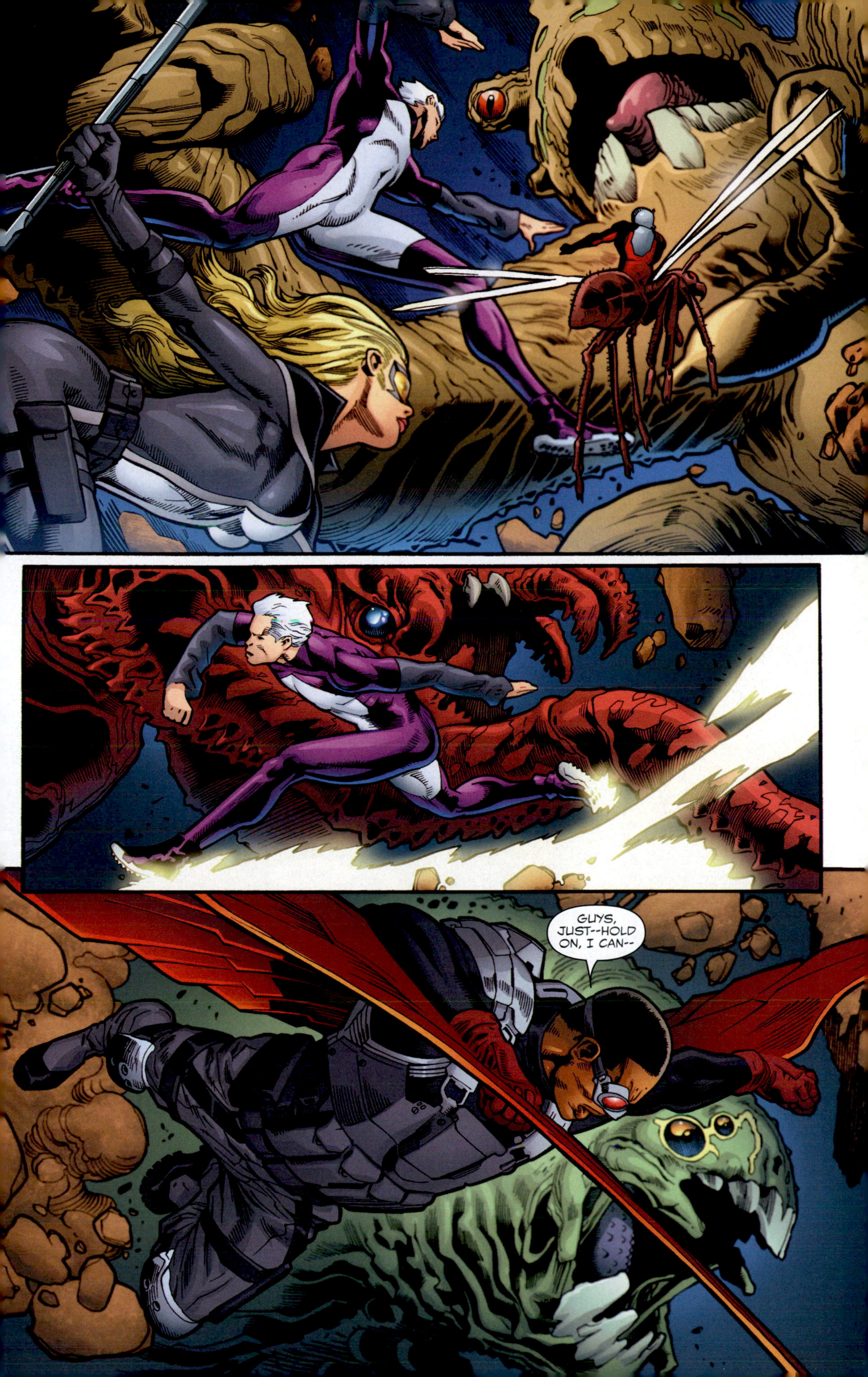
GUYS, JUST--HOLD ON, I CAN--

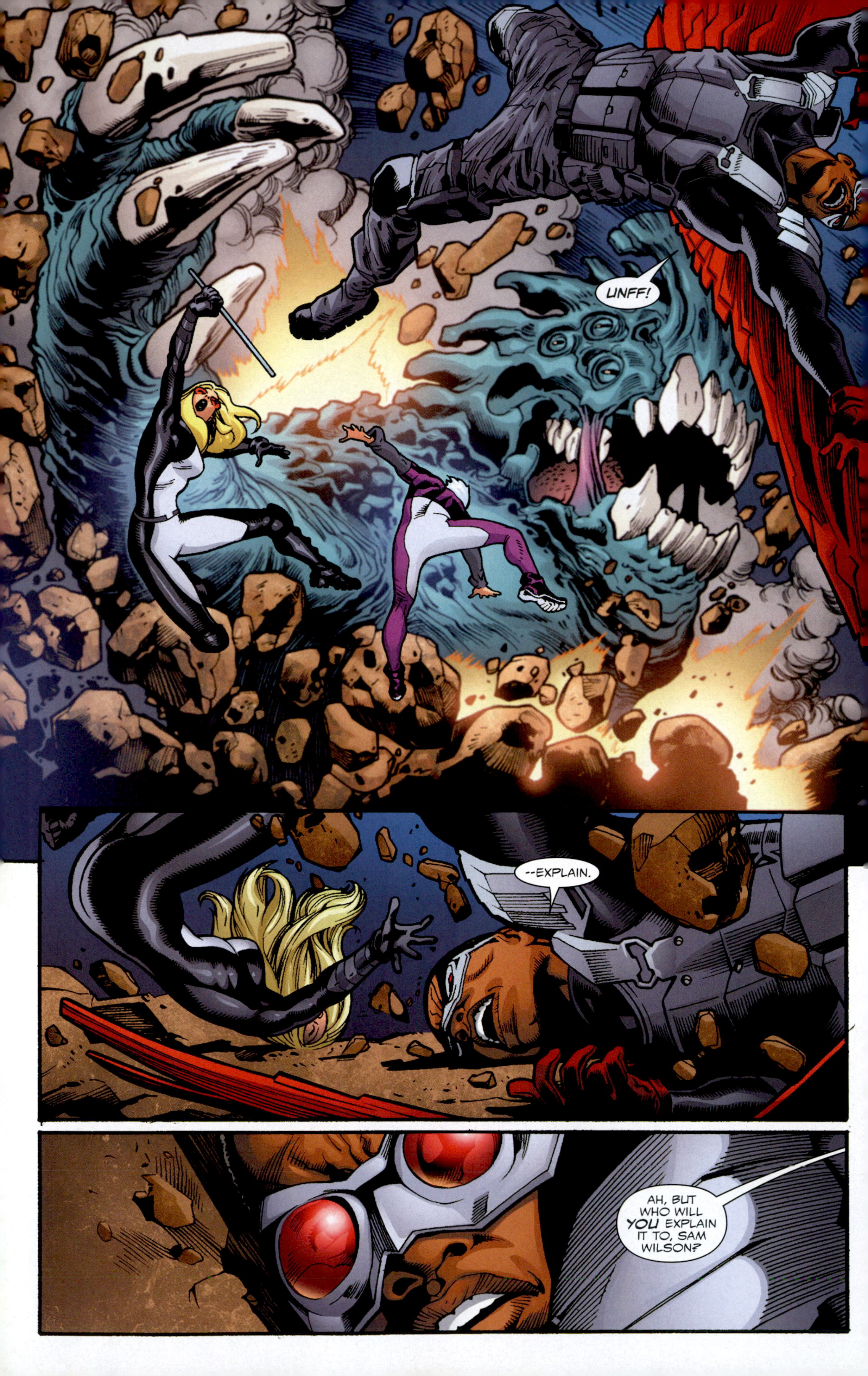
UNFF!
--EXPLAIN.
AH, BUT WHO WILL *YOU* EXPLAIN IT TO, SAM WILSON?

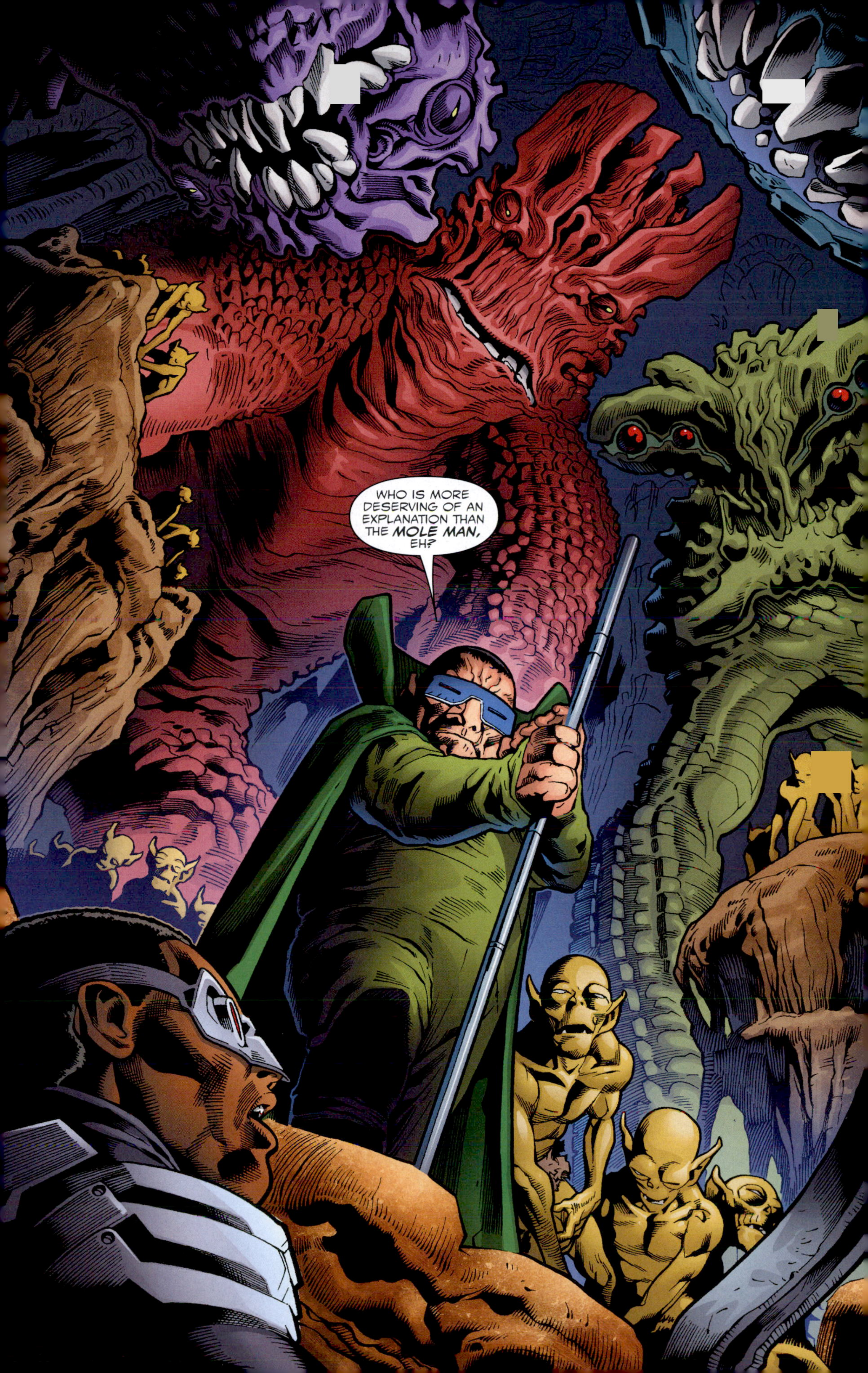
WHO IS MORE DESERVING OF AN EXPLANATION THAN THE MOLE MAN, EH?

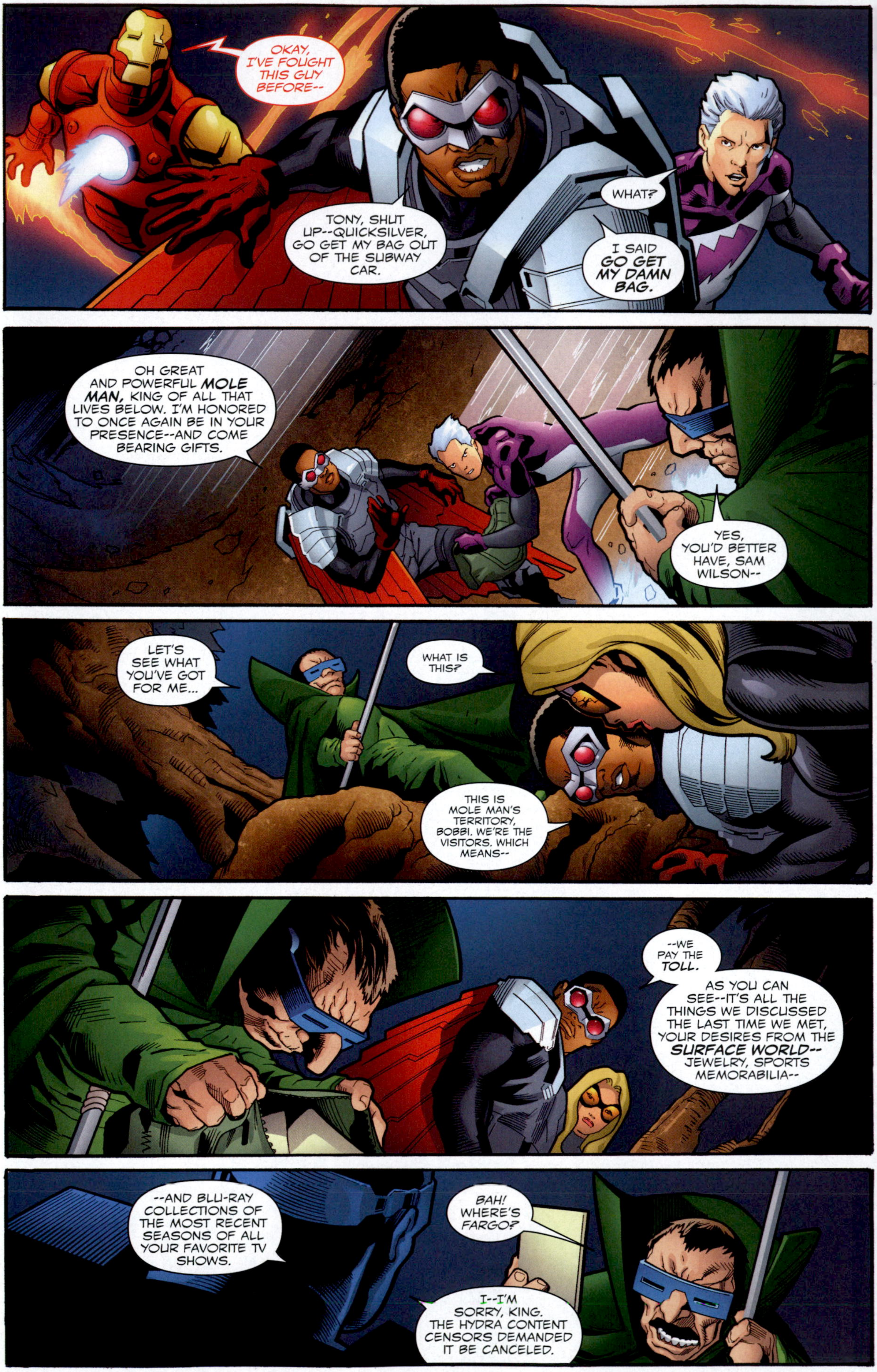
OKAY, I'VE FOUGHT THIS GUY BEFORE--
TONY, SHUT UP--QUICKSILVER, GO GET MY BAG OUT OF THE SUBWAY CAR.
WHAT?
I SAID **GO GET MY DAMN BAG.**
OH GREAT AND POWERFUL **MOLE MAN,** KING OF ALL THAT LIVES BELOW. I'M HONORED TO ONCE AGAIN BE IN YOUR PRESENCE--AND COME BEARING GIFTS.
YES, YOU'D BETTER HAVE, SAM WILSON--
LET'S SEE WHAT YOU'VE GOT FOR ME...
WHAT IS THIS?
THIS IS MOLE MAN'S TERRITORY, BOBBI. WE'RE THE VISITORS. WHICH MEANS--
--WE PAY THE **TOLL.**
AS YOU CAN SEE--IT'S ALL THE THINGS WE DISCUSSED THE LAST TIME WE MET, YOUR DESIRES FROM THE **SURFACE WORLD--** JEWELRY, SPORTS MEMORABILIA--
--AND BLU-RAY COLLECTIONS OF THE MOST RECENT SEASONS OF ALL YOUR FAVORITE TV SHOWS.
BAH! WHERE'S FARGO?
I--I'M SORRY, KING. THE HYDRA CONTENT CENSORS DEMANDED IT BE CANCELED.

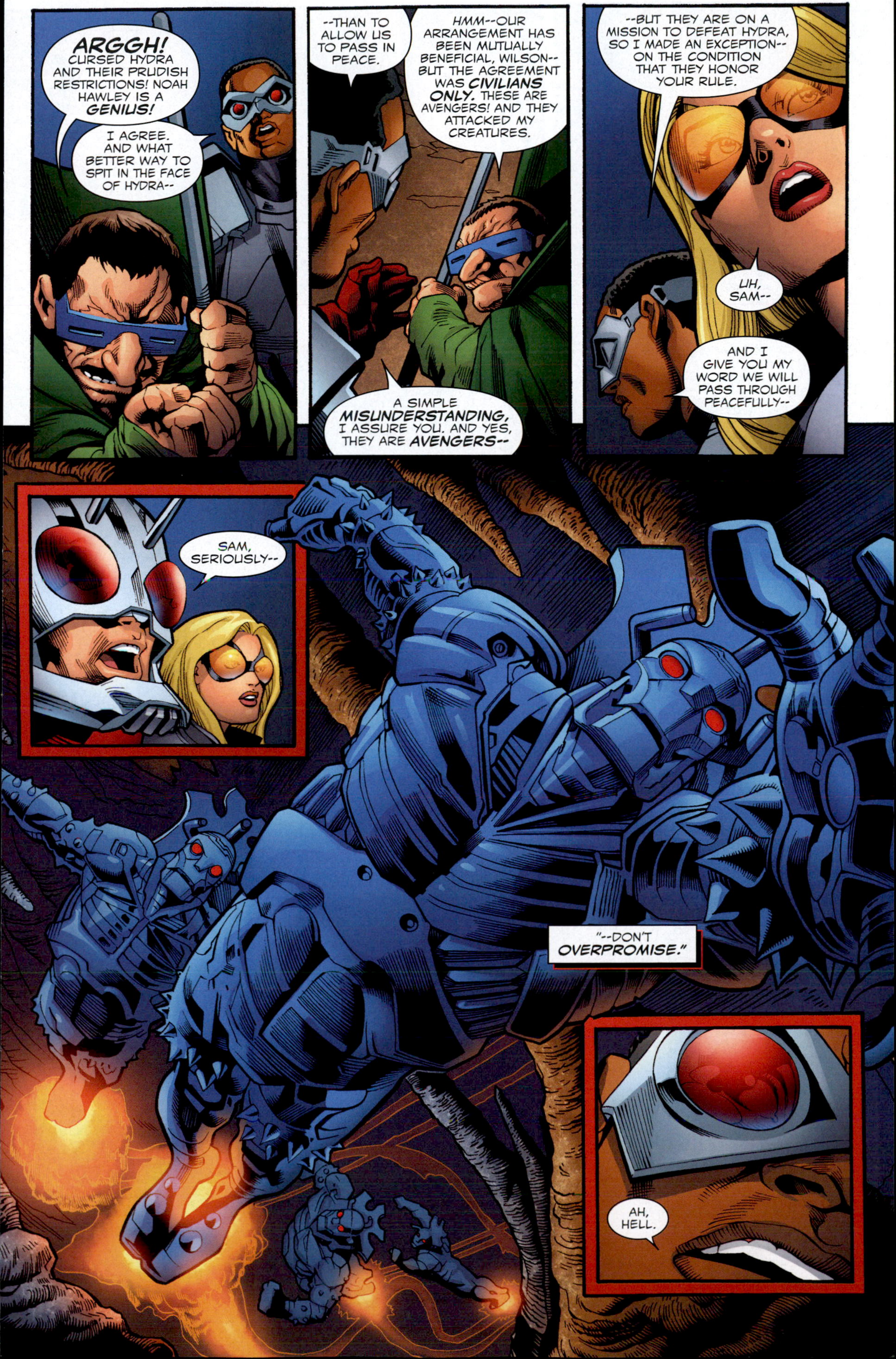
ARGGH! CURSED HYDRA AND THEIR PRUDISH RESTRICTIONS! NOAH HAWLEY IS A GENIUS!
I AGREE. AND WHAT BETTER WAY TO SPIT IN THE FACE OF HYDRA--
--THAN TO ALLOW US TO PASS IN PEACE.
HMM--OUR ARRANGEMENT HAS BEEN MUTUALLY BENEFICIAL, WILSON--BUT THE AGREEMENT WAS CIVILIANS ONLY. THESE ARE AVENGERS! AND THEY ATTACKED MY CREATURES.
A SIMPLE MISUNDERSTANDING, I ASSURE YOU. AND YES, THEY ARE AVENGERS--
--BUT THEY ARE ON A MISSION TO DEFEAT HYDRA, SO I MADE AN EXCEPTION--ON THE CONDITION THAT THEY HONOR YOUR RULE.
UH, SAM--
AND I GIVE YOU MY WORD WE WILL PASS THROUGH PEACEFULLY--
SAM, SERIOUSLY--
"--DON'T OVERPROMISE."
AH, HELL.

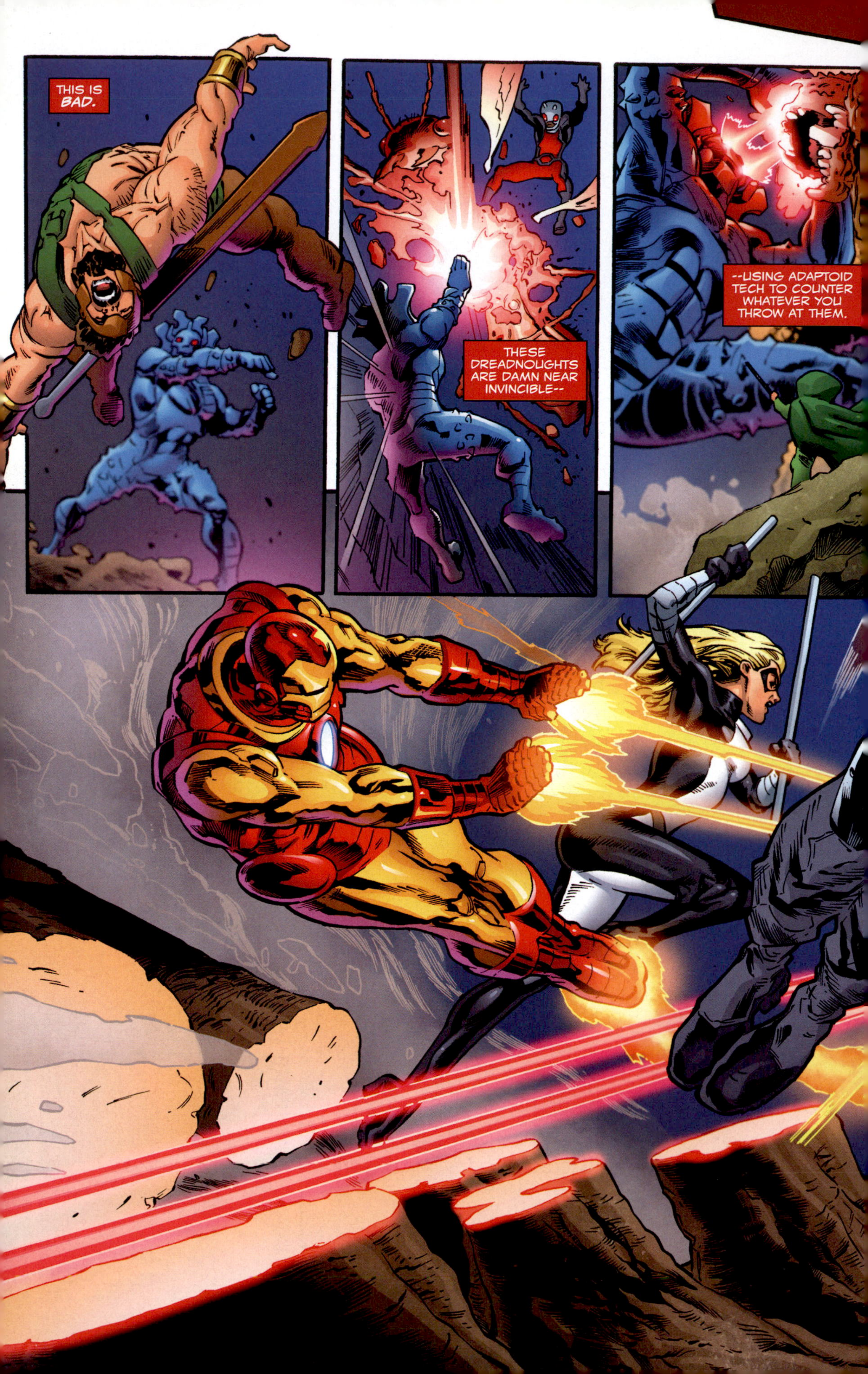
THIS IS BAD.
THESE DREADNOUGHTS ARE DAMN NEAR INVINCIBLE--
--USING ADAPTOID TECH TO COUNTER WHATEVER YOU THROW AT THEM.

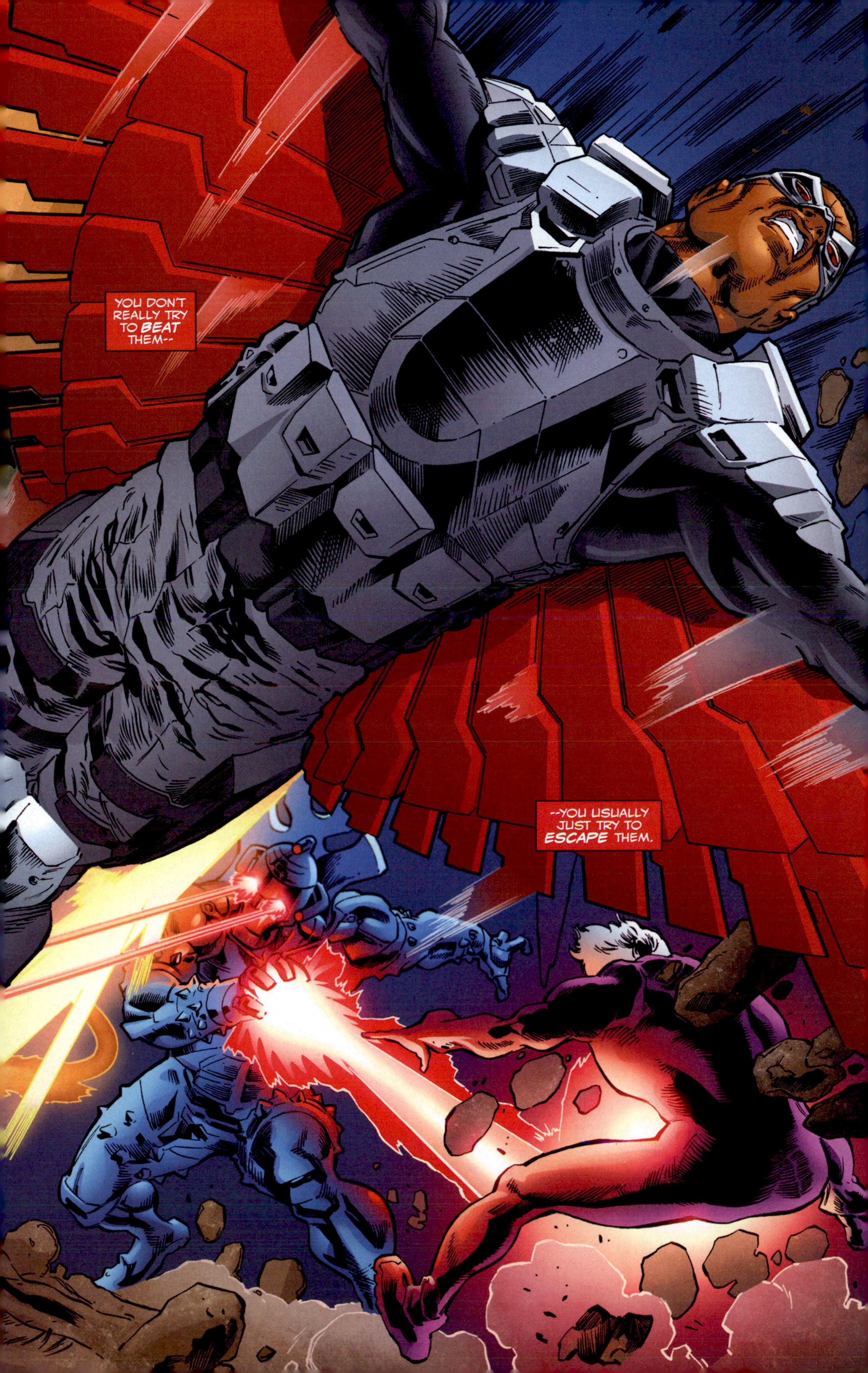

YOU DON'T REALLY TRY TO BEAT THEM--
--YOU USUALLY JUST TRY TO ESCAPE THEM.

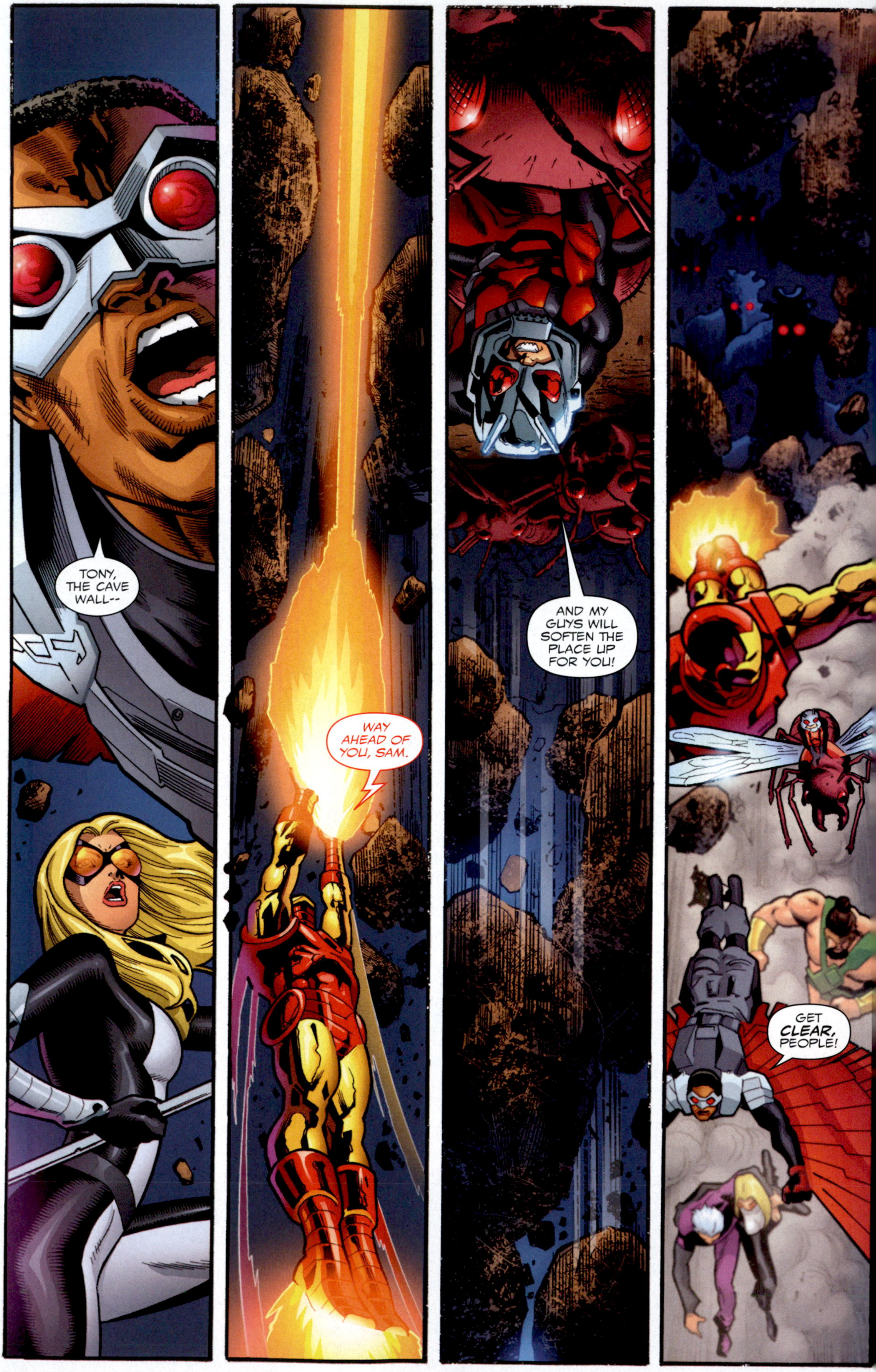
TONY, THE CAVE WALL--
WAY AHEAD OF YOU, SAM.
AND MY GUYS WILL SOFTEN THE PLACE UP FOR YOU!
GET CLEAR, PEOPLE!

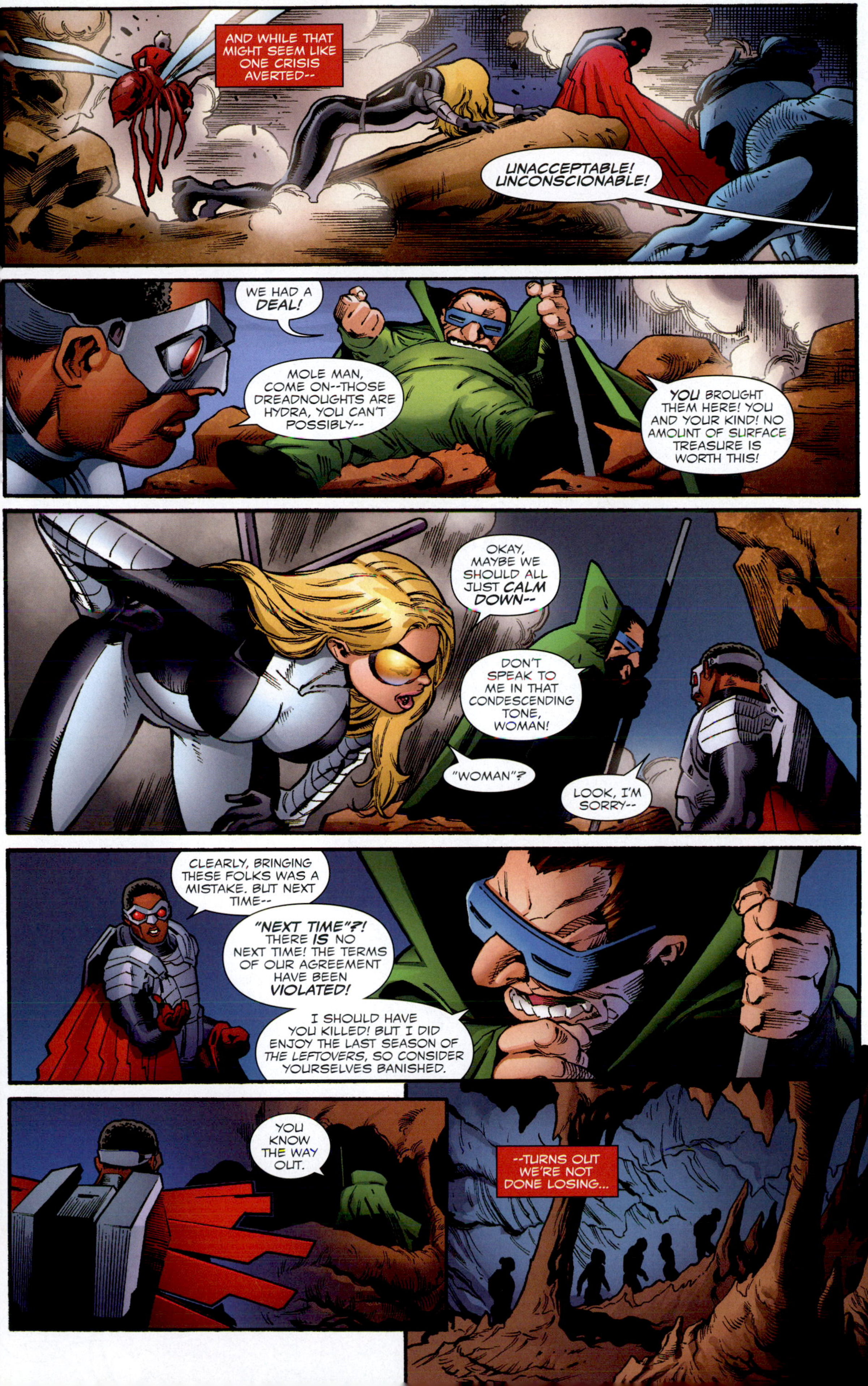
AND WHILE THAT MIGHT SEEM LIKE ONE CRISIS AVERTED--
UNACCEPTABLE! UNCONSCIONABLE!
WE HAD A DEAL!
MOLE MAN, COME ON--THOSE DREADNOUGHTS ARE HYDRA, YOU CAN'T POSSIBLY--
YOU BROUGHT THEM HERE! YOU AND YOUR KIND! NO AMOUNT OF SURFACE TREASURE IS WORTH THIS!
OKAY, MAYBE WE SHOULD ALL JUST CALM DOWN--
DON'T SPEAK TO ME IN THAT CONDESCENDING TONE, WOMAN!
"WOMAN"?
LOOK, I'M SORRY--
CLEARLY, BRINGING THESE FOLKS WAS A MISTAKE. BUT NEXT TIME--
"NEXT TIME"?! THERE IS NO NEXT TIME! THE TERMS OF OUR AGREEMENT HAVE BEEN VIOLATED!
I SHOULD HAVE YOU KILLED! BUT I DID ENJOY THE LAST SEASON OF THE LEFTOVERS, SO CONSIDER YOURSELVES BANISHED.
YOU KNOW THE WAY OUT.
--TURNS OUT WE'RE NOT DONE LOSING...

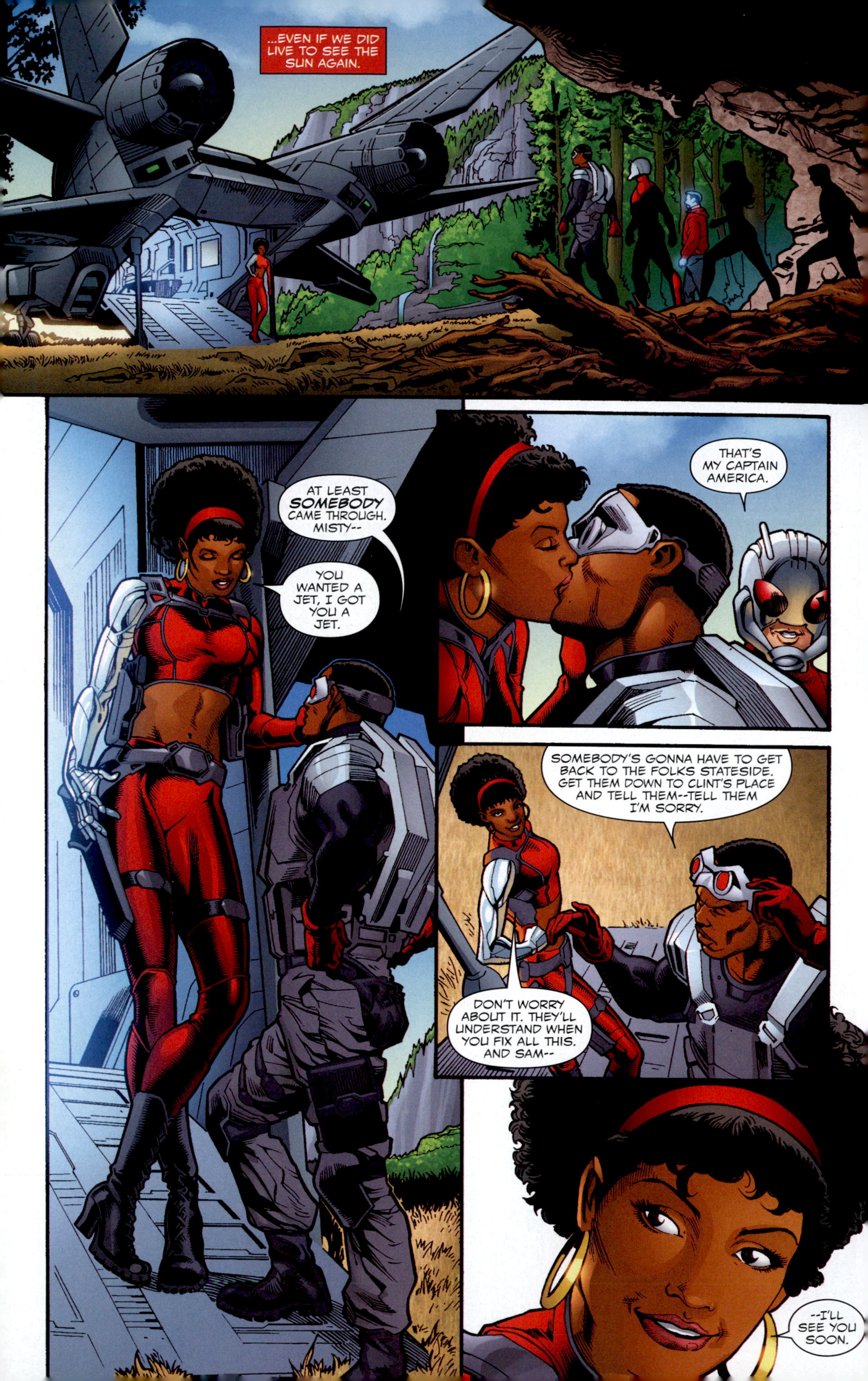
...EVEN IF WE DID LIVE TO SEE THE SUN AGAIN.
AT LEAST SOMEBODY CAME THROUGH. MISTY--
YOU WANTED A JET, I GOT YOU A JET.
THAT'S MY CAPTAIN AMERICA.
SOMEBODY'S GONNA HAVE TO GET BACK TO THE FOLKS STATESIDE. GET THEM DOWN TO CLINT'S PLACE AND TELL THEM--TELL THEM I'M SORRY.
DON'T WORRY ABOUT IT. THEY'LL UNDERSTAND WHEN YOU FIX ALL THIS. AND SAM--
--I'LL SEE YOU SOON.

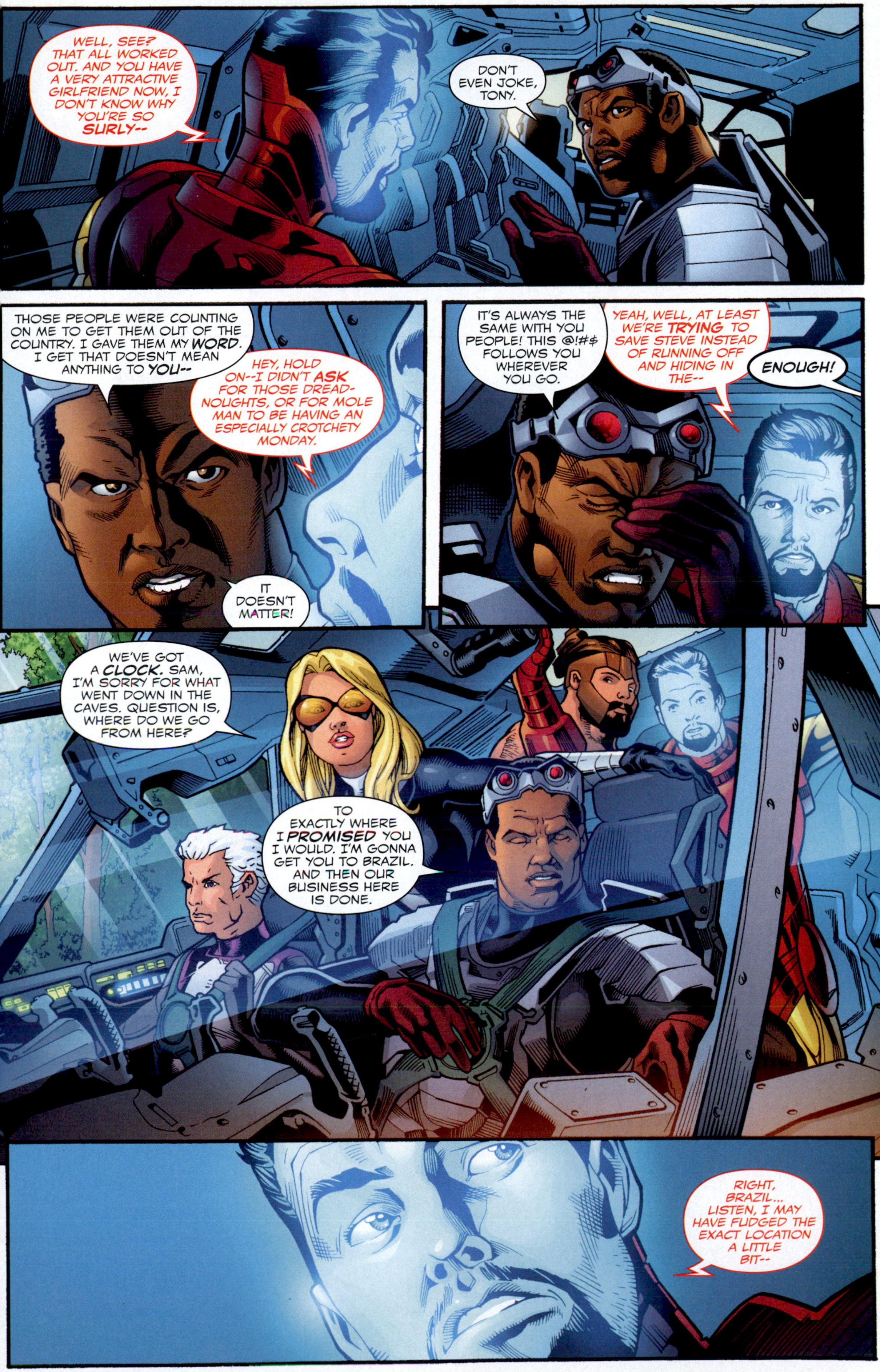
WELL, SEE? THAT ALL WORKED OUT. AND YOU HAVE A VERY ATTRACTIVE GIRLFRIEND NOW, I DON'T KNOW WHY YOU'RE SO SURLY--
DON'T EVEN JOKE, TONY.
THOSE PEOPLE WERE COUNTING ON ME TO GET THEM OUT OF THE COUNTRY. I GAVE THEM MY WORD. I GET THAT DOESN'T MEAN ANYTHING TO YOU--
HEY, HOLD ON--I DIDN'T ASK FOR THOSE DREADNOUGHTS, OR FOR MOLE MAN TO BE HAVING AN ESPECIALLY CROTCHETY MONDAY.
IT DOESN'T MATTER!
IT'S ALWAYS THE SAME WITH YOU PEOPLE! THIS @!#$ FOLLOWS YOU WHEREVER YOU GO.
YEAH, WELL, AT LEAST WE'RE TRYING TO SAVE STEVE INSTEAD OF RUNNING OFF AND HIDING IN THE--
ENOUGH!
WE'VE GOT A CLOCK. SAM, I'M SORRY FOR WHAT WENT DOWN IN THE CAVES. QUESTION IS, WHERE DO WE GO FROM HERE?
TO EXACTLY WHERE I PROMISED YOU I WOULD. I'M GONNA GET YOU TO BRAZIL. AND THEN OUR BUSINESS HERE IS DONE.
RIGHT, BRAZIL... LISTEN, I MAY HAVE FUDGED THE EXACT LOCATION A LITTLE BIT--

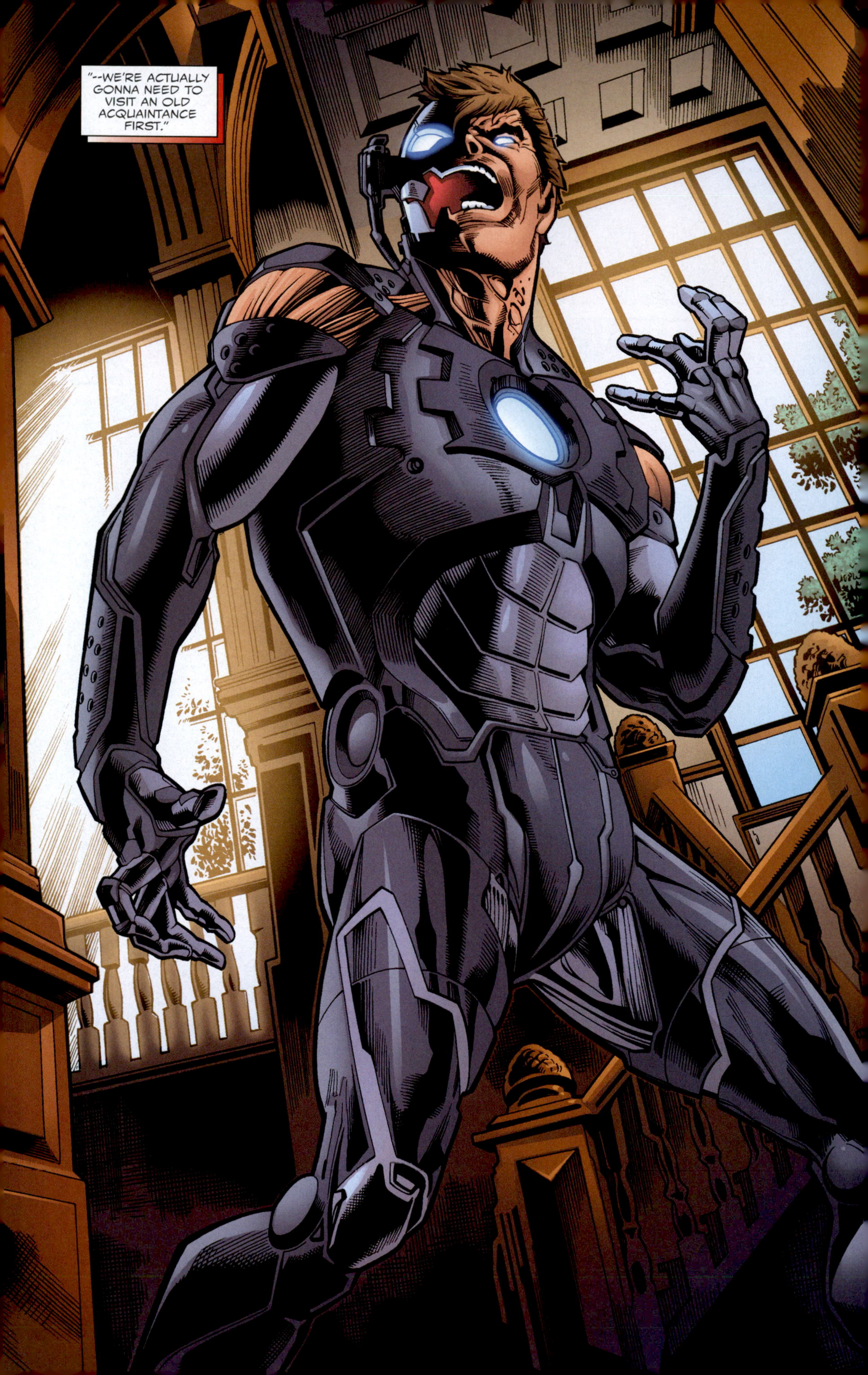
"--WE'RE ACTUALLY GONNA NEED TO VISIT AN OLD ACQUAINTANCE FIRST."

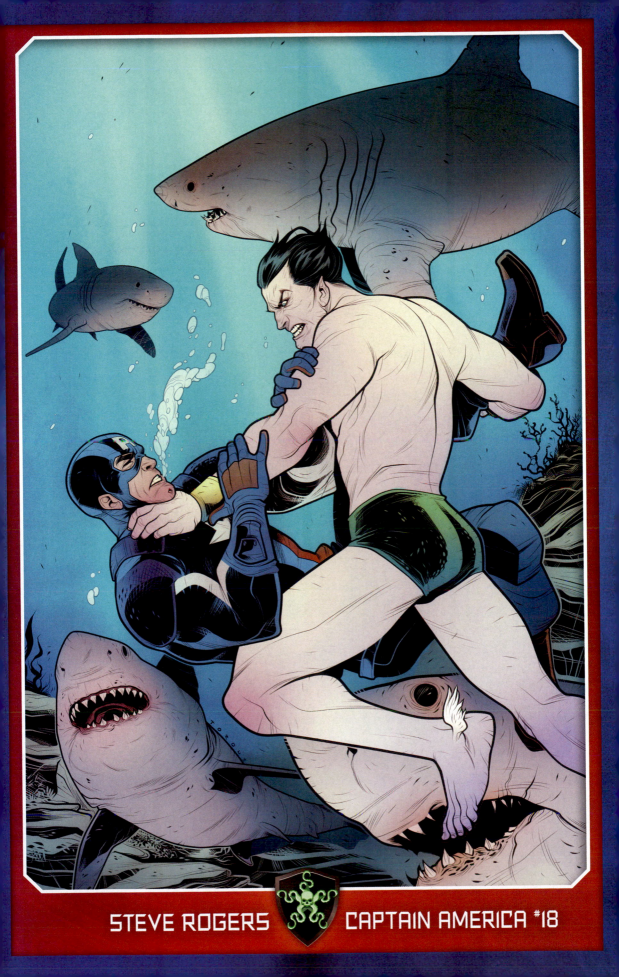

STEVE ROGERS   CAPTAIN AMERICA #18

Super-Soldier. Avenger. Agent of Hydra. He is...

Steve ★ Rogers
CAPTAIN AMERICA

A Cosmic Cube transformed Steve Rogers, Captain America, into the ultimate Hydra sleeper agent. After months of careful manipulation, Steve Rogers took control of S.H.I.E.L.D. and used a moment of international crisis to claim the United States for Hydra.

But with the shattered pieces of the Cosmic Cube hidden across the world, Steve hasn't been able to achieve his goal of rewriting reality in Hydra's image--and asserting Hydra's global dominance without its help is proving to be a challenge.

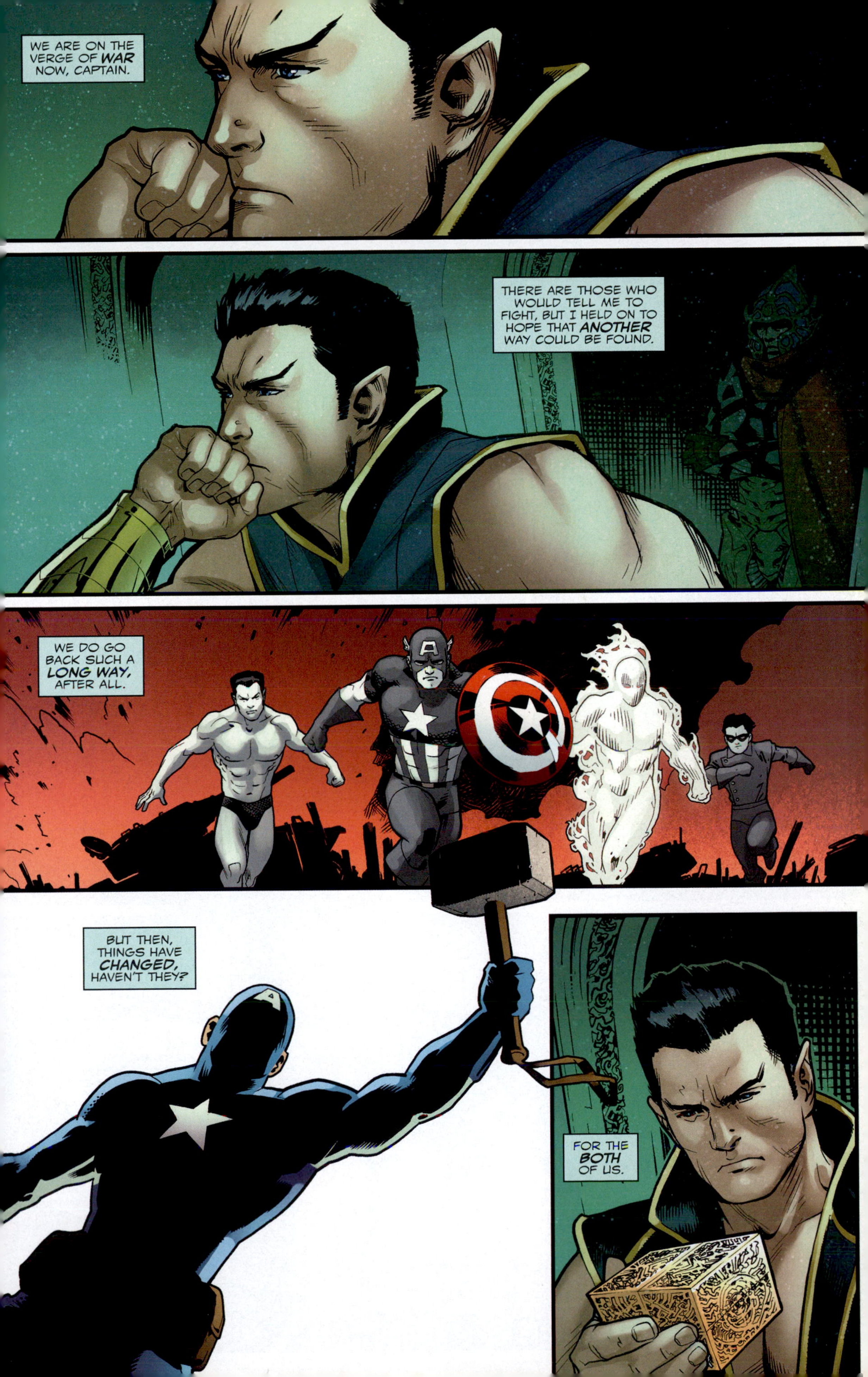

WE ARE ON THE VERGE OF WAR NOW, CAPTAIN.
THERE ARE THOSE WHO WOULD TELL ME TO FIGHT, BUT I HELD ON TO HOPE THAT ANOTHER WAY COULD BE FOUND.
WE DO GO BACK SUCH A LONG WAY, AFTER ALL.
BUT THEN, THINGS HAVE CHANGED, HAVEN'T THEY?
FOR THE BOTH OF US.

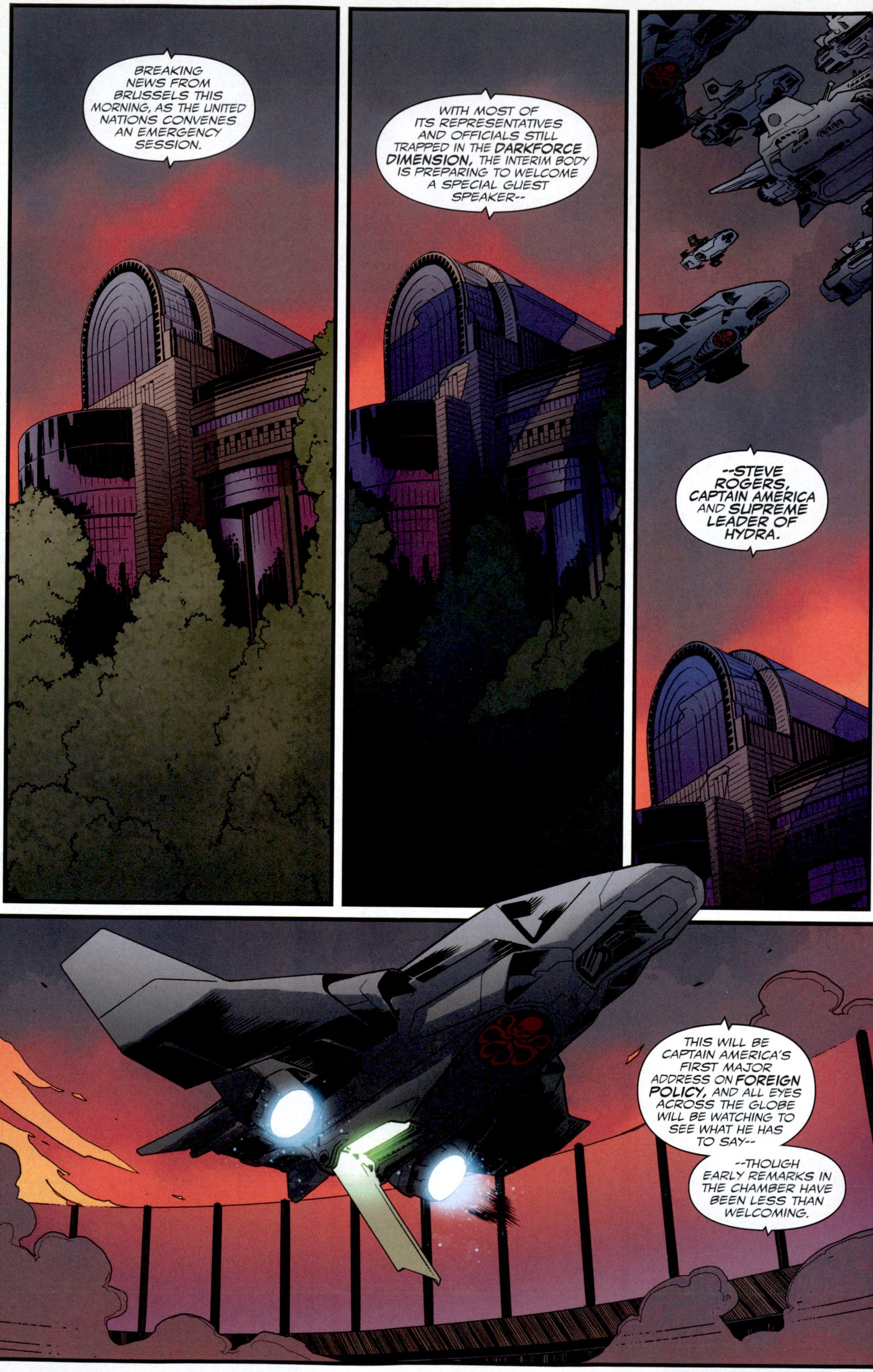
BREAKING NEWS FROM BRUSSELS THIS MORNING, AS THE UNITED NATIONS CONVENES AN EMERGENCY SESSION.
WITH MOST OF ITS REPRESENTATIVES AND OFFICIALS STILL TRAPPED IN THE DARKFORCE DIMENSION, THE INTERIM BODY IS PREPARING TO WELCOME A SPECIAL GUEST SPEAKER--
--STEVE ROGERS, CAPTAIN AMERICA AND SUPREME LEADER OF HYDRA.
THIS WILL BE CAPTAIN AMERICA'S FIRST MAJOR ADDRESS ON FOREIGN POLICY, AND ALL EYES ACROSS THE GLOBE WILL BE WATCHING TO SEE WHAT HE HAS TO SAY--
--THOUGH EARLY REMARKS IN THE CHAMBER HAVE BEEN LESS THAN WELCOMING.

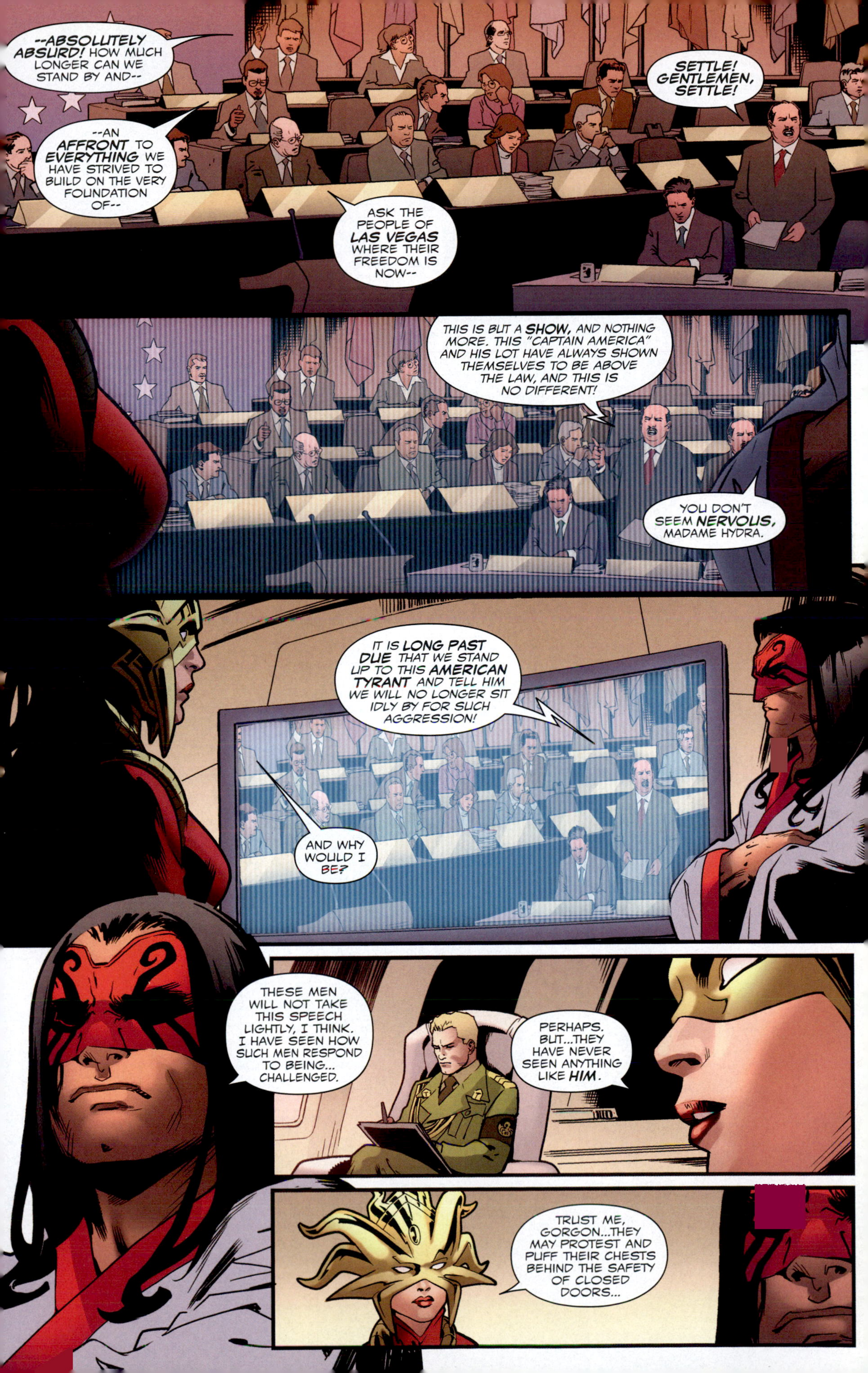

--ABSOLUTELY ABSURD! HOW MUCH LONGER CAN WE STAND BY AND--
--AN AFFRONT TO EVERYTHING WE HAVE STRIVED TO BUILD ON THE VERY FOUNDATION OF--
ASK THE PEOPLE OF LAS VEGAS WHERE THEIR FREEDOM IS NOW--
SETTLE! GENTLEMEN, SETTLE!
THIS IS BUT A SHOW, AND NOTHING MORE. THIS "CAPTAIN AMERICA" AND HIS LOT HAVE ALWAYS SHOWN THEMSELVES TO BE ABOVE THE LAW, AND THIS IS NO DIFFERENT!
YOU DON'T SEEM NERVOUS, MADAME HYDRA.
IT IS LONG PAST DUE THAT WE STAND UP TO THIS AMERICAN TYRANT AND TELL HIM WE WILL NO LONGER SIT IDLY BY FOR SUCH AGGRESSION!
AND WHY WOULD I BE?
THESE MEN WILL NOT TAKE THIS SPEECH LIGHTLY, I THINK. I HAVE SEEN HOW SUCH MEN RESPOND TO BEING... CHALLENGED.
PERHAPS. BUT...THEY HAVE NEVER SEEN ANYTHING LIKE HIM.
TRUST ME, GORGON...THEY MAY PROTEST AND PUFF THEIR CHESTS BEHIND THE SAFETY OF CLOSED DOORS...

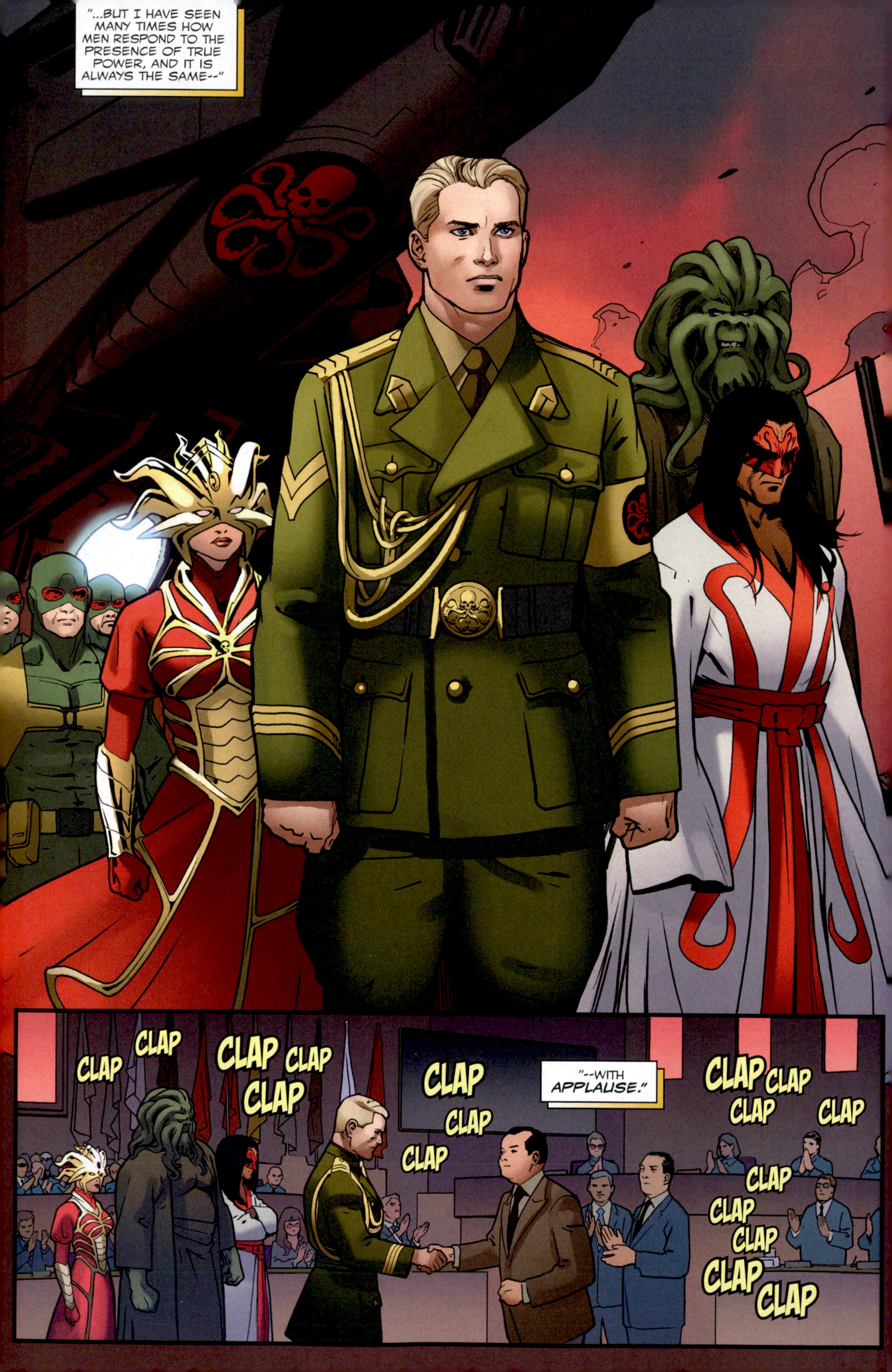
"...BUT I HAVE SEEN MANY TIMES HOW MEN RESPOND TO THE PRESENCE OF TRUE POWER, AND IT IS ALWAYS THE SAME--"
CLAP
CLAP
CLAP
CLAP
CLAP
CLAP
CLAP
CLAP
"--WITH APPLAUSE."
CLAP
CLAP
CLAP
CLAP
CLAP
CLAP
CLAP
CLAP
CLAP

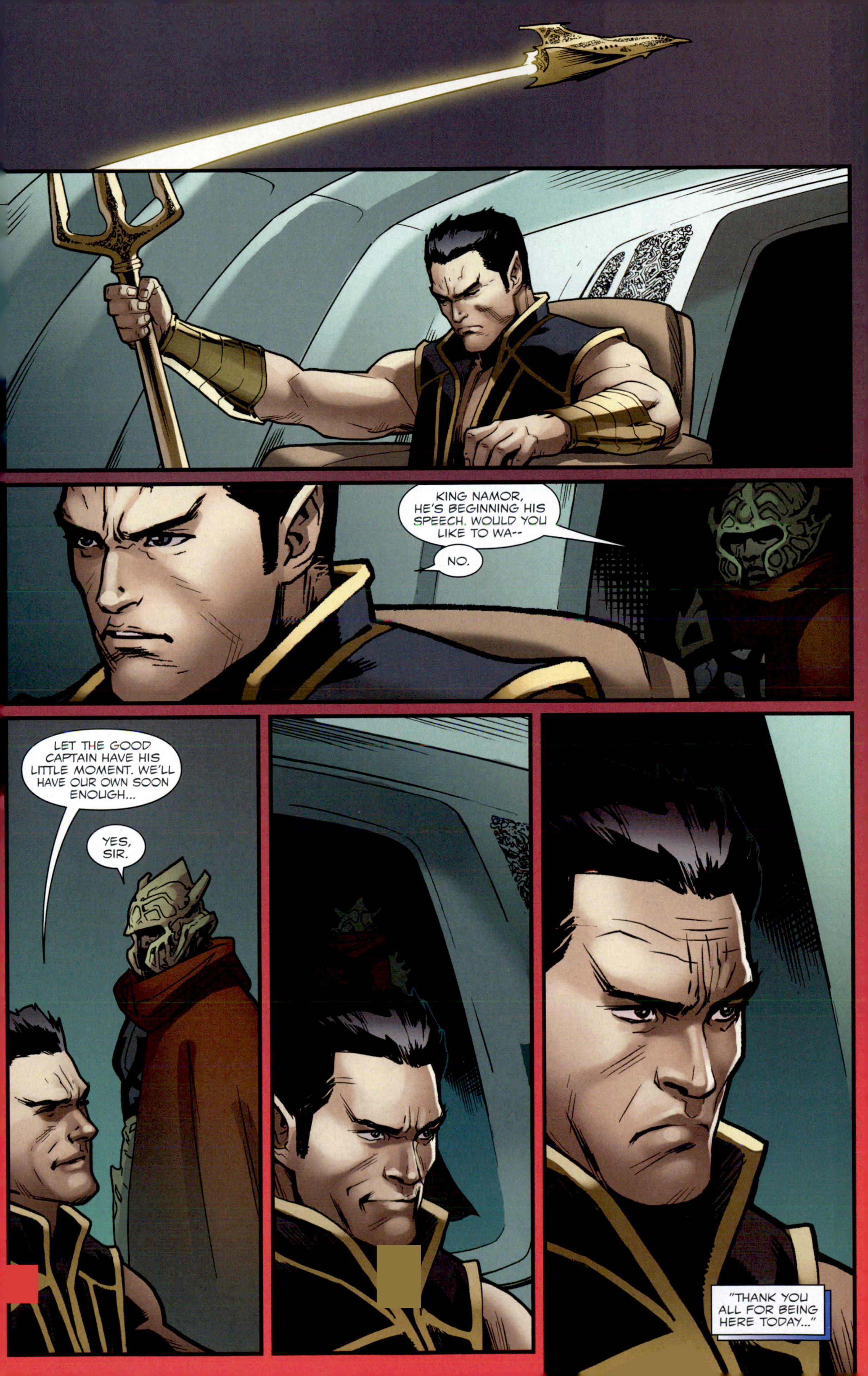
KING NAMOR, HE'S BEGINNING HIS SPEECH. WOULD YOU LIKE TO WA--
NO.
LET THE GOOD CAPTAIN HAVE HIS LITTLE MOMENT. WE'LL HAVE OUR OWN SOON ENOUGH...
YES, SIR.
"THANK YOU ALL FOR BEING HERE TODAY..."

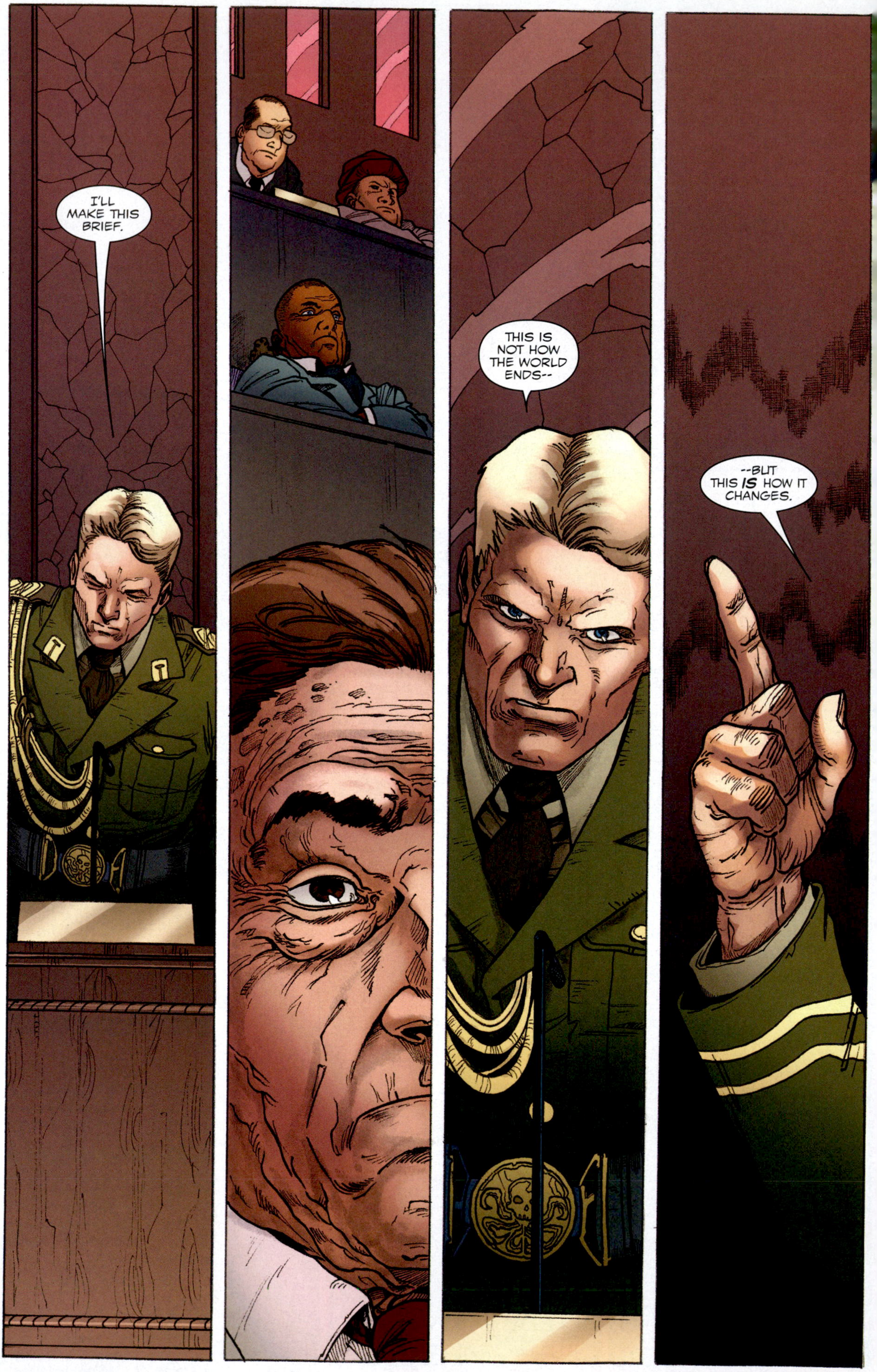
I'LL MAKE THIS BRIEF.
THIS IS NOT HOW THE WORLD ENDS--
--BUT THIS IS HOW IT CHANGES.

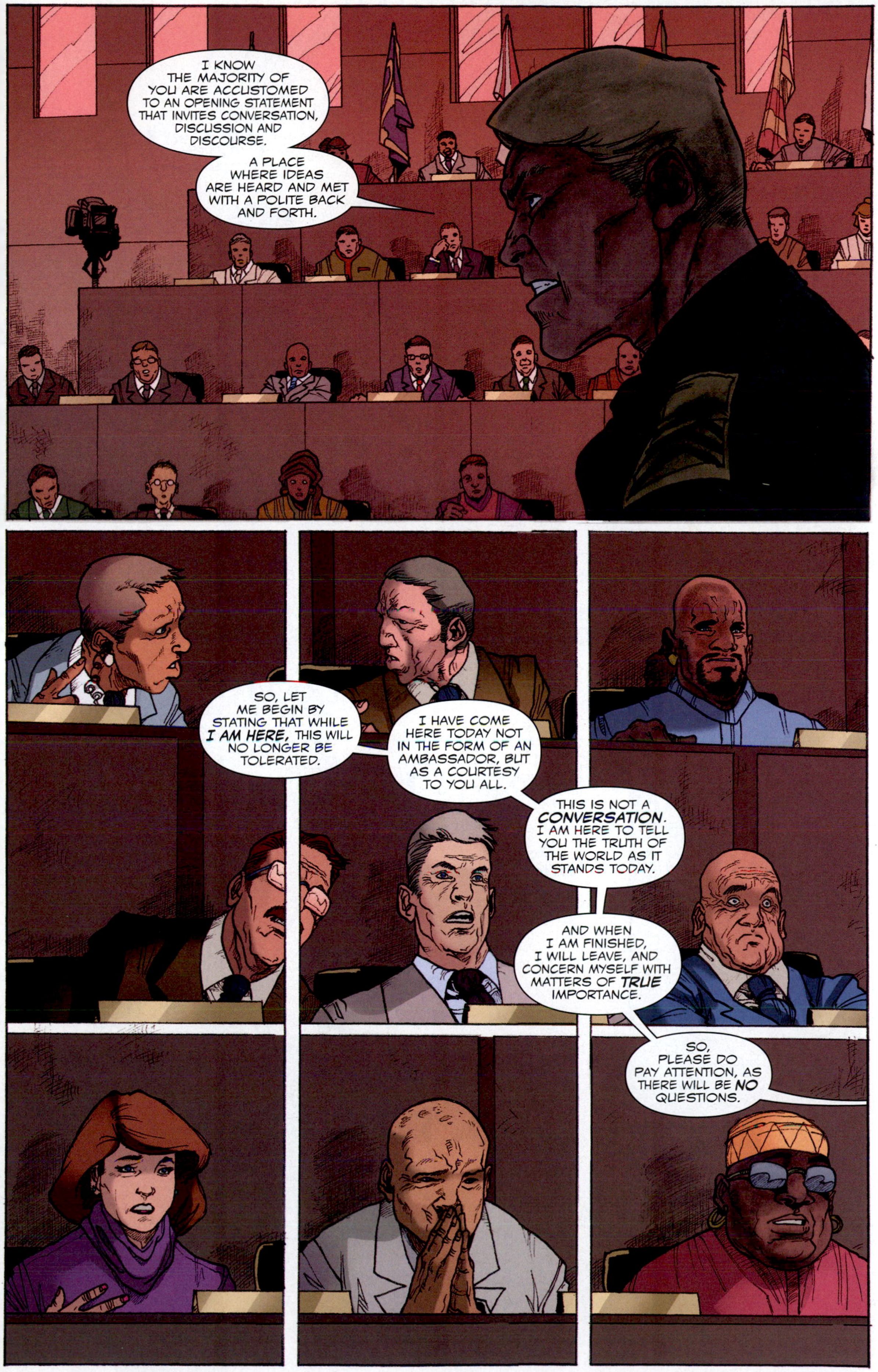
I KNOW THE MAJORITY OF YOU ARE ACCUSTOMED TO AN OPENING STATEMENT THAT INVITES CONVERSATION, DISCUSSION AND DISCOURSE.
A PLACE WHERE IDEAS ARE HEARD AND MET WITH A POLITE BACK AND FORTH.
SO, LET ME BEGIN BY STATING THAT WHILE *I AM HERE,* THIS WILL NO LONGER BE TOLERATED.
I HAVE COME HERE TODAY NOT IN THE FORM OF AN AMBASSADOR, BUT AS A COURTESY TO YOU ALL.
THIS IS NOT A *CONVERSATION*. I AM HERE TO TELL YOU THE TRUTH OF THE WORLD AS IT STANDS TODAY.
AND WHEN I AM FINISHED, I WILL LEAVE, AND CONCERN MYSELF WITH MATTERS OF *TRUE* IMPORTANCE.
SO, PLEASE DO PAY ATTENTION, AS THERE WILL BE *NO* QUESTIONS.

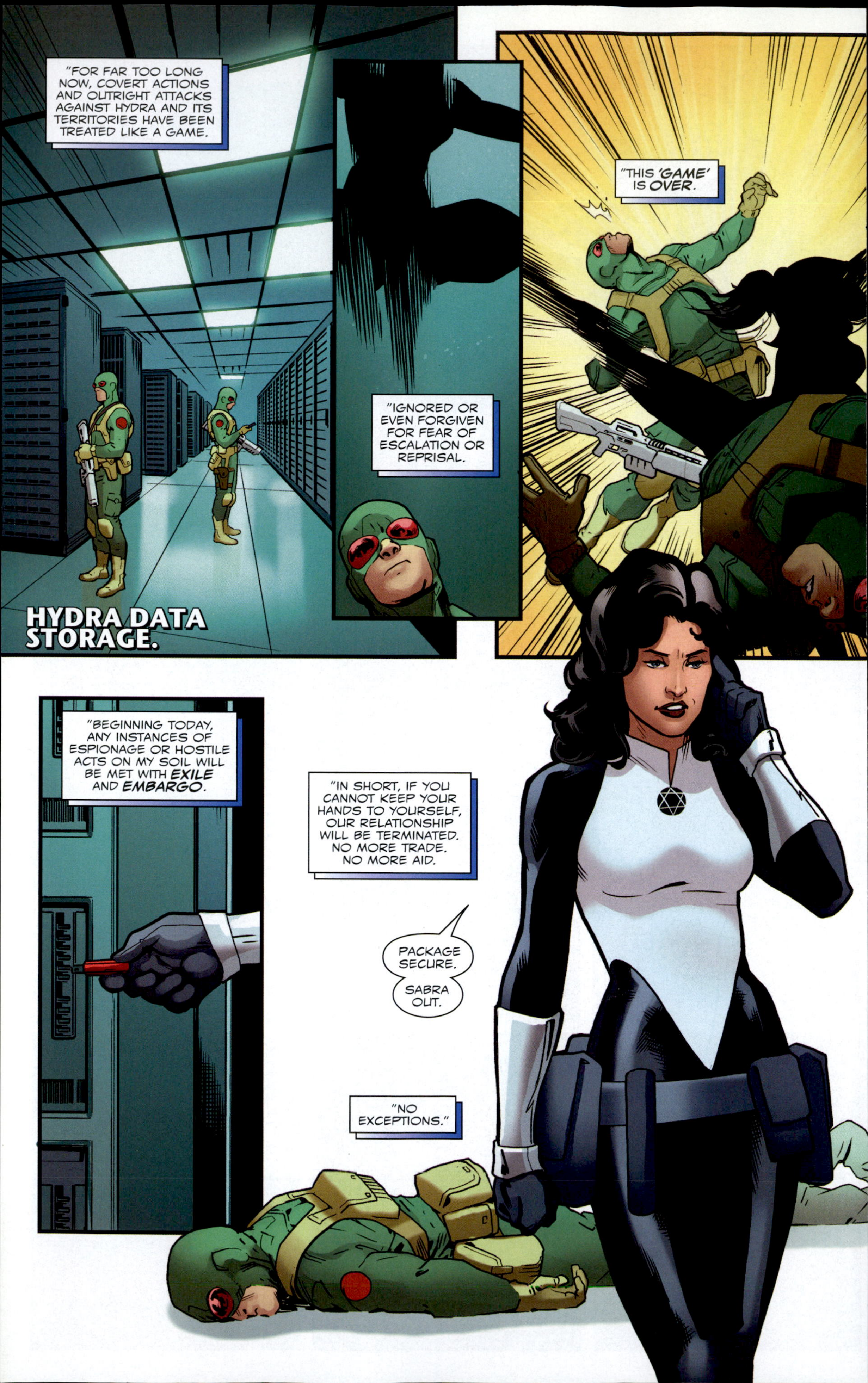
"FOR FAR TOO LONG NOW, COVERT ACTIONS AND OUTRIGHT ATTACKS AGAINST HYDRA AND ITS TERRITORIES HAVE BEEN TREATED LIKE A GAME.
HYDRA DATA STORAGE.
"IGNORED OR EVEN FORGIVEN FOR FEAR OF ESCALATION OR REPRISAL.
"THIS 'GAME' IS OVER.
"BEGINNING TODAY, ANY INSTANCES OF ESPIONAGE OR HOSTILE ACTS ON MY SOIL WILL BE MET WITH EXILE AND EMBARGO.
"IN SHORT, IF YOU CANNOT KEEP YOUR HANDS TO YOURSELF, OUR RELATIONSHIP WILL BE TERMINATED. NO MORE TRADE. NO MORE AID.
PACKAGE SECURE.
SABRA OUT.
"NO EXCEPTIONS."

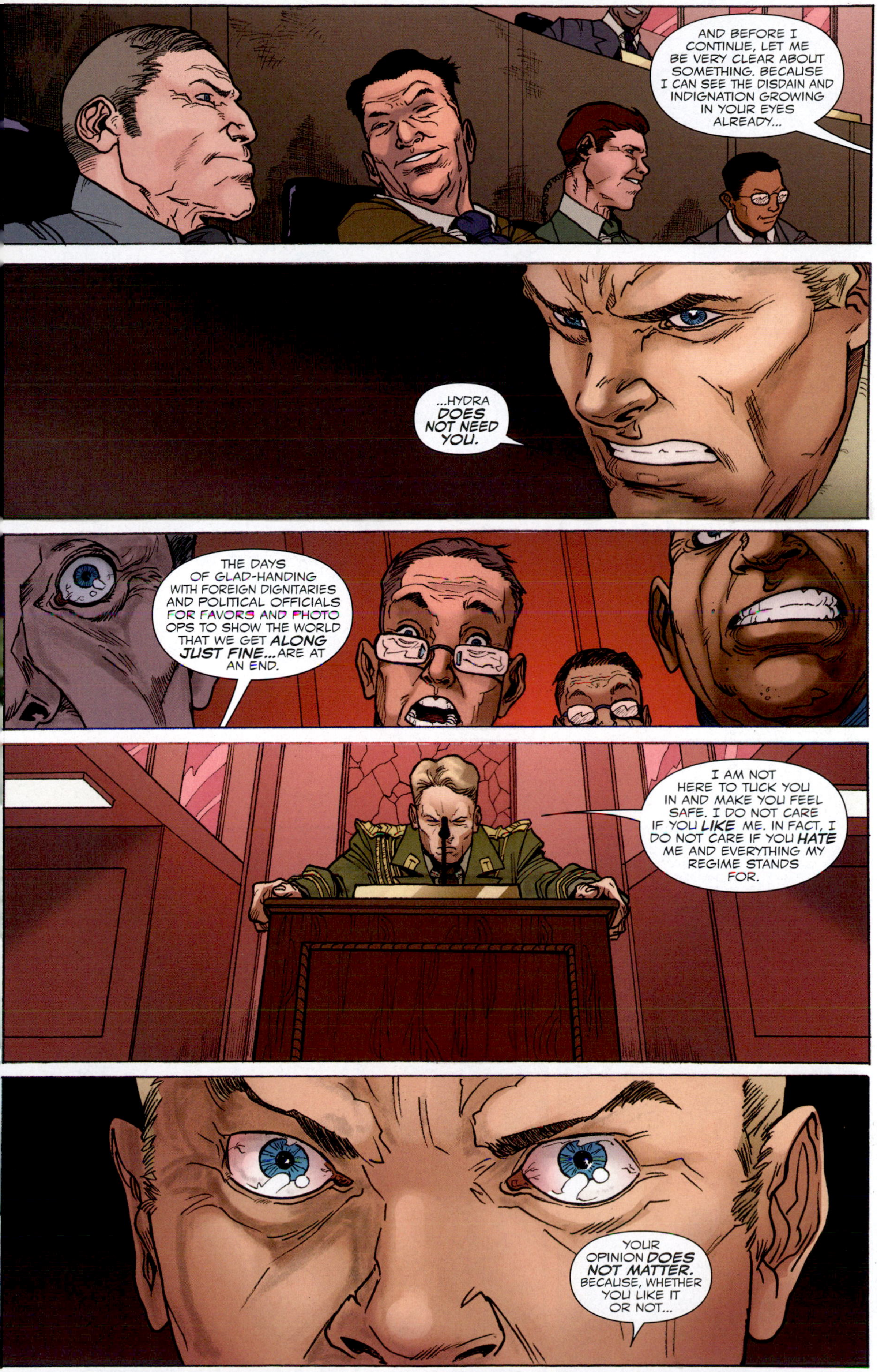
AND BEFORE I CONTINUE, LET ME BE VERY CLEAR ABOUT SOMETHING. BECAUSE I CAN SEE THE DISDAIN AND INDIGNATION GROWING IN YOUR EYES ALREADY...
...HYDRA DOES NOT NEED YOU.
THE DAYS OF GLAD-HANDING WITH FOREIGN DIGNITARIES AND POLITICAL OFFICIALS FOR FAVORS AND PHOTO OPS TO SHOW THE WORLD THAT WE GET ALONG JUST FINE...ARE AT AN END.
I AM NOT HERE TO TUCK YOU IN AND MAKE YOU FEEL SAFE. I DO NOT CARE IF YOU LIKE ME. IN FACT, I DO NOT CARE IF YOU HATE ME AND EVERYTHING MY REGIME STANDS FOR.
YOUR OPINION DOES NOT MATTER. BECAUSE, WHETHER YOU LIKE IT OR NOT...

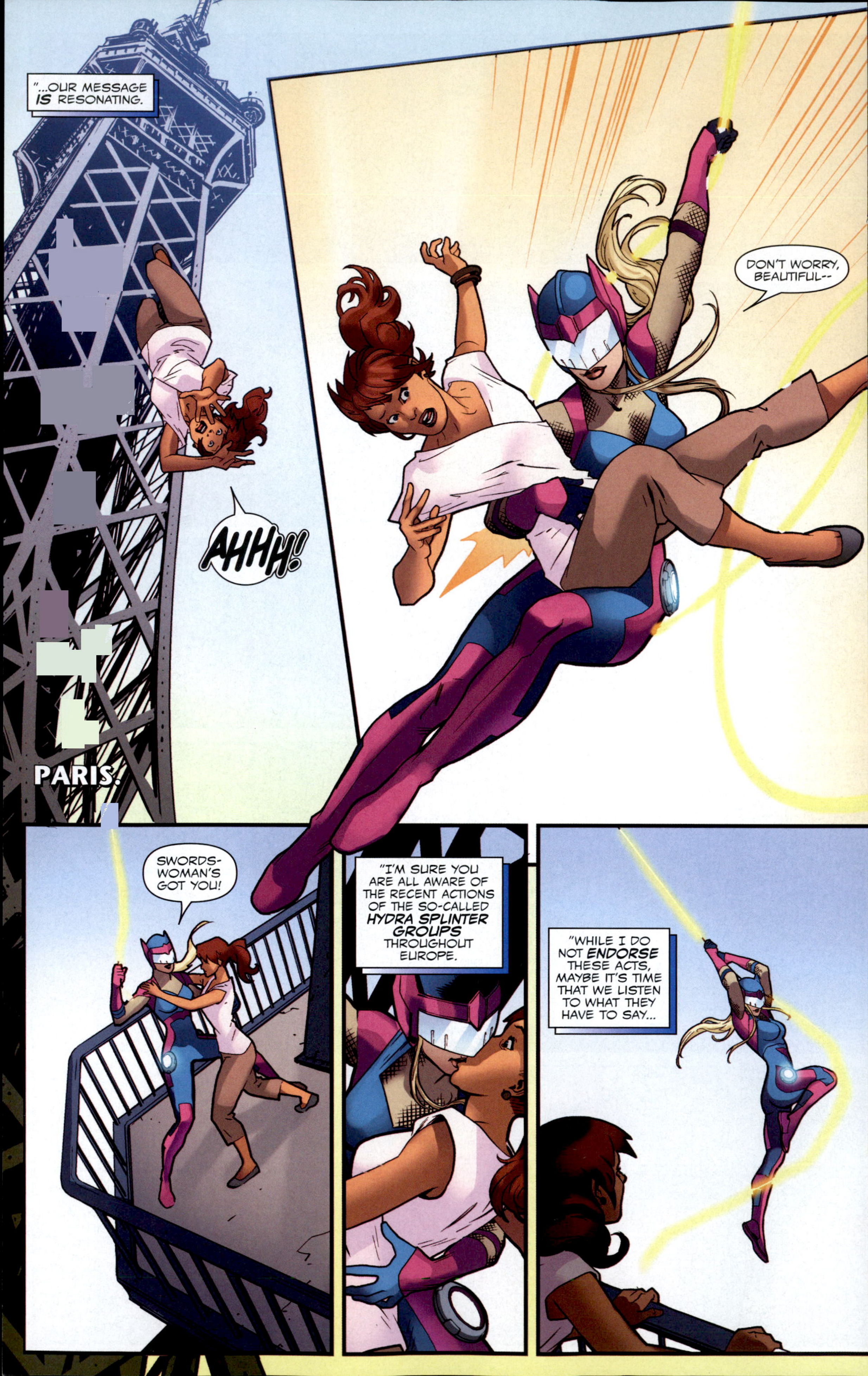
"...OUR MESSAGE IS RESONATING.
PARIS.
AHHH!
DON'T WORRY, BEAUTIFUL--
SWORDS-WOMAN'S GOT YOU!
"I'M SURE YOU ARE ALL AWARE OF THE RECENT ACTIONS OF THE SO-CALLED HYDRA SPLINTER GROUPS THROUGHOUT EUROPE.
"WHILE I DO NOT ENDORSE THESE ACTS, MAYBE IT'S TIME THAT WE LISTEN TO WHAT THEY HAVE TO SAY...

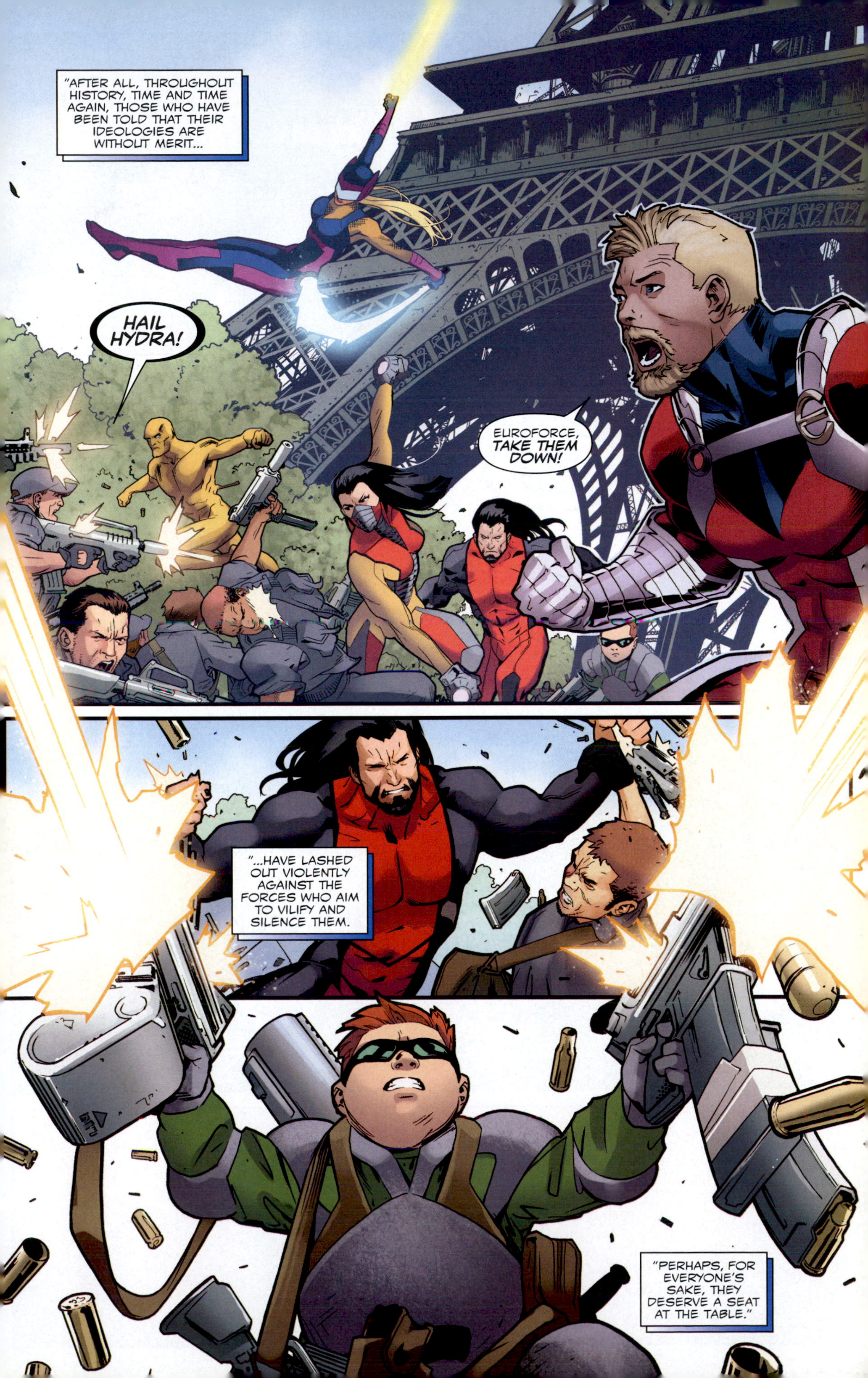
"AFTER ALL, THROUGHOUT HISTORY, TIME AND TIME AGAIN, THOSE WHO HAVE BEEN TOLD THAT THEIR IDEOLOGIES ARE WITHOUT MERIT...
HAIL HYDRA!
EUROFORCE, TAKE THEM DOWN!
"...HAVE LASHED OUT VIOLENTLY AGAINST THE FORCES WHO AIM TO VILIFY AND SILENCE THEM.
"PERHAPS, FOR EVERYONE'S SAKE, THEY DESERVE A SEAT AT THE TABLE."

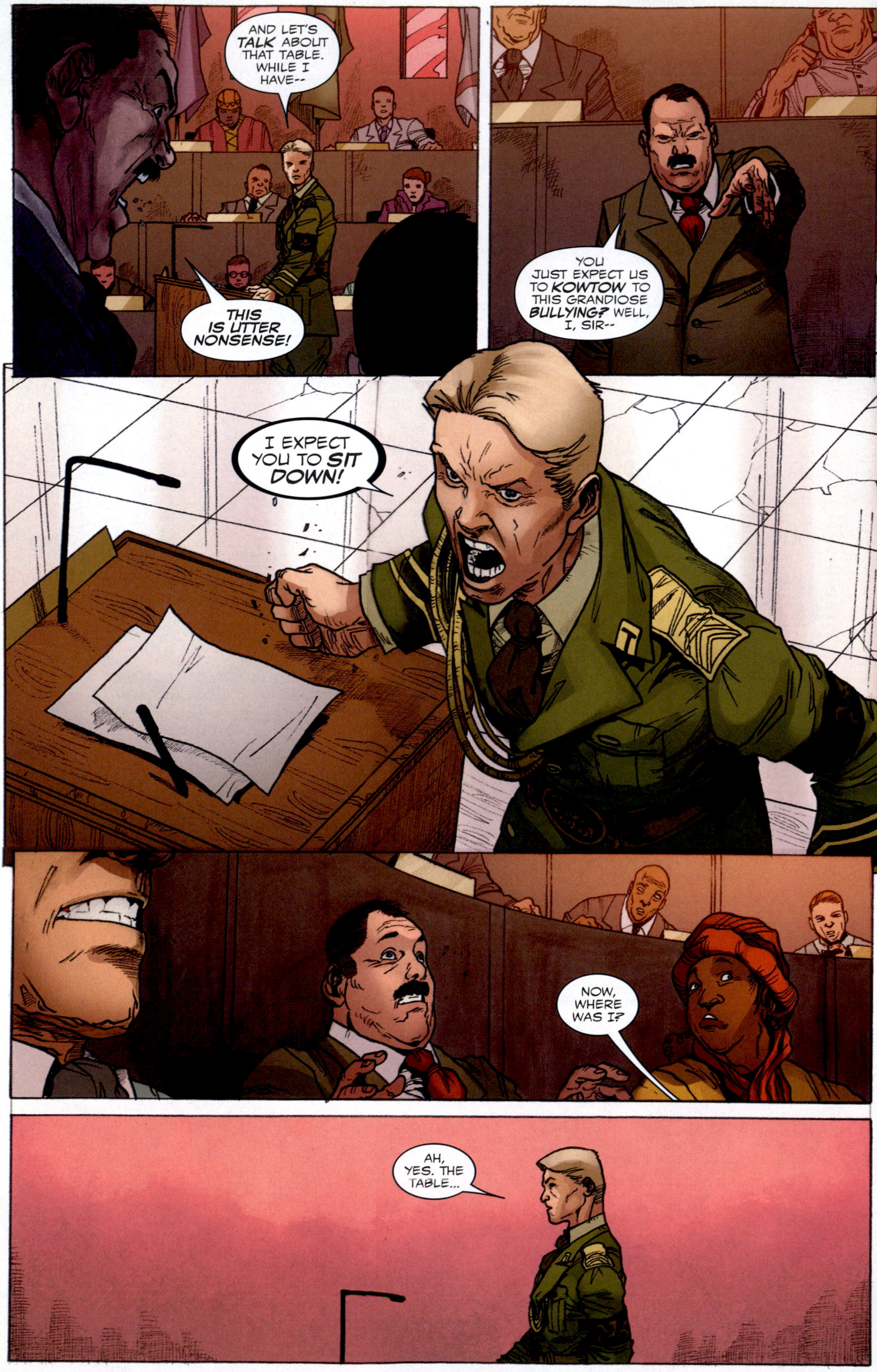
AND LET'S TALK ABOUT THAT TABLE. WHILE I HAVE--
THIS IS UTTER NONSENSE!
YOU JUST EXPECT US TO KOWTOW TO THIS GRANDIOSE BULLYING? WELL, I, SIR--
I EXPECT YOU TO SIT DOWN!
NOW, WHERE WAS I?
AH, YES. THE TABLE...

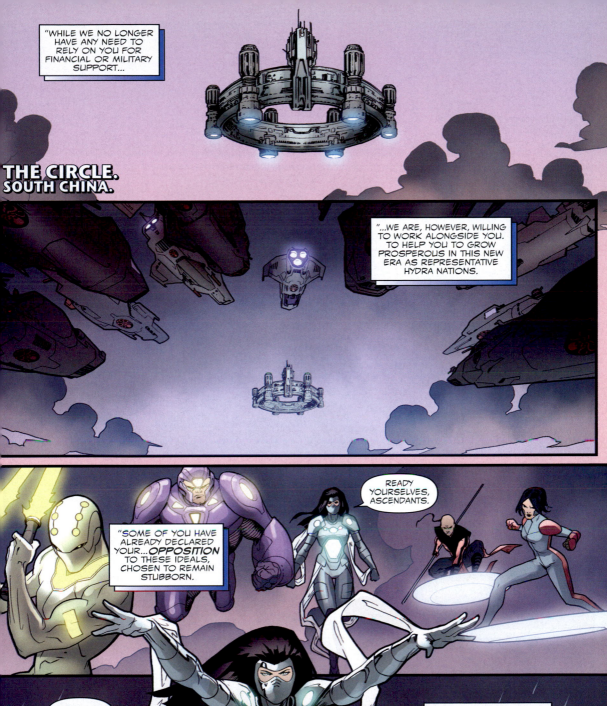

"WHILE WE NO LONGER HAVE ANY NEED TO RELY ON YOU FOR FINANCIAL OR MILITARY SUPPORT...

THE CIRCLE.
SOUTH CHINA.

"...WE ARE, HOWEVER, WILLING TO WORK ALONGSIDE YOU. TO HELP YOU TO GROW PROSPEROUS IN THIS NEW ERA AS REPRESENTATIVE HYDRA NATIONS.

READY YOURSELVES, ASCENDANTS.

"SOME OF YOU HAVE ALREADY DECLARED YOUR...*OPPOSITION* TO THESE IDEALS, CHOSEN TO REMAIN STUBBORN.

HYDRA WILL *NOT* TAKE THE CIRCLE.

"TO CONTINUE TO PLAY OUT YOUR ABSURD BORDER DISPUTES AND CLING TO YOUR FORMER SOVEREIGNTY.

"IT IS MY GREATEST WISH THAT YOU RECONSIDER THIS STANCE..."

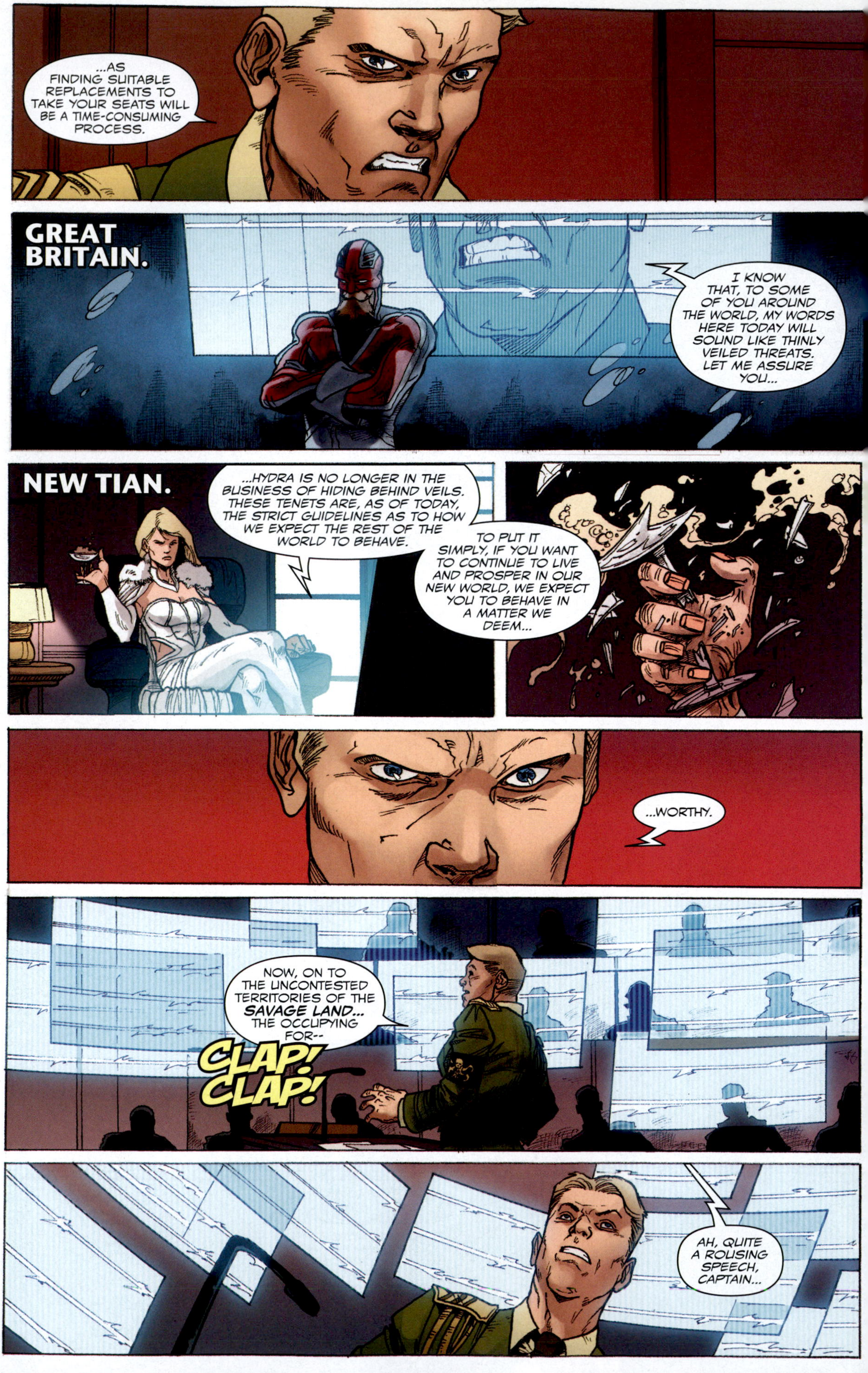
...AS FINDING SUITABLE REPLACEMENTS TO TAKE YOUR SEATS WILL BE A TIME-CONSUMING PROCESS.
GREAT BRITAIN.
I KNOW THAT, TO SOME OF YOU AROUND THE WORLD, MY WORDS HERE TODAY WILL SOUND LIKE THINLY VEILED THREATS. LET ME ASSURE YOU...
NEW TIAN.
...HYDRA IS NO LONGER IN THE BUSINESS OF HIDING BEHIND VEILS. THESE TENETS ARE, AS OF TODAY, THE STRICT GUIDELINES AS TO HOW WE EXPECT THE REST OF THE WORLD TO BEHAVE.
TO PUT IT SIMPLY, IF YOU WANT TO CONTINUE TO LIVE AND PROSPER IN OUR NEW WORLD, WE EXPECT YOU TO BEHAVE IN A MATTER WE DEEM...
...WORTHY.
NOW, ON TO THE UNCONTESTED TERRITORIES OF THE SAVAGE LAND... THE OCCUPYING FOR--
CLAP! CLAP!
AH, QUITE A ROUSING SPEECH, CAPTAIN...

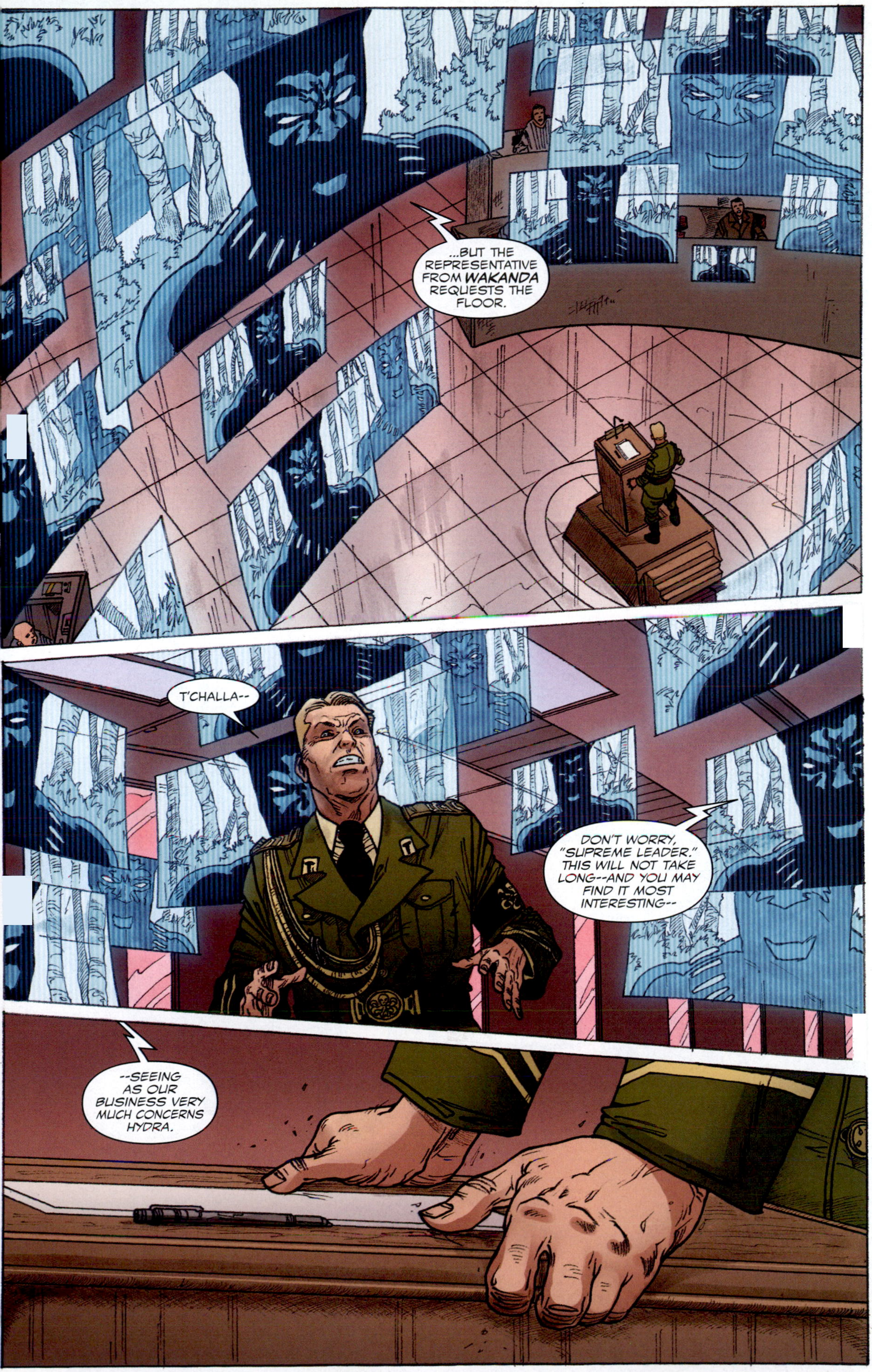
...BUT THE REPRESENTATIVE FROM WAKANDA REQUESTS THE FLOOR.
T'CHALLA--
DON'T WORRY, "SUPREME LEADER." THIS WILL NOT TAKE LONG--AND YOU MAY FIND IT MOST INTERESTING--
--SEEING AS OUR BUSINESS VERY MUCH CONCERNS HYDRA.

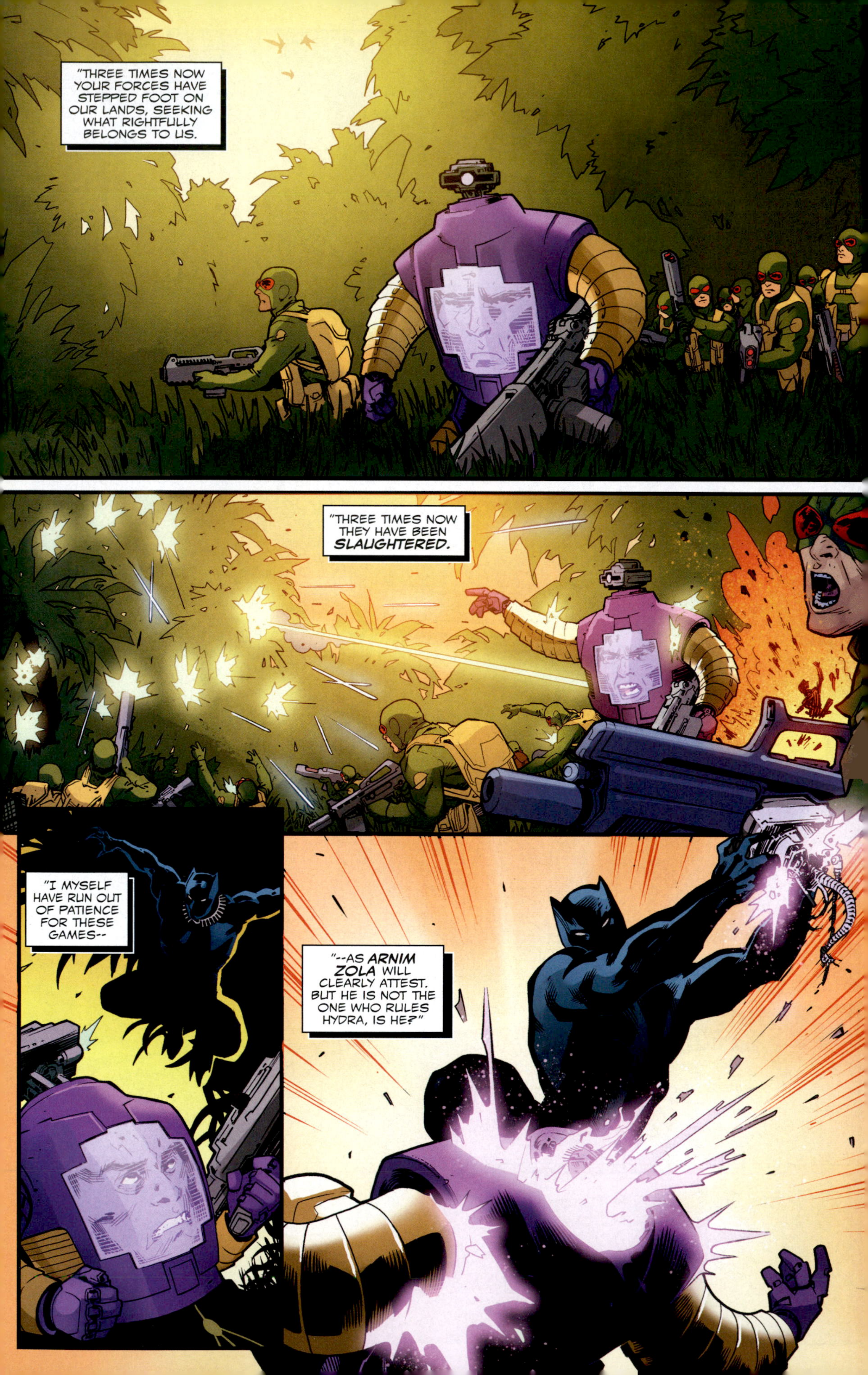
"THREE TIMES NOW YOUR FORCES HAVE STEPPED FOOT ON OUR LANDS, SEEKING WHAT RIGHTFULLY BELONGS TO US.
"THREE TIMES NOW THEY HAVE BEEN SLAUGHTERED.
"I MYSELF HAVE RUN OUT OF PATIENCE FOR THESE GAMES--
"--AS ARNIM ZOLA WILL CLEARLY ATTEST. BUT HE IS NOT THE ONE WHO RULES HYDRA, IS HE?"

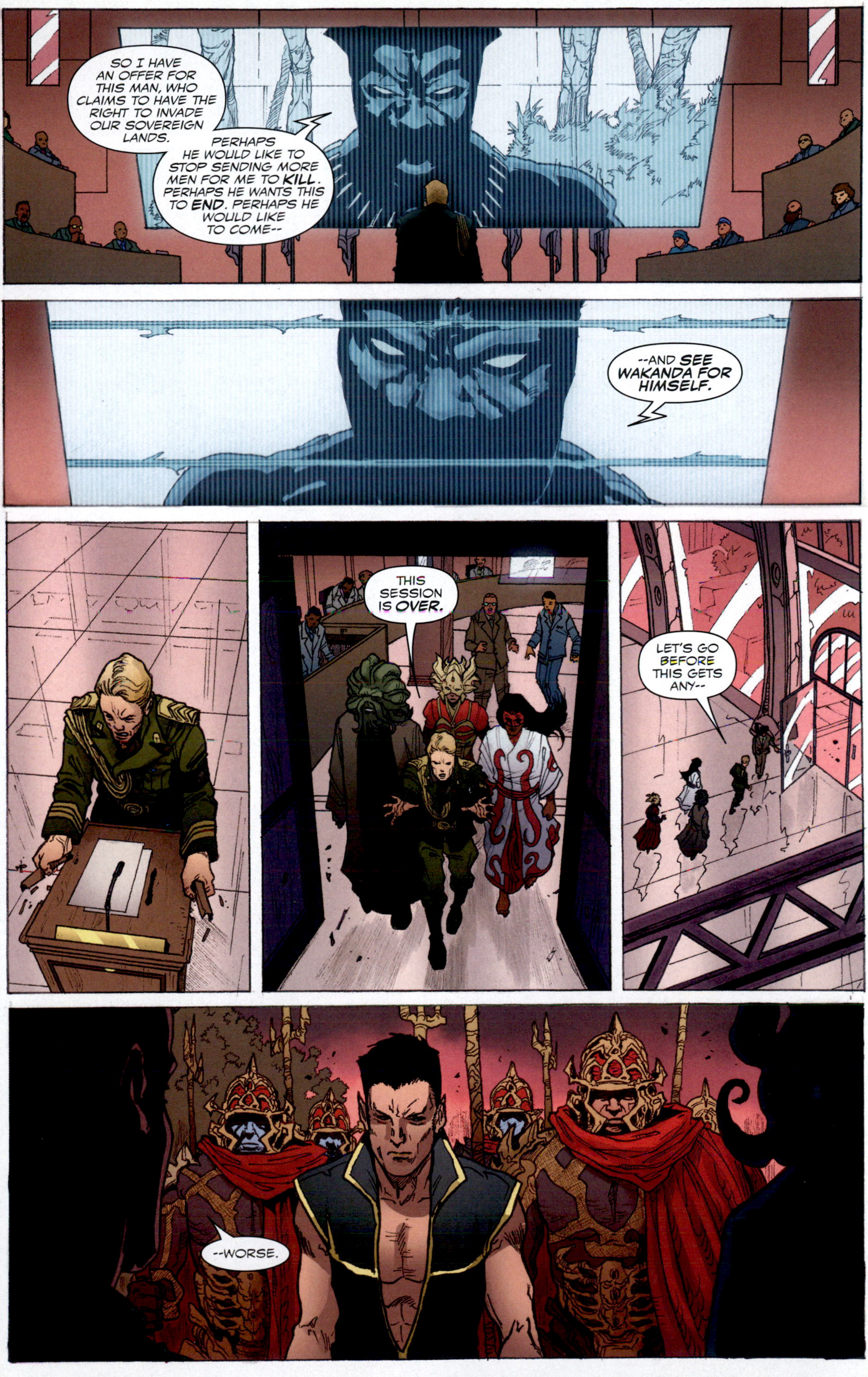
SO I HAVE AN OFFER FOR THIS MAN, WHO CLAIMS TO HAVE THE RIGHT TO INVADE OUR SOVEREIGN LANDS.
PERHAPS HE WOULD LIKE TO STOP SENDING MORE MEN FOR ME TO KILL. PERHAPS HE WANTS THIS TO END. PERHAPS HE WOULD LIKE TO COME--
--AND SEE WAKANDA FOR HIMSELF.
THIS SESSION IS OVER.
LET'S GO BEFORE THIS GETS ANY--
--WORSE.

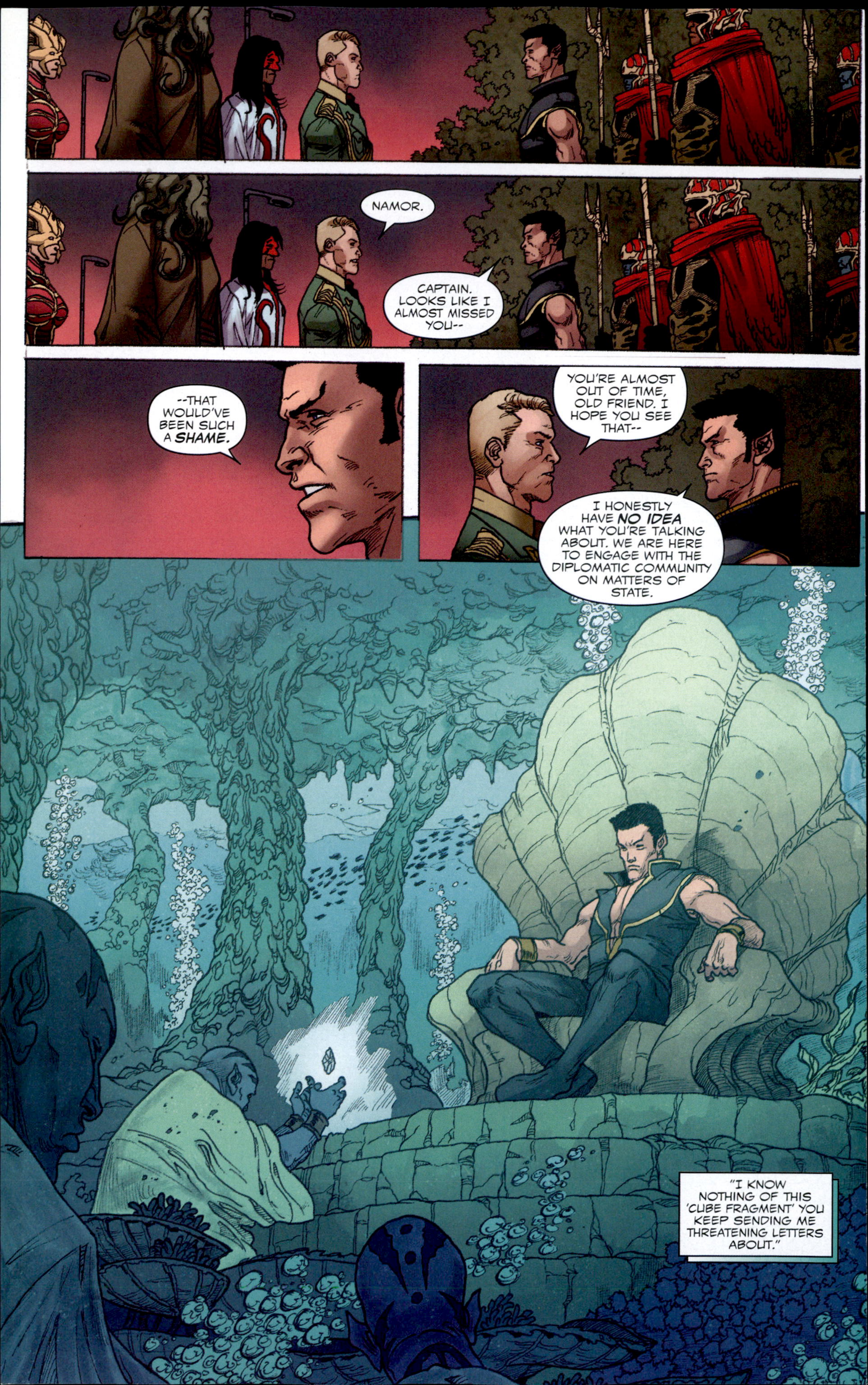
NAMOR.
CAPTAIN. LOOKS LIKE I ALMOST MISSED YOU--
--THAT WOULD'VE BEEN SUCH A SHAME.
YOU'RE ALMOST OUT OF TIME, OLD FRIEND. I HOPE YOU SEE THAT--
I HONESTLY HAVE NO IDEA WHAT YOU'RE TALKING ABOUT. WE ARE HERE TO ENGAGE WITH THE DIPLOMATIC COMMUNITY ON MATTERS OF STATE.
"I KNOW NOTHING OF THIS 'CUBE FRAGMENT' YOU KEEP SENDING ME THREATENING LETTERS ABOUT."

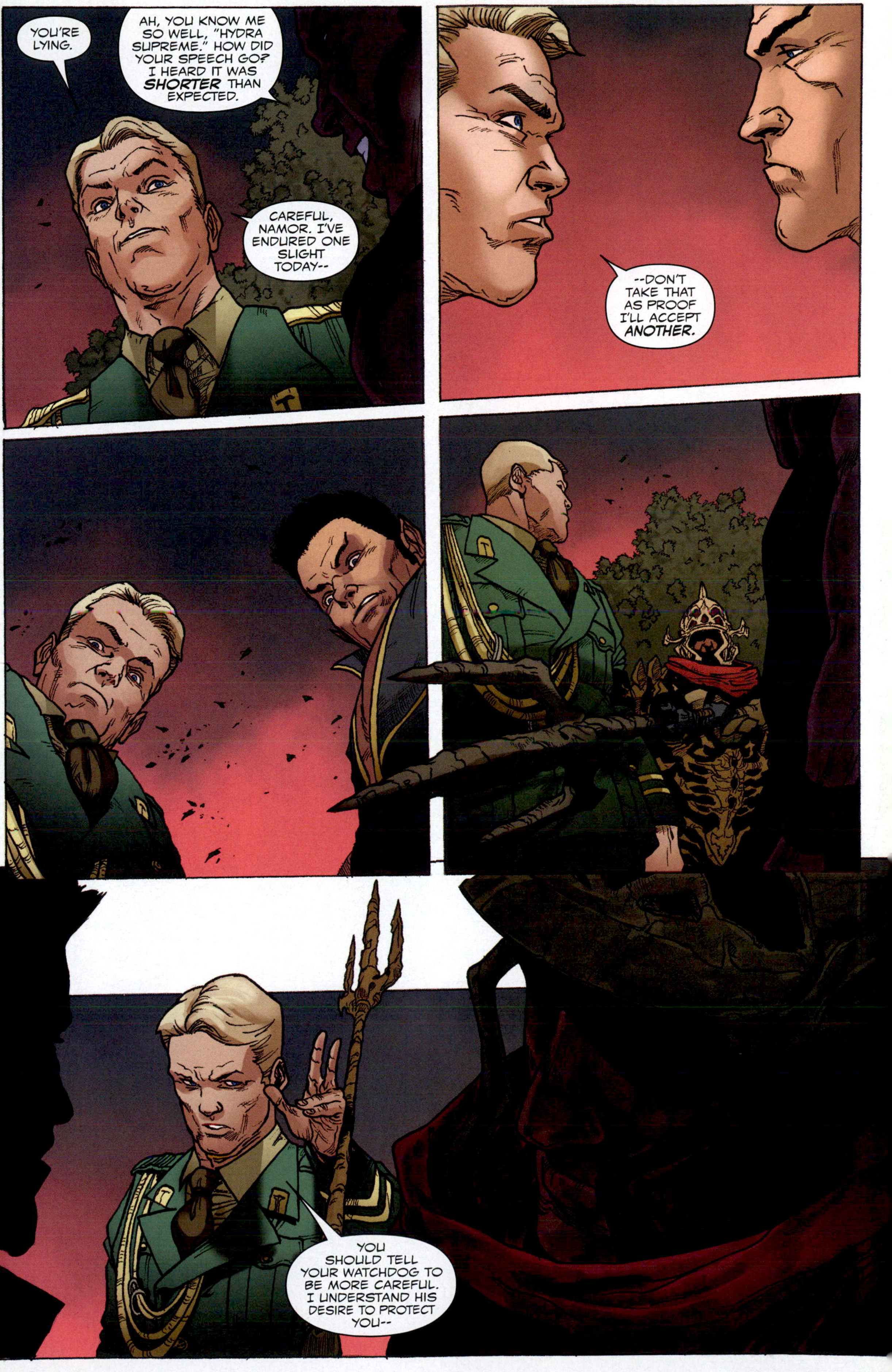
YOU'RE LYING.
AH, YOU KNOW ME SO WELL, "HYDRA SUPREME." HOW DID YOUR SPEECH GO? I HEARD IT WAS SHORTER THAN EXPECTED.
CAREFUL, NAMOR. I'VE ENDURED ONE SLIGHT TODAY--
--DON'T TAKE THAT AS PROOF I'LL ACCEPT ANOTHER.
YOU SHOULD TELL YOUR WATCHDOG TO BE MORE CAREFUL. I UNDERSTAND HIS DESIRE TO PROTECT YOU--

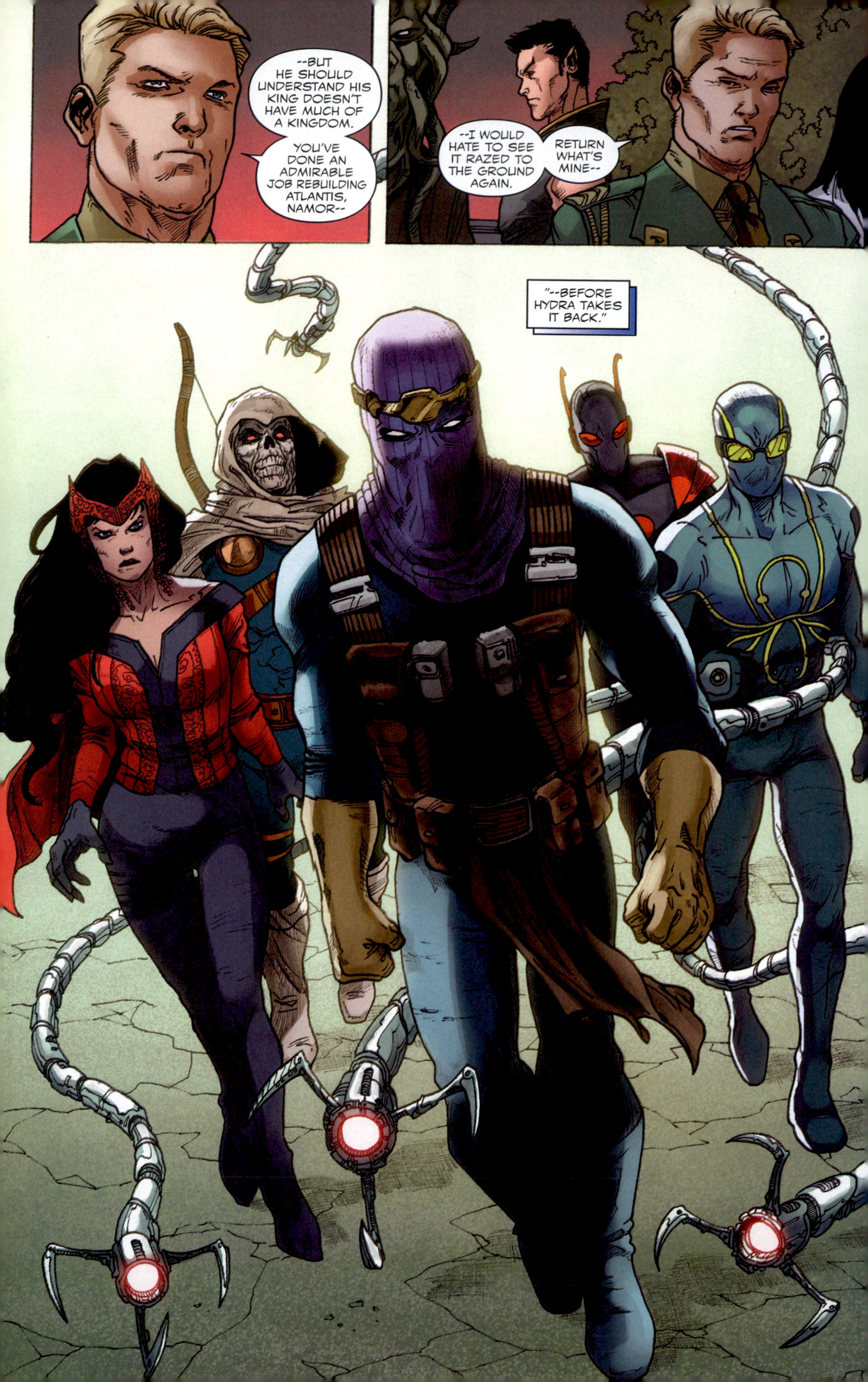
--BUT HE SHOULD UNDERSTAND HIS KING DOESN'T HAVE MUCH OF A KINGDOM.
YOU'VE DONE AN ADMIRABLE JOB REBUILDING ATLANTIS, NAMOR--
RETURN WHAT'S MINE--
--I WOULD HATE TO SEE IT RAZED TO THE GROUND AGAIN.
"--BEFORE HYDRA TAKES IT BACK."

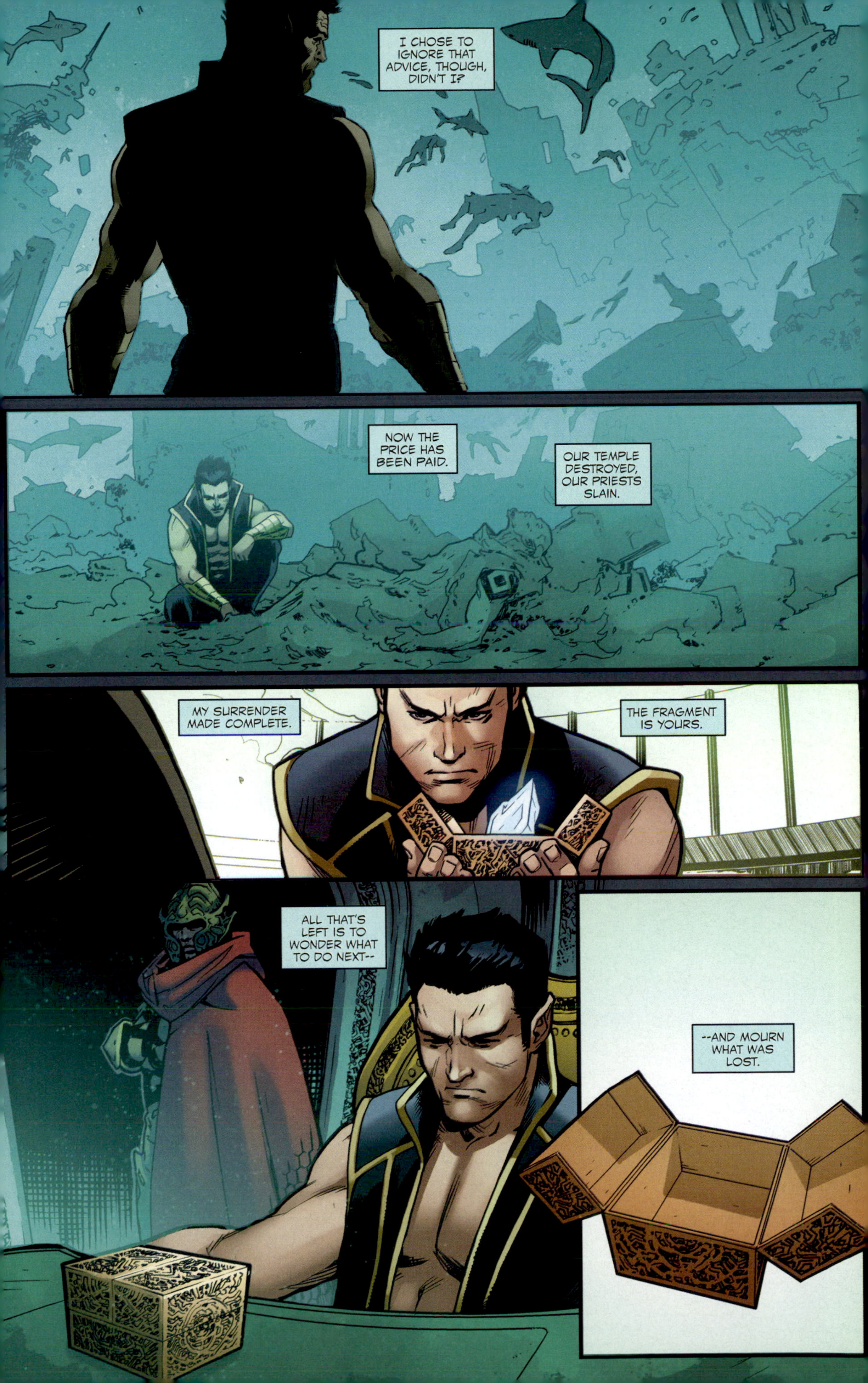

I CHOSE TO IGNORE THAT ADVICE, THOUGH, DIDN'T I?
NOW THE PRICE HAS BEEN PAID.
OUR TEMPLE DESTROYED, OUR PRIESTS SLAIN.
MY SURRENDER MADE COMPLETE.
THE FRAGMENT IS YOURS.
ALL THAT'S LEFT IS TO WONDER WHAT TO DO NEXT--
--AND MOURN WHAT WAS LOST.

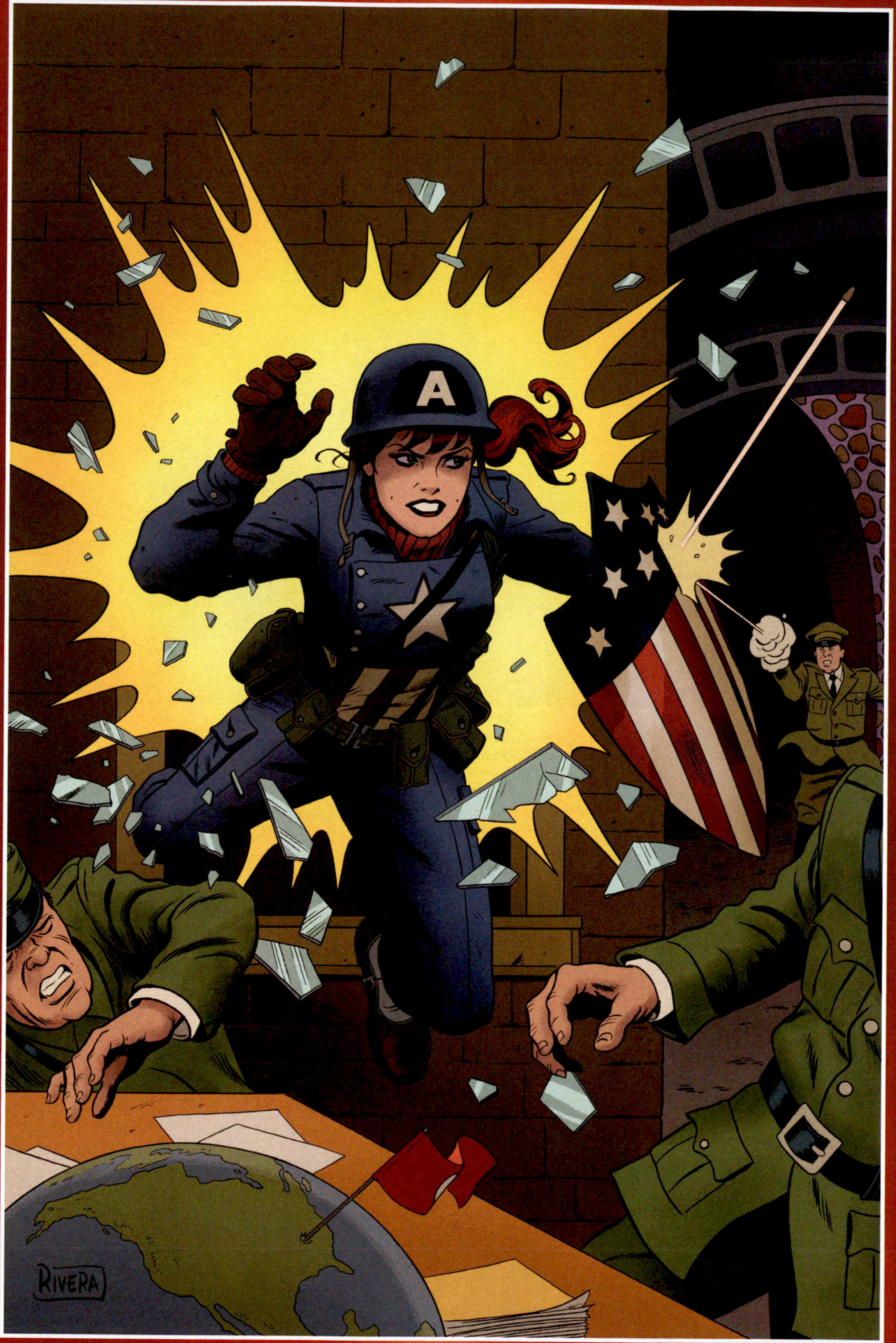
RIVERA

Paolo Rivera

CAPTAIN AMERICA: STEVE ROGERS #18 MARY JANE VARIANT

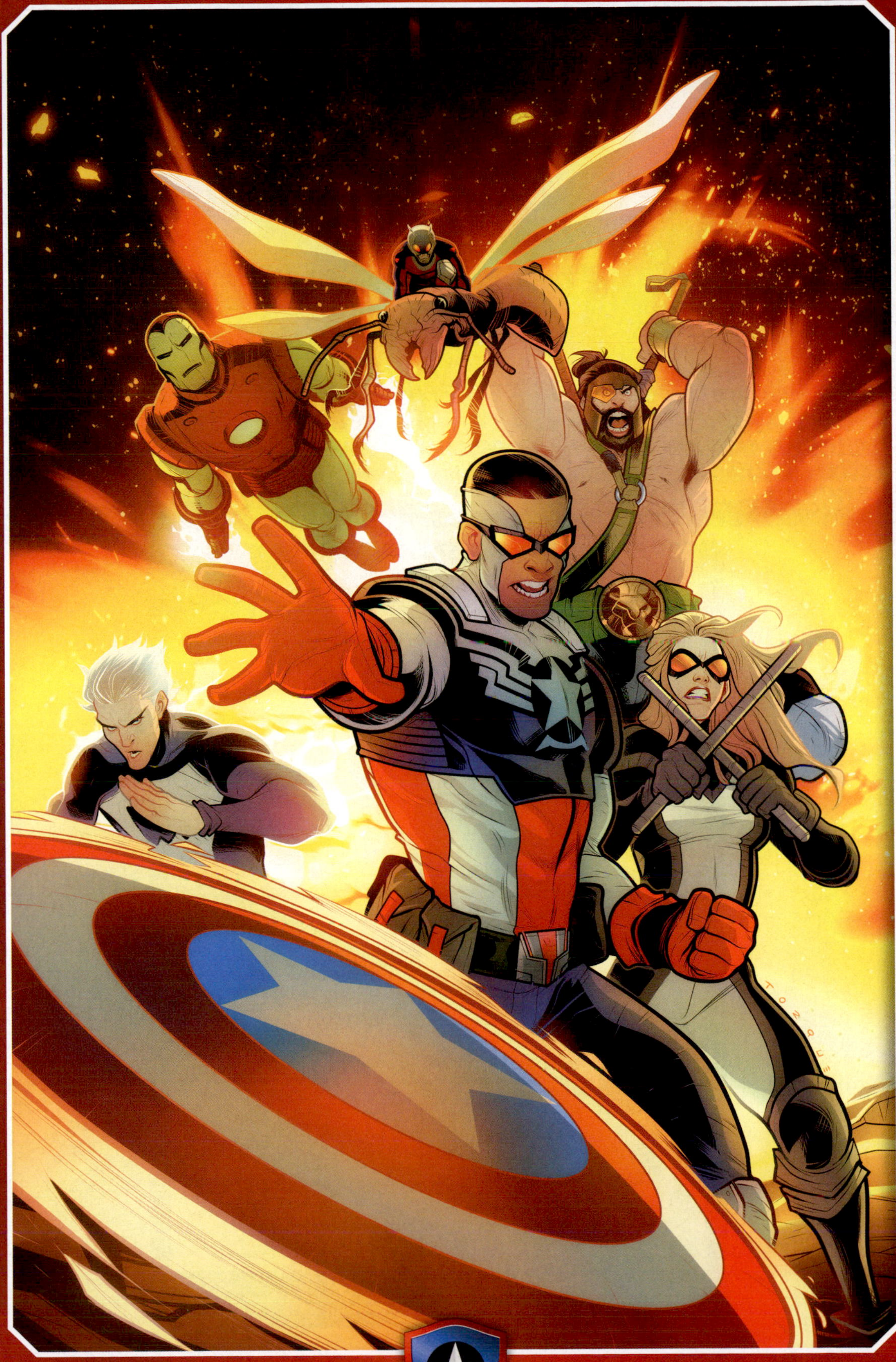

SAM WILSON CAPTAIN AMERICA #24

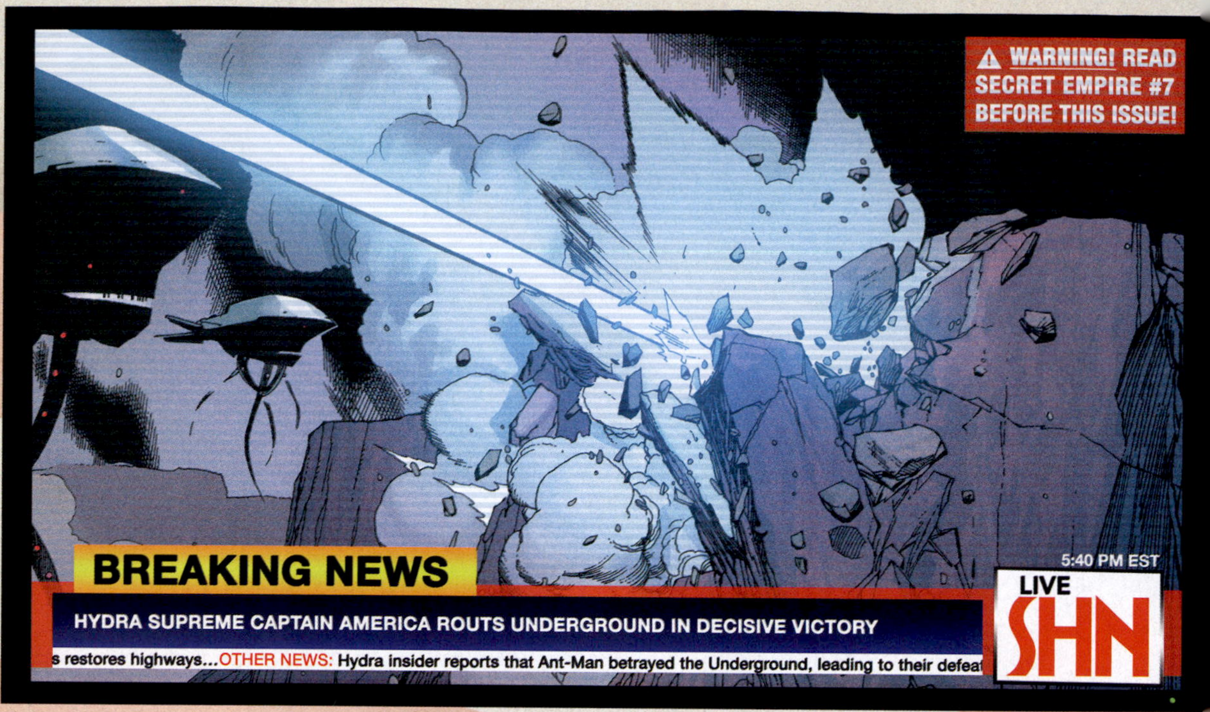
⚠ WARNING! READ SECRET EMPIRE #7 BEFORE THIS ISSUE!
BREAKING NEWS
HYDRA SUPREME CAPTAIN AMERICA ROUTS UNDERGROUND IN DECISIVE VICTORY
s restores highways...OTHER NEWS: Hydra insider reports that Ant-Man betrayed the Underground, leading to their defea
5:40 PM EST
LIVE
SHN

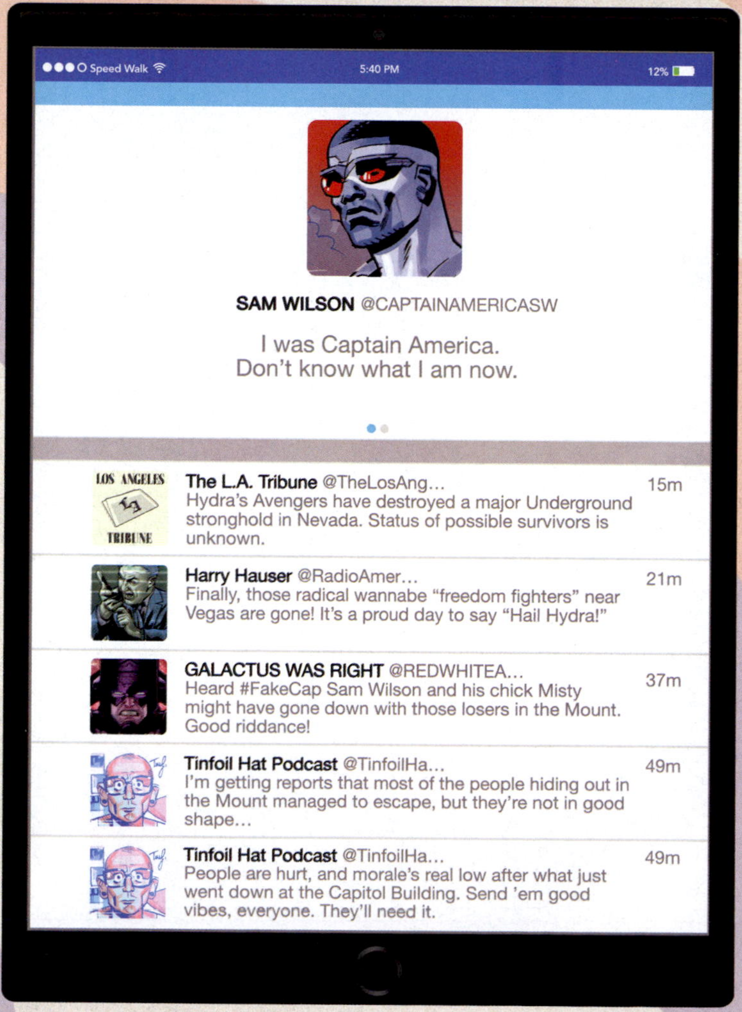
Speed Walk
5:40 PM
12%
SAM WILSON @CAPTAINAMERICASW
I was Captain America.
Don't know what I am now.
LOS ANGELES TRIBUNE
The L.A. Tribune @TheLosAng... 15m
Hydra's Avengers have destroyed a major Underground stronghold in Nevada. Status of possible survivors is unknown.
Harry Hauser @RadioAmer... 21m
Finally, those radical wannabe "freedom fighters" near Vegas are gone! It's a proud day to say "Hail Hydra!"
GALACTUS WAS RIGHT @REDWHITEA... 37m
Heard #FakeCap Sam Wilson and his chick Misty might have gone down with those losers in the Mount. Good riddance!
Tinfoil Hat Podcast @TinfoilHa... 49m
I'm getting reports that most of the people hiding out in the Mount managed to escape, but they're not in good shape...
Tinfoil Hat Podcast @TinfoilHa... 49m
People are hurt, and morale's real low after what just went down at the Capitol Building. Send 'em good vibes, everyone. They'll need it.

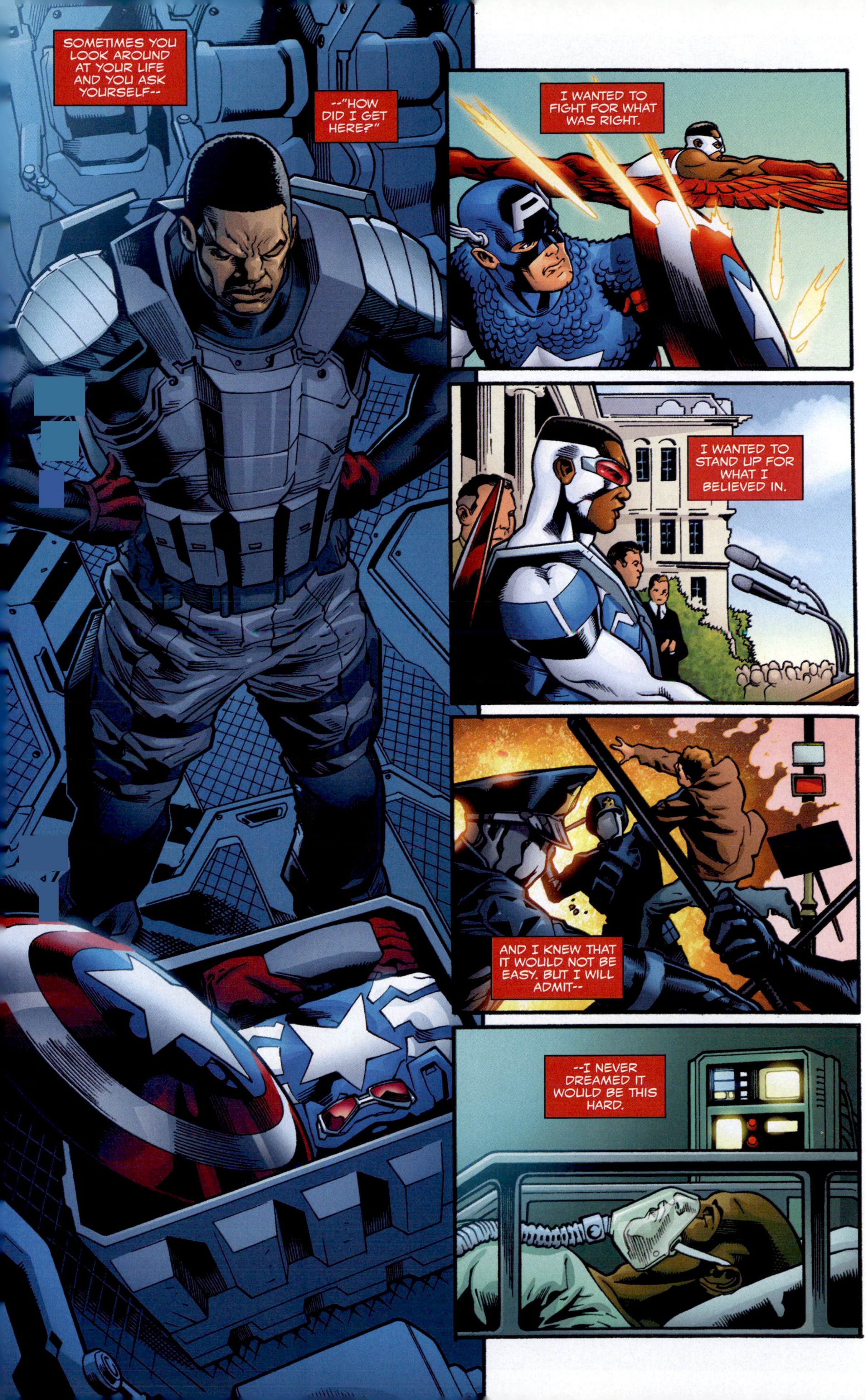
SOMETIMES YOU LOOK AROUND AT YOUR LIFE AND YOU ASK YOURSELF--
--"HOW DID I GET HERE?"
I WANTED TO FIGHT FOR WHAT WAS RIGHT.
I WANTED TO STAND UP FOR WHAT I BELIEVED IN.
AND I KNEW THAT IT WOULD NOT BE EASY. BUT I WILL ADMIT--
--I NEVER DREAMED IT WOULD BE THIS HARD.

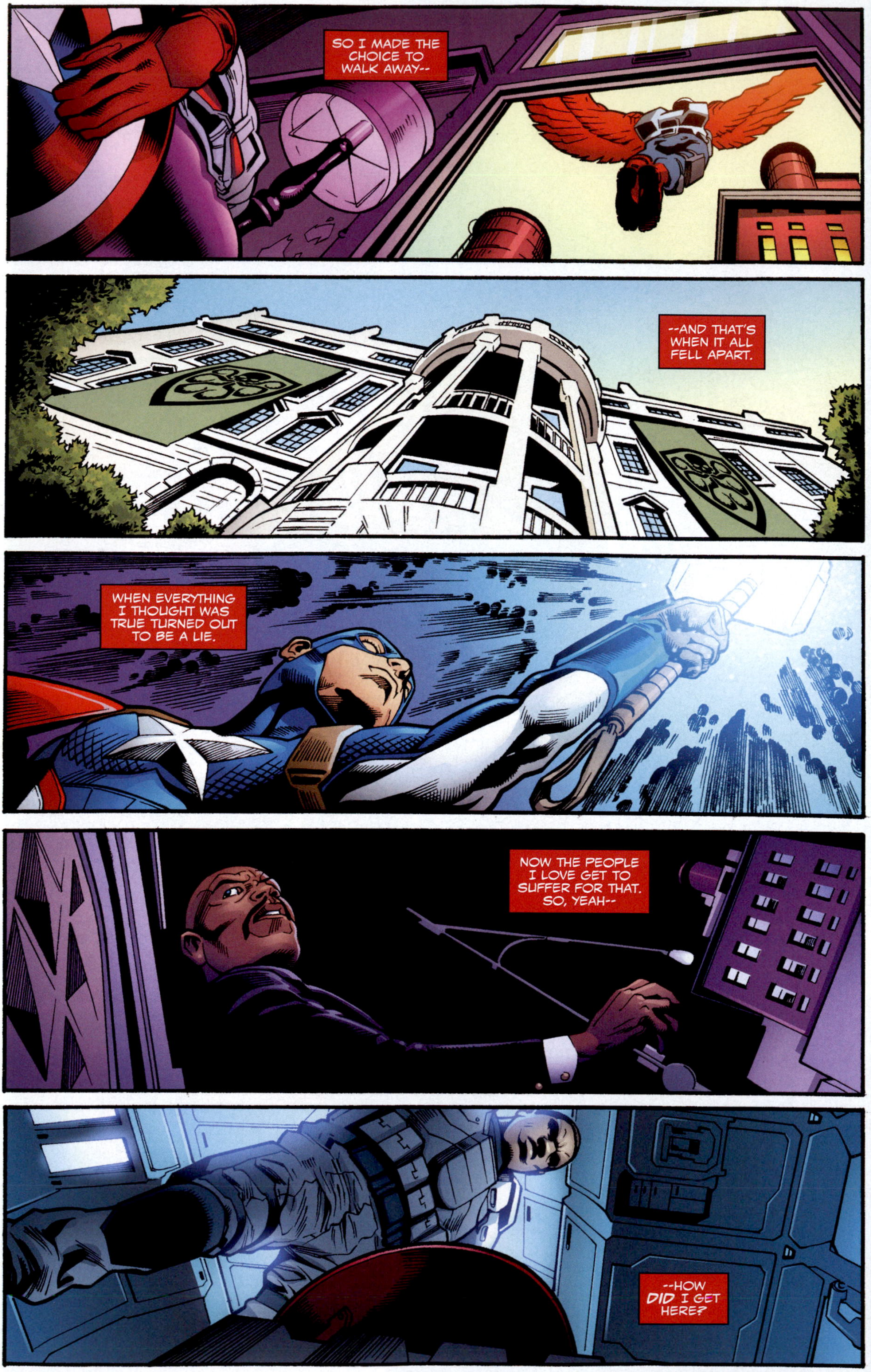

SO I MADE THE CHOICE TO WALK AWAY--
--AND THAT'S WHEN IT ALL FELL APART.
WHEN EVERYTHING I THOUGHT WAS TRUE TURNED OUT TO BE A LIE.
NOW THE PEOPLE I LOVE GET TO SUFFER FOR THAT. SO, YEAH--
--HOW *DID* I GET HERE?

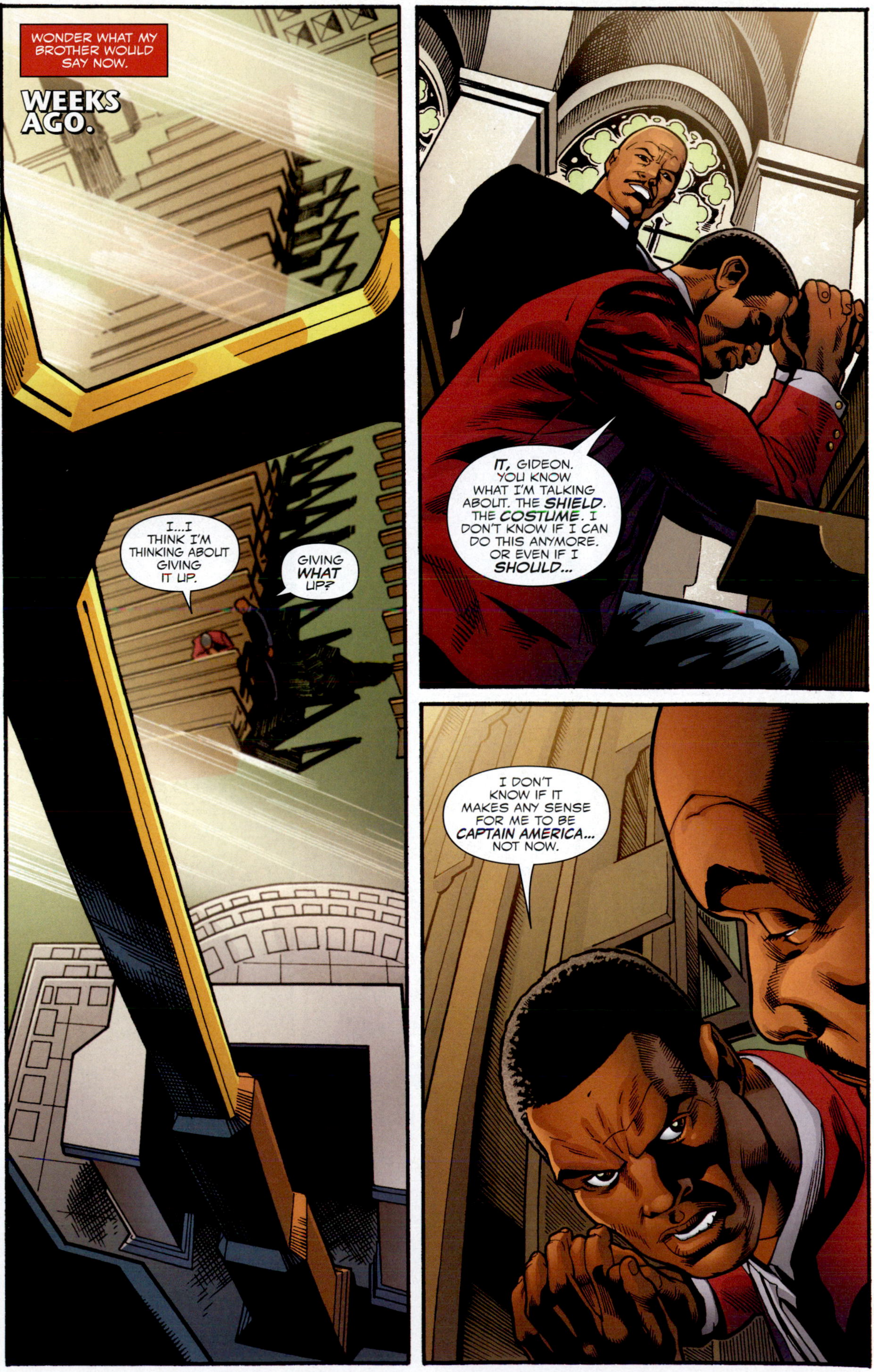

WONDER WHAT MY BROTHER WOULD SAY NOW.
WEEKS AGO.
I...I THINK I'M THINKING ABOUT GIVING IT UP.
GIVING WHAT UP?
IT, GIDEON. YOU KNOW WHAT I'M TALKING ABOUT. THE SHIELD. THE COSTUME. I DON'T KNOW IF I CAN DO THIS ANYMORE. OR EVEN IF I SHOULD...
I DON'T KNOW IF IT MAKES ANY SENSE FOR ME TO BE CAPTAIN AMERICA... NOT NOW.

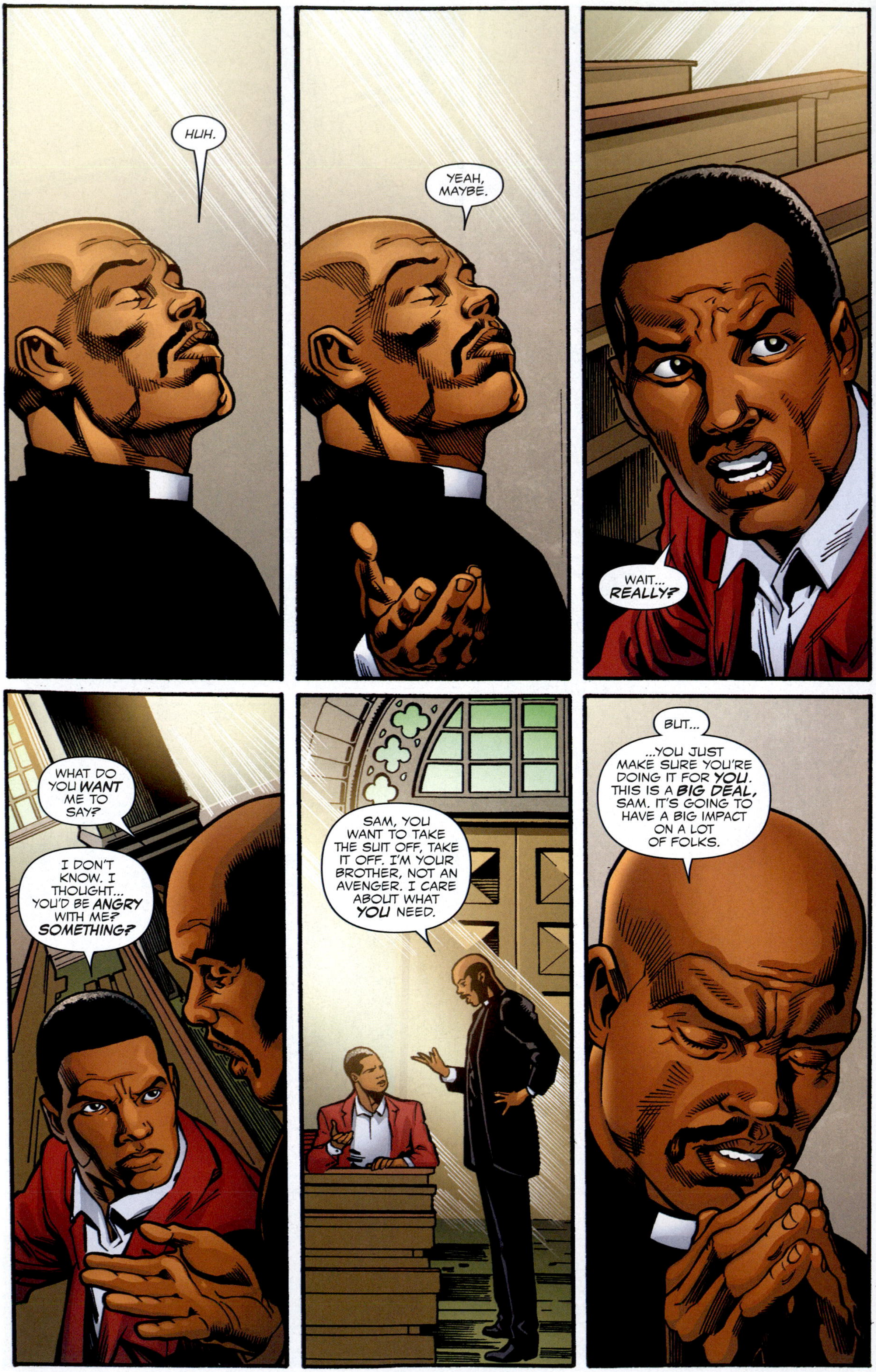
HUH.
YEAH, MAYBE.
WAIT... REALLY?
WHAT DO YOU WANT ME TO SAY?
I DON'T KNOW. I THOUGHT... YOU'D BE ANGRY WITH ME? SOMETHING?
SAM, YOU WANT TO TAKE THE SUIT OFF, TAKE IT OFF. I'M YOUR BROTHER, NOT AN AVENGER. I CARE ABOUT WHAT YOU NEED.
BUT...
...YOU JUST MAKE SURE YOU'RE DOING IT FOR YOU. THIS IS A BIG DEAL, SAM. IT'S GOING TO HAVE A BIG IMPACT ON A LOT OF FOLKS.

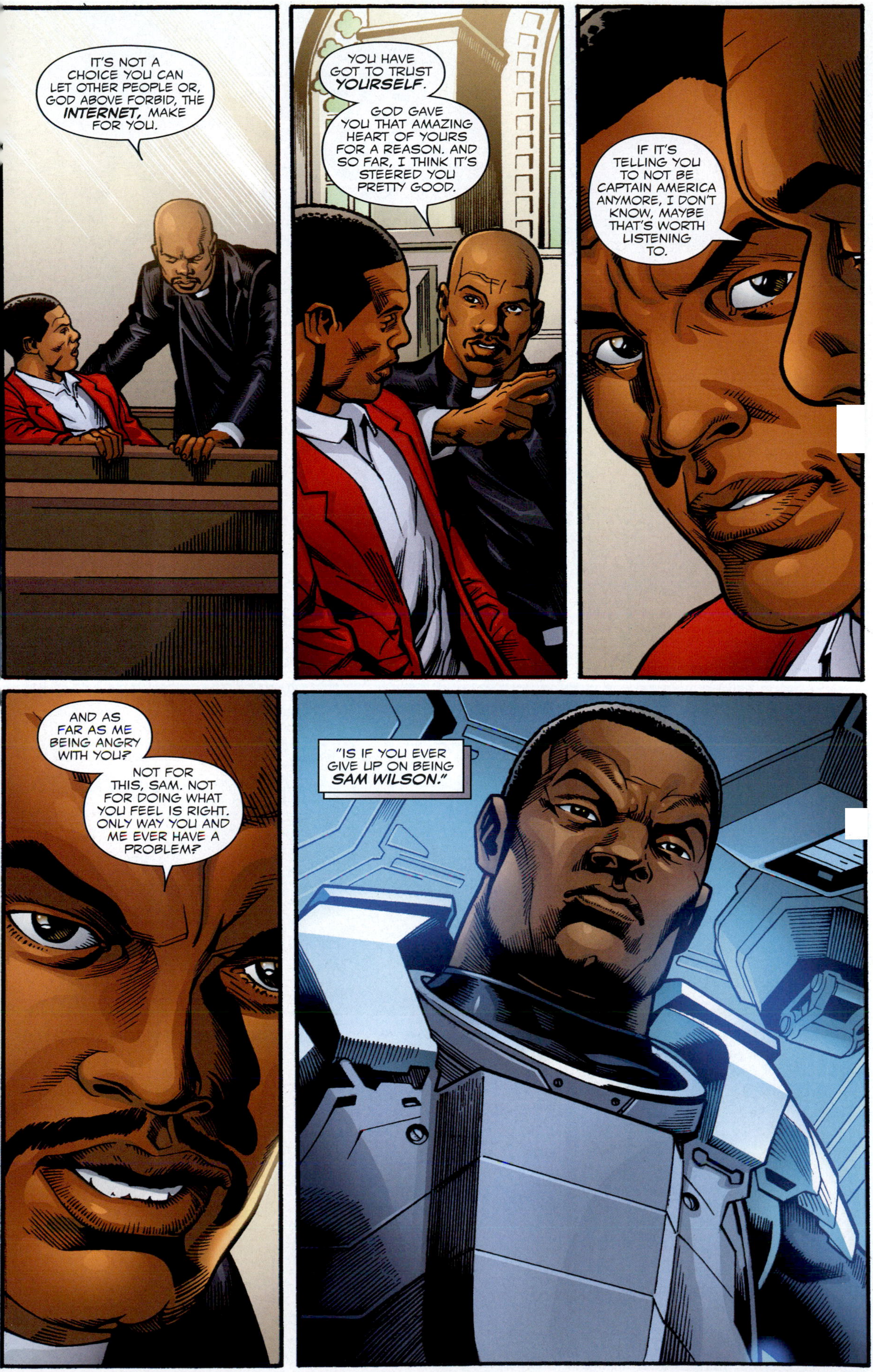
IT'S NOT A CHOICE YOU CAN LET OTHER PEOPLE OR, GOD ABOVE FORBID, THE **INTERNET,** MAKE FOR YOU.
YOU HAVE GOT TO TRUST **YOURSELF**.
GOD GAVE YOU THAT AMAZING HEART OF YOURS FOR A REASON. AND SO FAR, I THINK IT'S STEERED YOU PRETTY GOOD.
IF IT'S TELLING YOU TO NOT BE CAPTAIN AMERICA ANYMORE, I DON'T KNOW, MAYBE THAT'S WORTH LISTENING TO.
AND AS FAR AS ME BEING ANGRY WITH YOU?
NOT FOR THIS, SAM. NOT FOR DOING WHAT YOU FEEL IS RIGHT. ONLY WAY YOU AND ME EVER HAVE A PROBLEM?
"IS IF YOU EVER GIVE UP ON BEING **SAM WILSON.**"

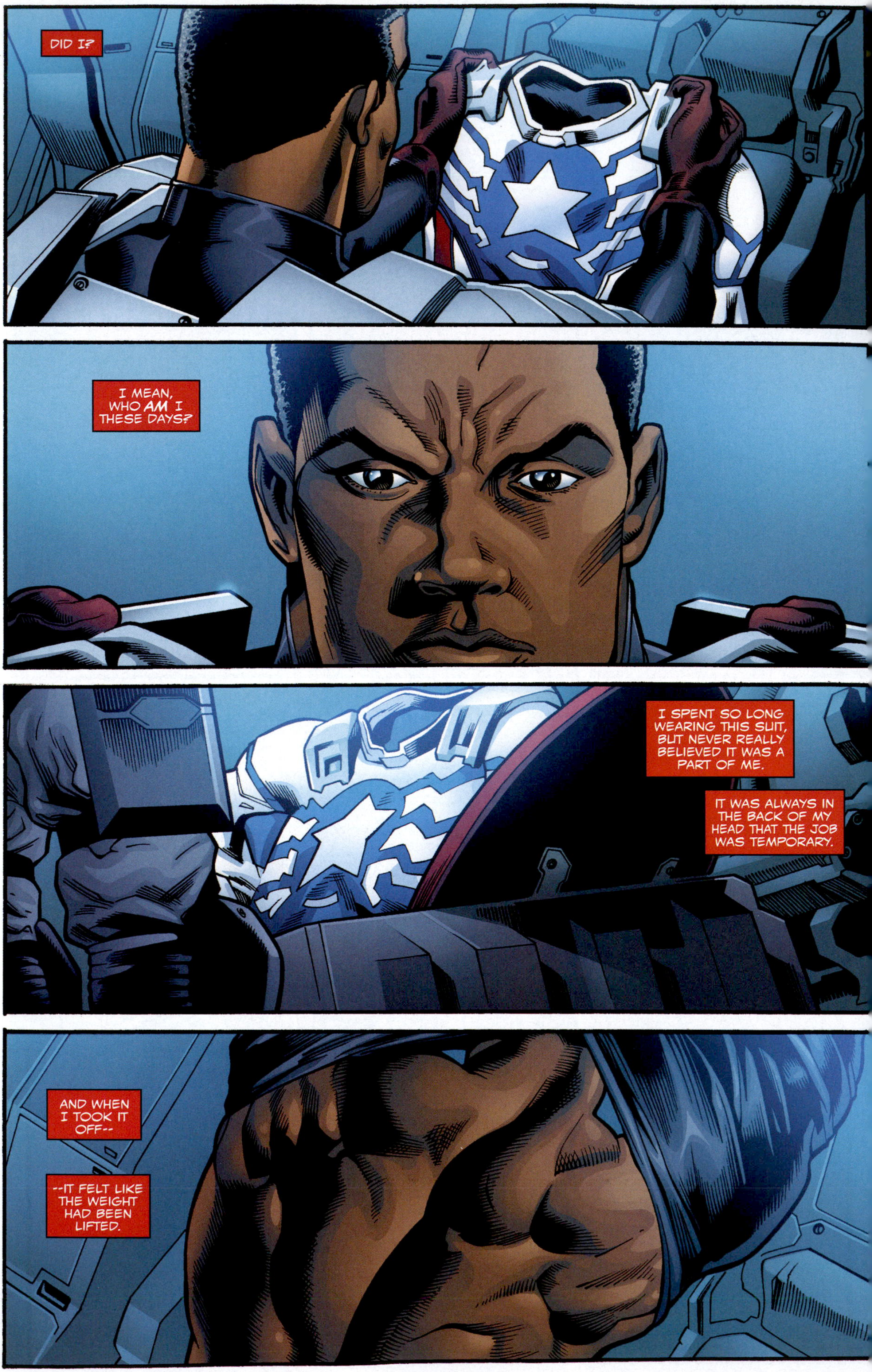
DID I?
I MEAN, WHO *AM* I THESE DAYS?
I SPENT SO LONG WEARING THIS SUIT, BUT NEVER REALLY BELIEVED IT WAS A PART OF ME.
IT WAS ALWAYS IN THE BACK OF MY HEAD THAT THE JOB WAS TEMPORARY.
AND WHEN I TOOK IT OFF--
--IT FELT LIKE THE WEIGHT HAD BEEN LIFTED.

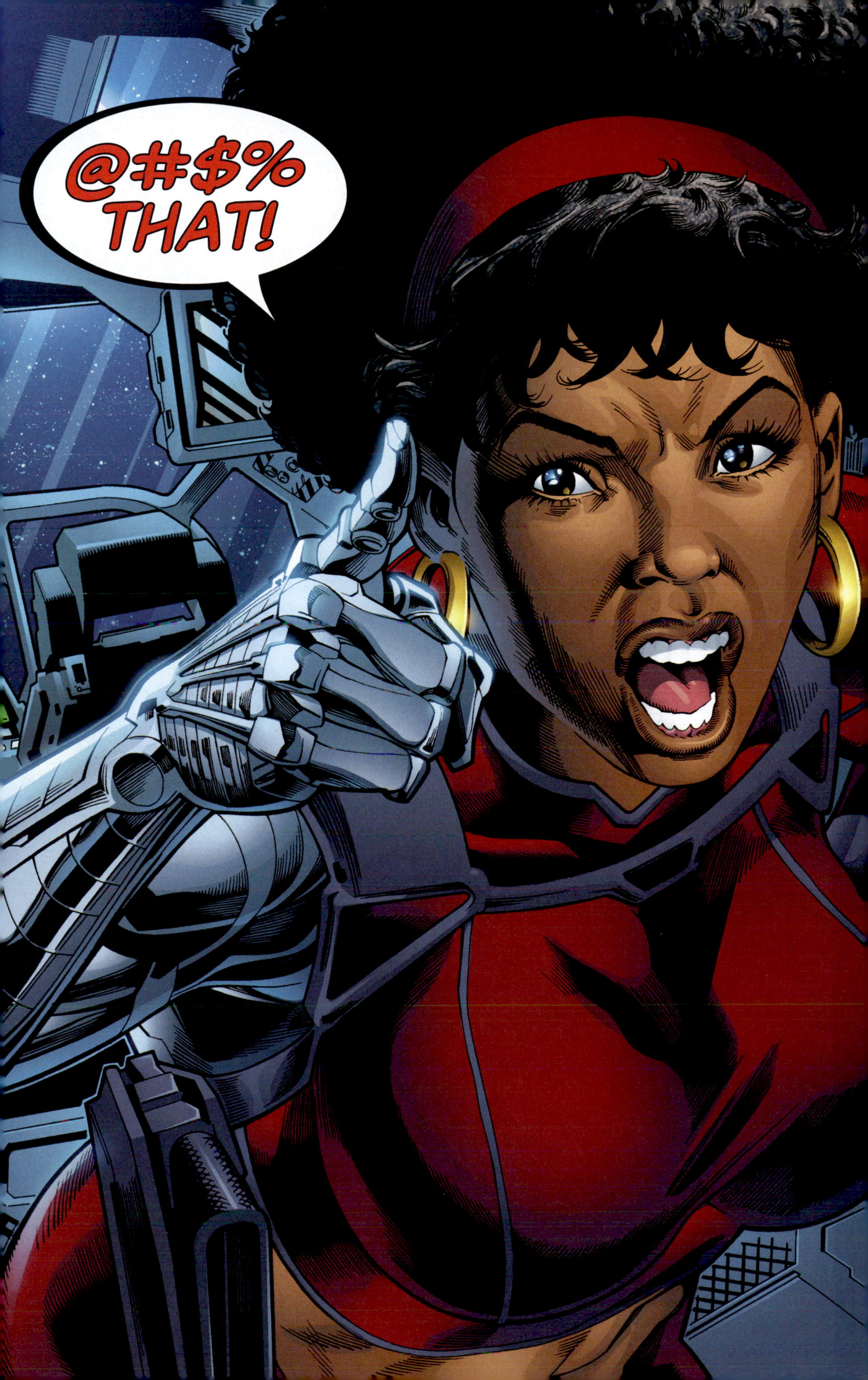
@#$% THAT!

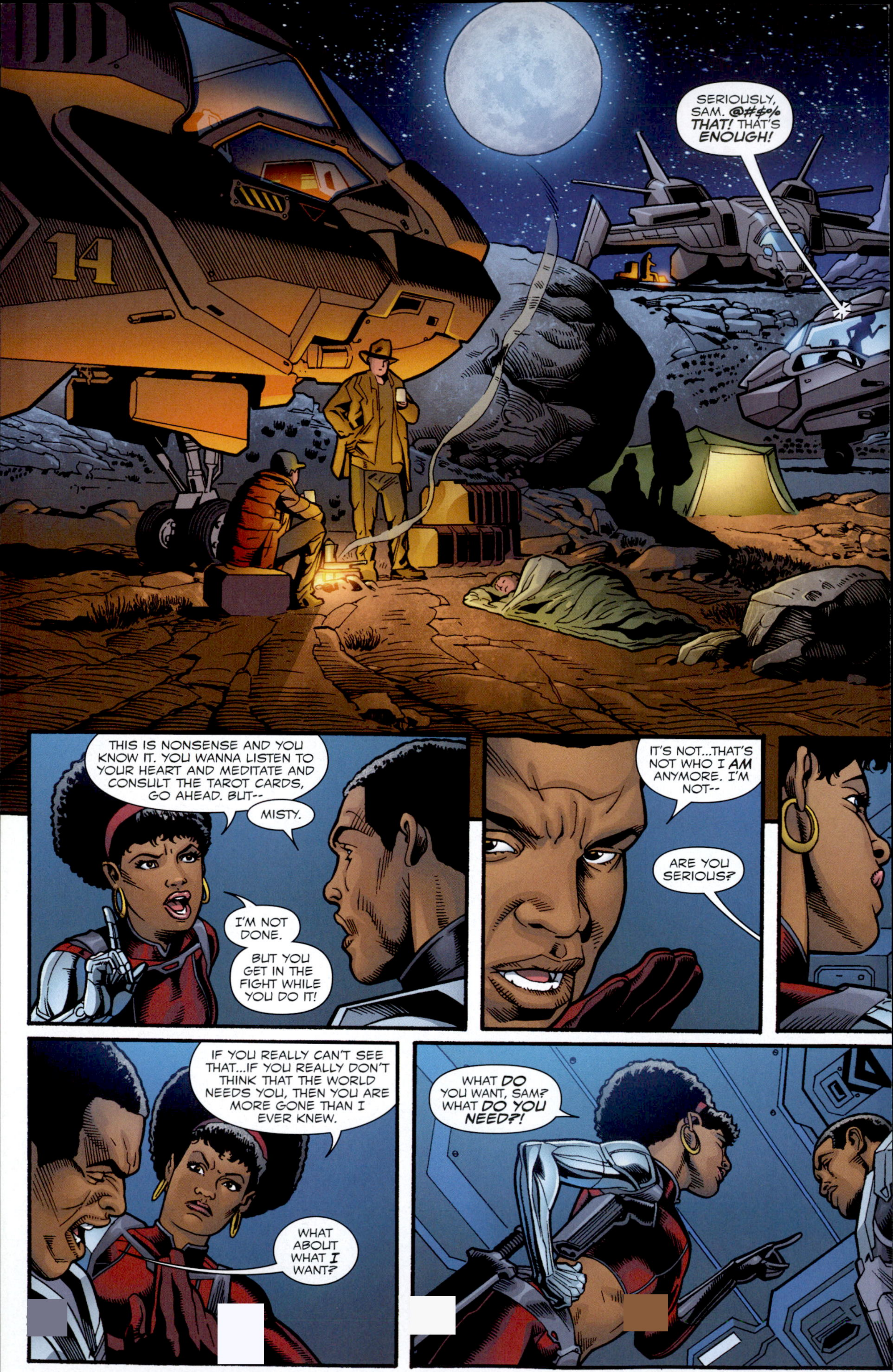
SERIOUSLY, SAM. @#$%% THAT! THAT'S ENOUGH!
THIS IS NONSENSE AND YOU KNOW IT. YOU WANNA LISTEN TO YOUR HEART AND MEDITATE AND CONSULT THE TAROT CARDS, GO AHEAD. BUT--
MISTY.
I'M NOT DONE.
BUT YOU GET IN THE FIGHT WHILE YOU DO IT!
IT'S NOT...THAT'S NOT WHO I AM ANYMORE. I'M NOT--
ARE YOU SERIOUS?
IF YOU REALLY CAN'T SEE THAT...IF YOU REALLY DON'T THINK THAT THE WORLD NEEDS YOU, THEN YOU ARE MORE GONE THAN I EVER KNEW.
WHAT ABOUT WHAT I WANT?
WHAT DO YOU WANT, SAM? WHAT DO YOU NEED?!

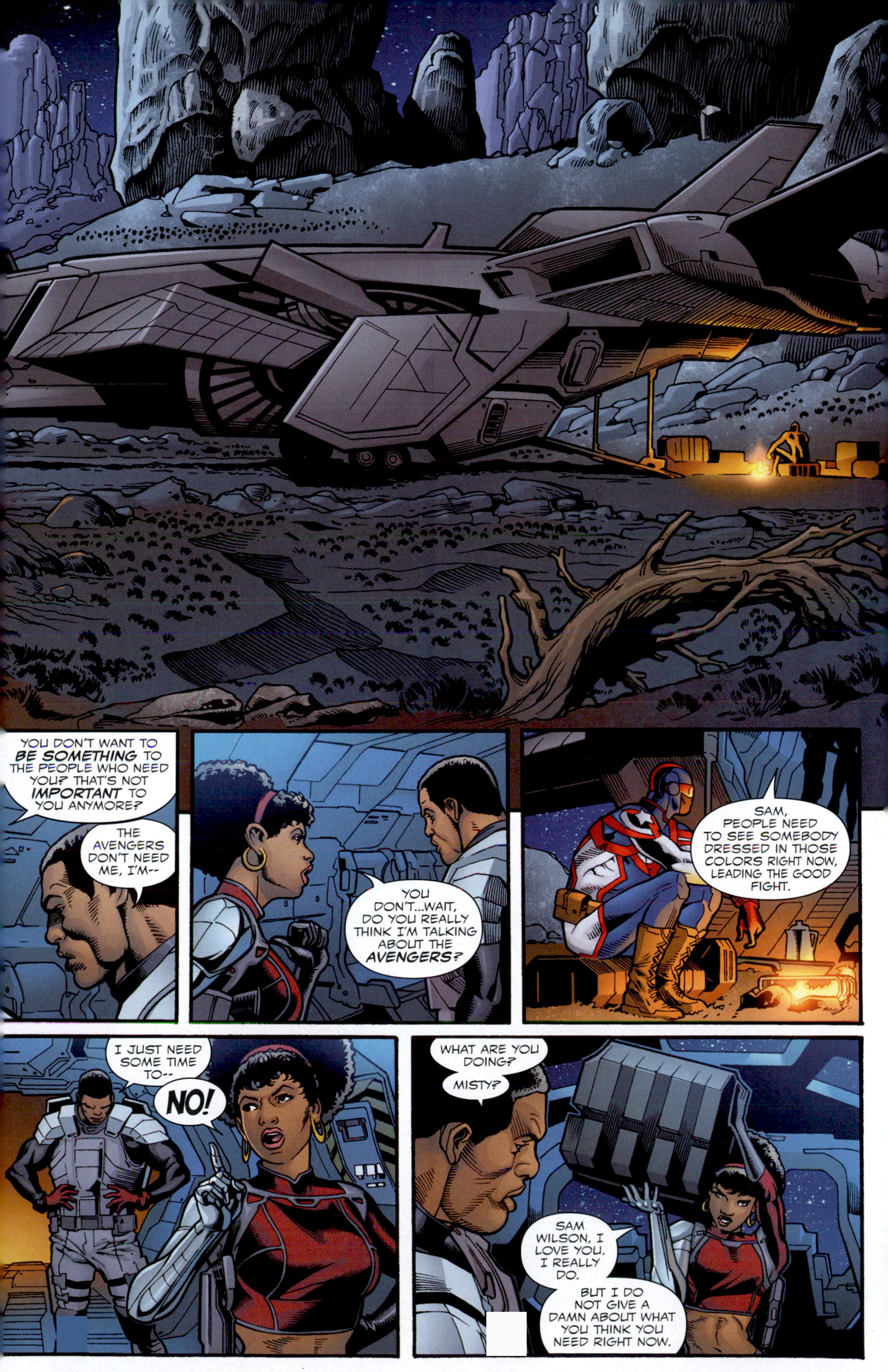
YOU DON'T WANT TO BE SOMETHING TO THE PEOPLE WHO NEED YOU? THAT'S NOT IMPORTANT TO YOU ANYMORE?
THE AVENGERS DON'T NEED ME, I'M--
YOU DON'T...WAIT, DO YOU REALLY THINK I'M TALKING ABOUT THE AVENGERS?
SAM, PEOPLE NEED TO SEE SOMEBODY DRESSED IN THOSE COLORS RIGHT NOW, LEADING THE GOOD FIGHT.
I JUST NEED SOME TIME TO--
NO!
WHAT ARE YOU DOING?
MISTY?
SAM WILSON, I LOVE YOU. I REALLY DO.
BUT I DO NOT GIVE A DAMN ABOUT WHAT YOU THINK YOU NEED RIGHT NOW.

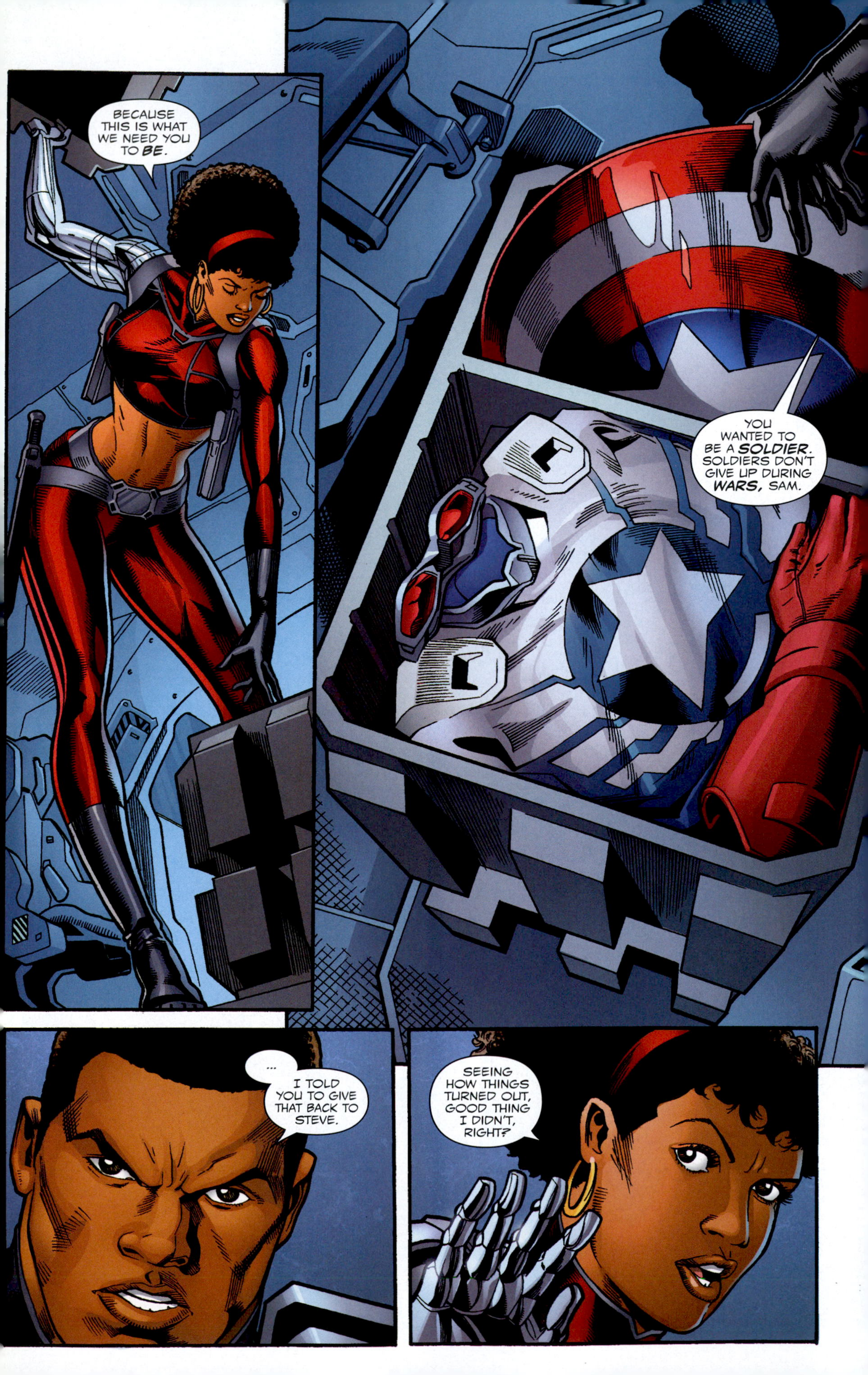

BECAUSE THIS IS WHAT WE NEED YOU TO BE.
YOU WANTED TO BE A SOLDIER. SOLDIERS DON'T GIVE UP DURING WARS, SAM.
... I TOLD YOU TO GIVE THAT BACK TO STEVE.
SEEING HOW THINGS TURNED OUT, GOOD THING I DIDN'T, RIGHT?

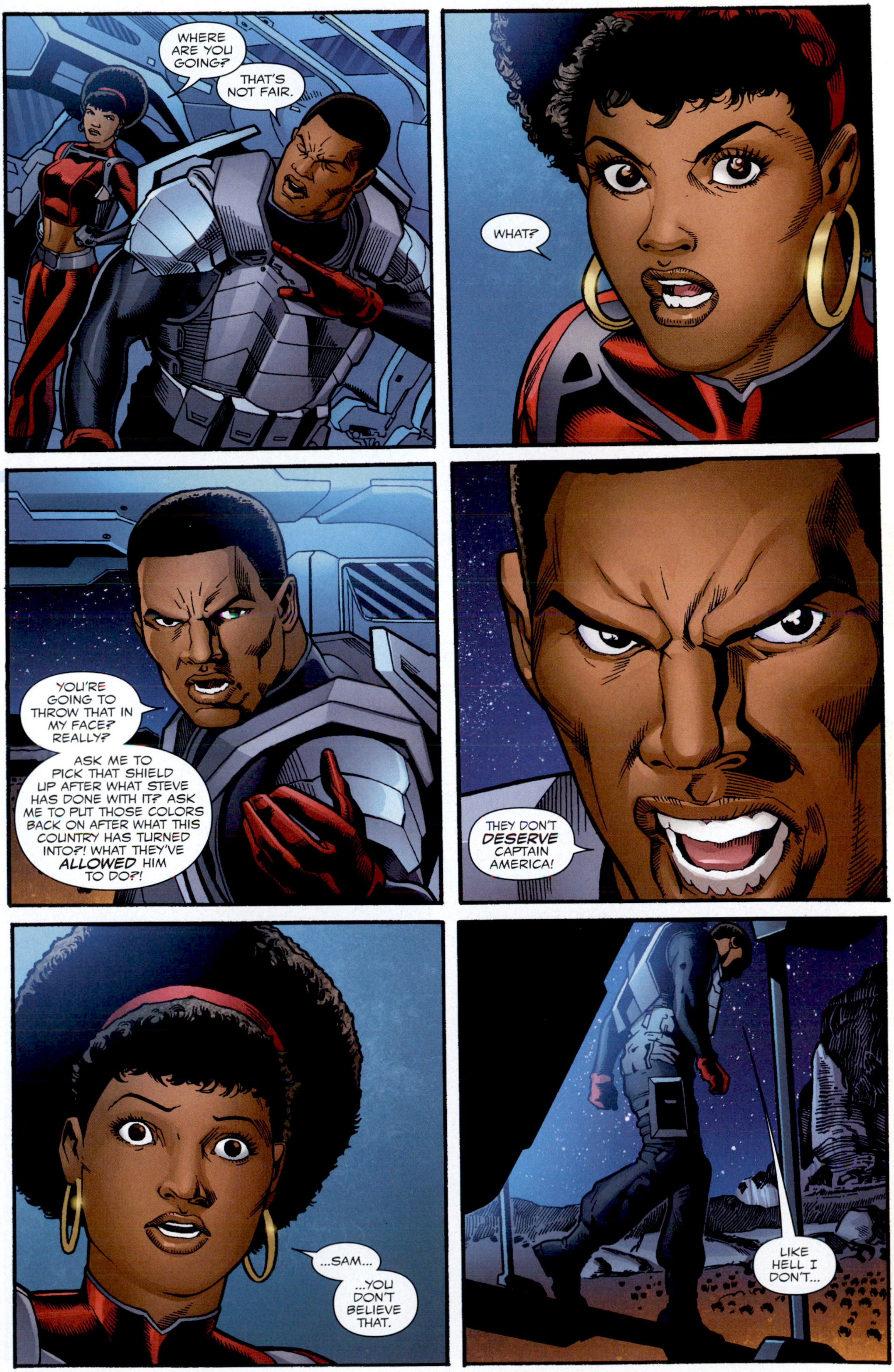
WHERE ARE YOU GOING?
THAT'S NOT FAIR.
WHAT?
YOU'RE GOING TO THROW THAT IN MY FACE? REALLY?
ASK ME TO PICK THAT SHIELD UP AFTER WHAT STEVE HAS DONE WITH IT? ASK ME TO PUT THOSE COLORS BACK ON AFTER WHAT THIS COUNTRY HAS TURNED INTO?! WHAT THEY'VE ALLOWED HIM TO DO?!
THEY DON'T DESERVE CAPTAIN AMERICA!
...SAM...
...YOU DON'T BELIEVE THAT.
LIKE HELL I DON'T...

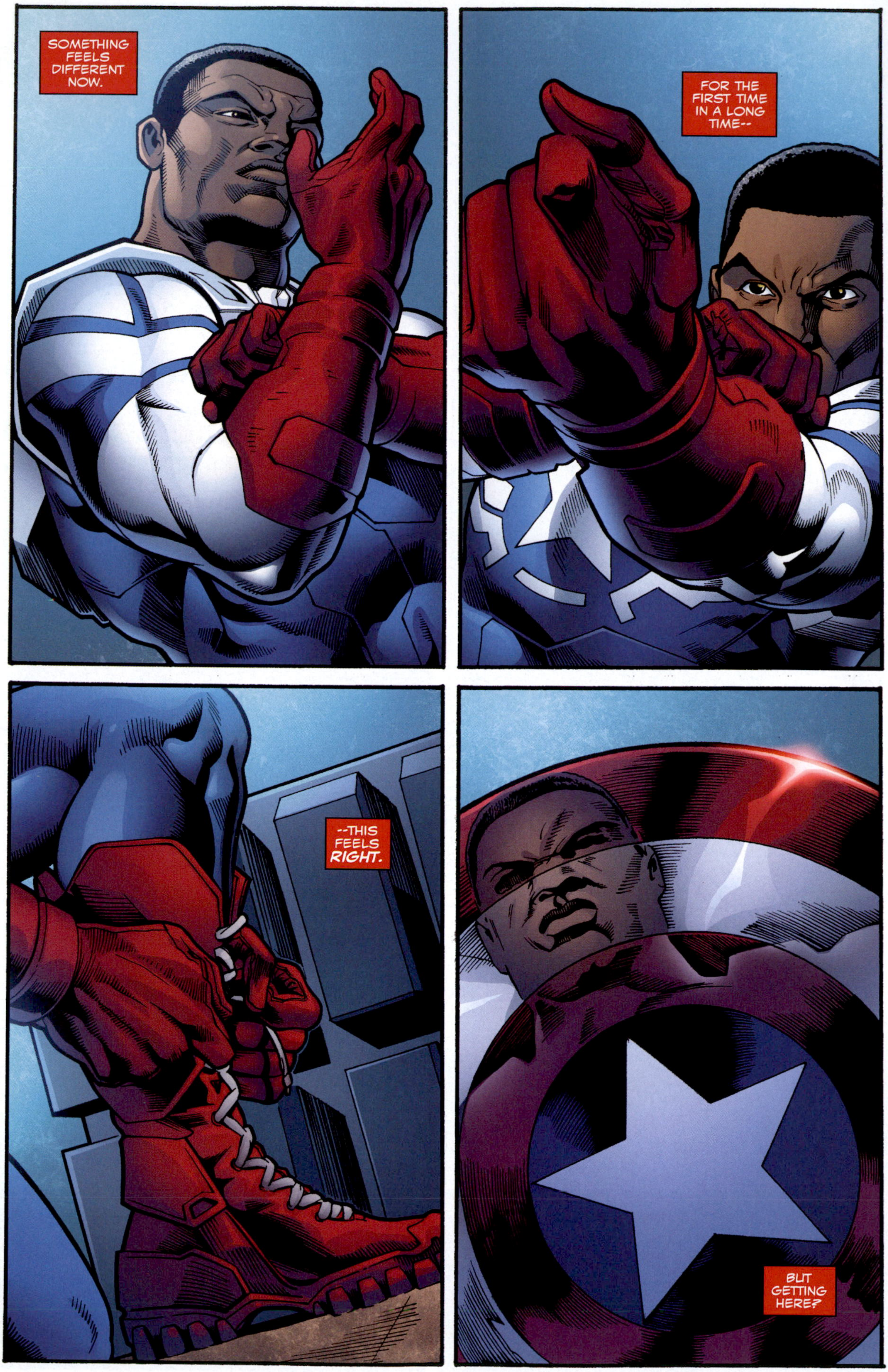
SOMETHING FEELS DIFFERENT NOW.
FOR THE FIRST TIME IN A LONG TIME--
--THIS FEELS RIGHT.
BUT GETTING HERE?

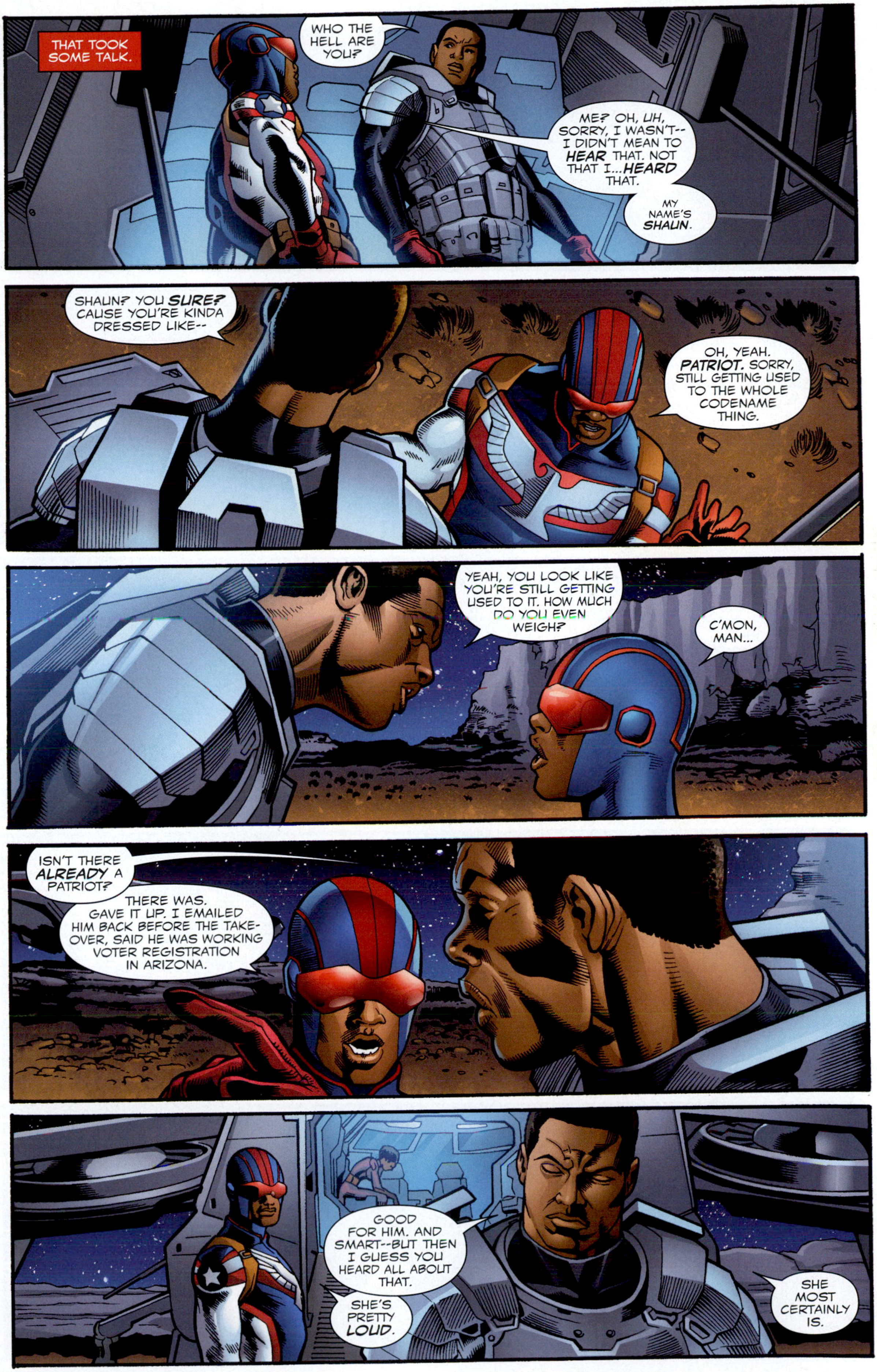
THAT TOOK SOME TALK.
WHO THE HELL ARE YOU?
ME? OH, UH, SORRY, I WASN'T-- I DIDN'T MEAN TO HEAR THAT. NOT THAT I...HEARD THAT.
MY NAME'S SHAUN.
SHAUN? YOU SURE? CAUSE YOU'RE KINDA DRESSED LIKE--
OH, YEAH. PATRIOT. SORRY, STILL GETTING USED TO THE WHOLE CODENAME THING.
YEAH, YOU LOOK LIKE YOU'RE STILL GETTING USED TO IT. HOW MUCH DO YOU EVEN WEIGH?
C'MON, MAN...
ISN'T THERE ALREADY A PATRIOT?
THERE WAS. GAVE IT UP. I EMAILED HIM BACK BEFORE THE TAKE-OVER, SAID HE WAS WORKING VOTER REGISTRATION IN ARIZONA.
GOOD FOR HIM. AND SMART--BUT THEN I GUESS YOU HEARD ALL ABOUT THAT.
SHE'S PRETTY LOUD.
SHE MOST CERTAINLY IS.

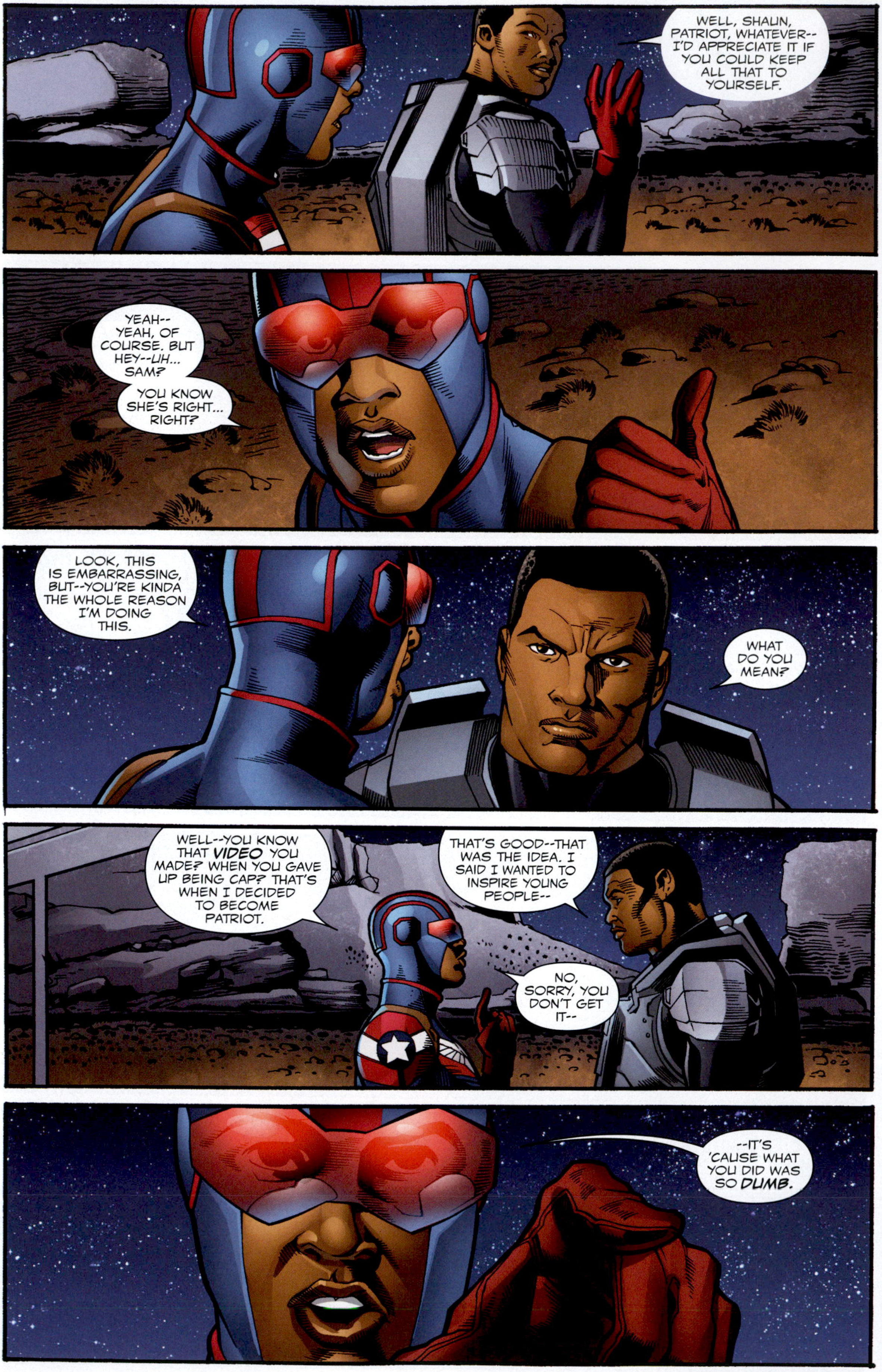
WELL, SHAUN, PATRIOT, WHATEVER-- I'D APPRECIATE IT IF YOU COULD KEEP ALL THAT TO YOURSELF.
YEAH-- YEAH, OF COURSE. BUT HEY--UH... SAM?
YOU KNOW SHE'S RIGHT... RIGHT?
LOOK, THIS IS EMBARRASSING, BUT--YOU'RE KINDA THE WHOLE REASON I'M DOING THIS.
WHAT DO YOU MEAN?
WELL--YOU KNOW THAT VIDEO YOU MADE? WHEN YOU GAVE UP BEING CAP? THAT'S WHEN I DECIDED TO BECOME PATRIOT.
THAT'S GOOD--THAT WAS THE IDEA. I SAID I WANTED TO INSPIRE YOUNG PEOPLE--
NO, SORRY, YOU DON'T GET IT--
--IT'S 'CAUSE WHAT YOU DID WAS SO DUMB.

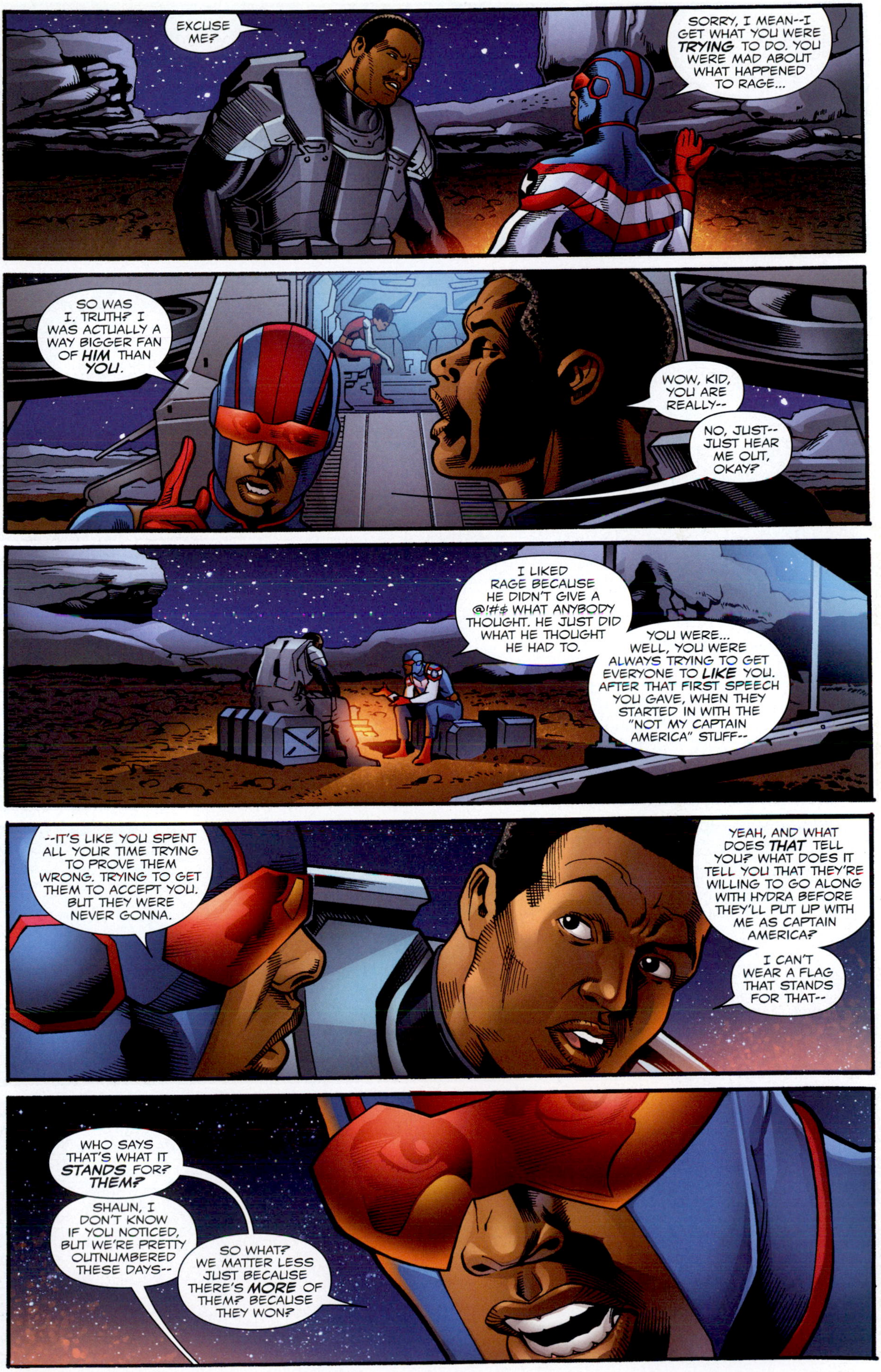
EXCUSE ME?
SORRY, I MEAN--I GET WHAT YOU WERE TRYING TO DO. YOU WERE MAD ABOUT WHAT HAPPENED TO RAGE...
SO WAS I. TRUTH? I WAS ACTUALLY A WAY BIGGER FAN OF HIM THAN YOU.
WOW, KID, YOU ARE REALLY--
NO, JUST-- JUST HEAR ME OUT, OKAY?
I LIKED RAGE BECAUSE HE DIDN'T GIVE A @!#$ WHAT ANYBODY THOUGHT. HE JUST DID WHAT HE THOUGHT HE HAD TO.
YOU WERE... WELL, YOU WERE ALWAYS TRYING TO GET EVERYONE TO LIKE YOU. AFTER THAT FIRST SPEECH YOU GAVE, WHEN THEY STARTED IN WITH THE "NOT MY CAPTAIN AMERICA" STUFF--
--IT'S LIKE YOU SPENT ALL YOUR TIME TRYING TO PROVE THEM WRONG. TRYING TO GET THEM TO ACCEPT YOU. BUT THEY WERE NEVER GONNA.
YEAH, AND WHAT DOES THAT TELL YOU? WHAT DOES IT TELL YOU THAT THEY'RE WILLING TO GO ALONG WITH HYDRA BEFORE THEY'LL PUT UP WITH ME AS CAPTAIN AMERICA?
I CAN'T WEAR A FLAG THAT STANDS FOR THAT--
WHO SAYS THAT'S WHAT IT STANDS FOR? THEM?
SHAUN, I DON'T KNOW IF YOU NOTICED, BUT WE'RE PRETTY OUTNUMBERED THESE DAYS--
SO WHAT? WE MATTER LESS JUST BECAUSE THERE'S MORE OF THEM? BECAUSE THEY WON?

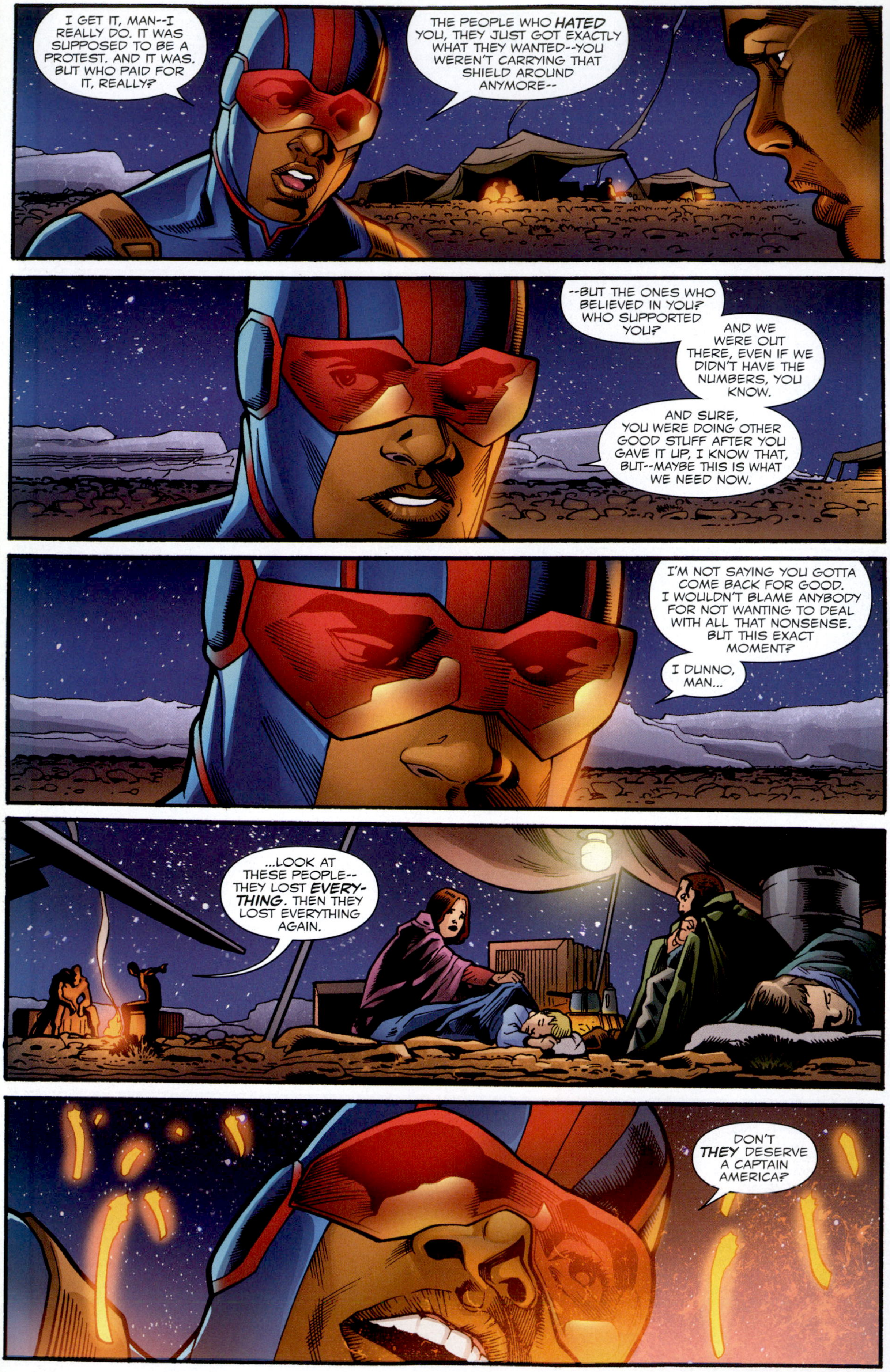
I GET IT, MAN--I REALLY DO. IT WAS SUPPOSED TO BE A PROTEST. AND IT WAS. BUT WHO PAID FOR IT, REALLY?
THE PEOPLE WHO HATED YOU, THEY JUST GOT EXACTLY WHAT THEY WANTED--YOU WEREN'T CARRYING THAT SHIELD AROUND ANYMORE--
--BUT THE ONES WHO BELIEVED IN YOU? WHO SUPPORTED YOU?
AND WE WERE OUT THERE, EVEN IF WE DIDN'T HAVE THE NUMBERS, YOU KNOW.
AND SURE, YOU WERE DOING OTHER GOOD STUFF AFTER YOU GAVE IT UP, I KNOW THAT, BUT--MAYBE THIS IS WHAT WE NEED NOW.
I'M NOT SAYING YOU GOTTA COME BACK FOR GOOD. I WOULDN'T BLAME ANYBODY FOR NOT WANTING TO DEAL WITH ALL THAT NONSENSE. BUT THIS EXACT MOMENT?
I DUNNO, MAN...
...LOOK AT THESE PEOPLE--THEY LOST EVERYTHING. THEN THEY LOST EVERYTHING AGAIN.
DON'T THEY DESERVE A CAPTAIN AMERICA?

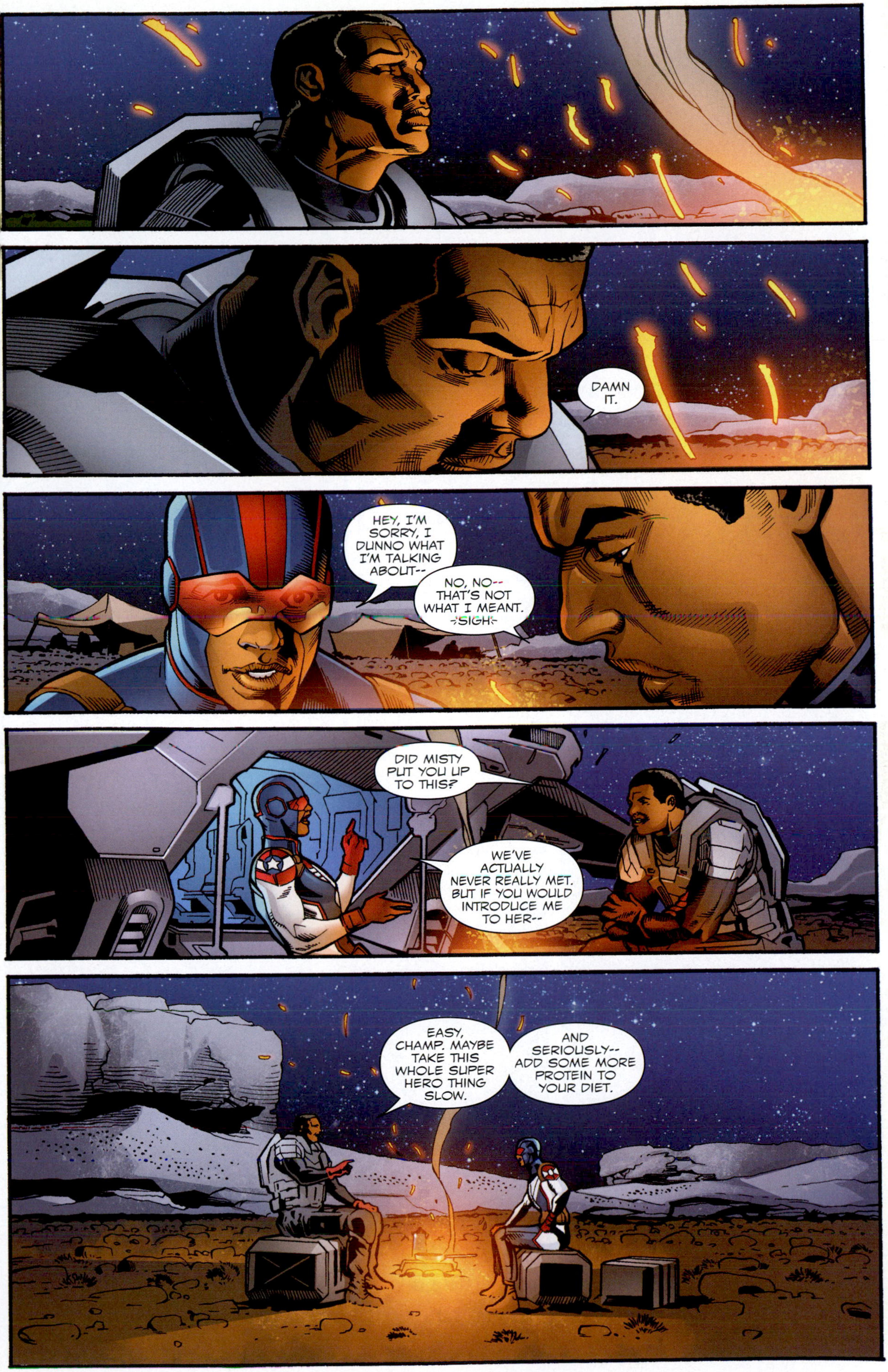
DAMN IT.
HEY, I'M SORRY, I DUNNO WHAT I'M TALKING ABOUT--
NO, NO-- THAT'S NOT WHAT I MEANT. -SIGH-
DID MISTY PUT YOU UP TO THIS?
WE'VE ACTUALLY NEVER REALLY MET. BUT IF YOU WOULD INTRODUCE ME TO HER--
EASY, CHAMP. MAYBE TAKE THIS WHOLE SUPER HERO THING SLOW.
AND SERIOUSLY-- ADD SOME MORE PROTEIN TO YOUR DIET.

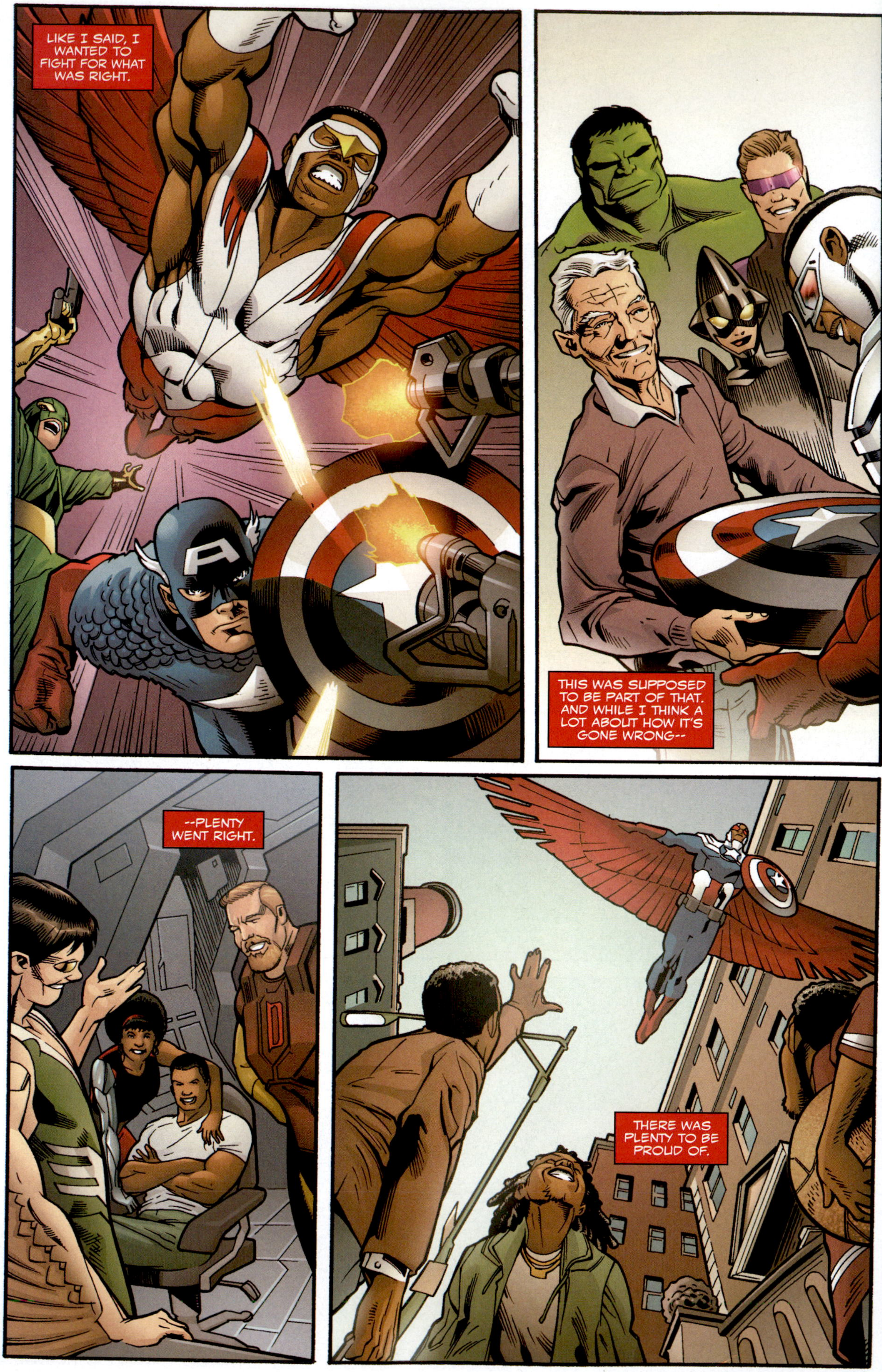
LIKE I SAID, I WANTED TO FIGHT FOR WHAT WAS RIGHT.
THIS WAS SUPPOSED TO BE PART OF THAT. AND WHILE I THINK A LOT ABOUT HOW IT'S GONE WRONG--
--PLENTY WENT RIGHT.
THERE WAS PLENTY TO BE PROUD OF.

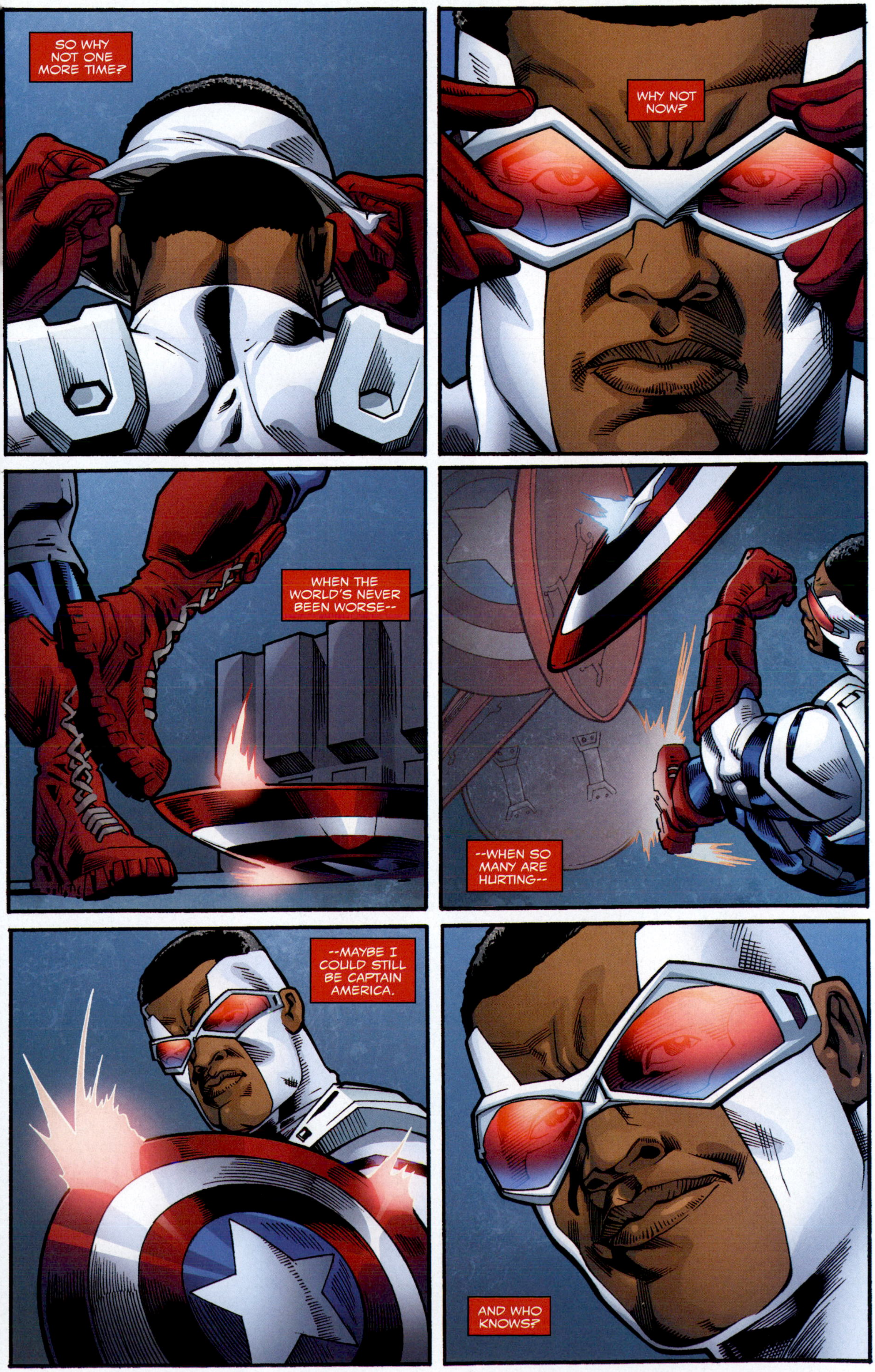
SO WHY NOT ONE MORE TIME?
WHY NOT NOW?
WHEN THE WORLD'S NEVER BEEN WORSE--
--WHEN SO MANY ARE HURTING--
--MAYBE I COULD STILL BE CAPTAIN AMERICA.
AND WHO KNOWS?

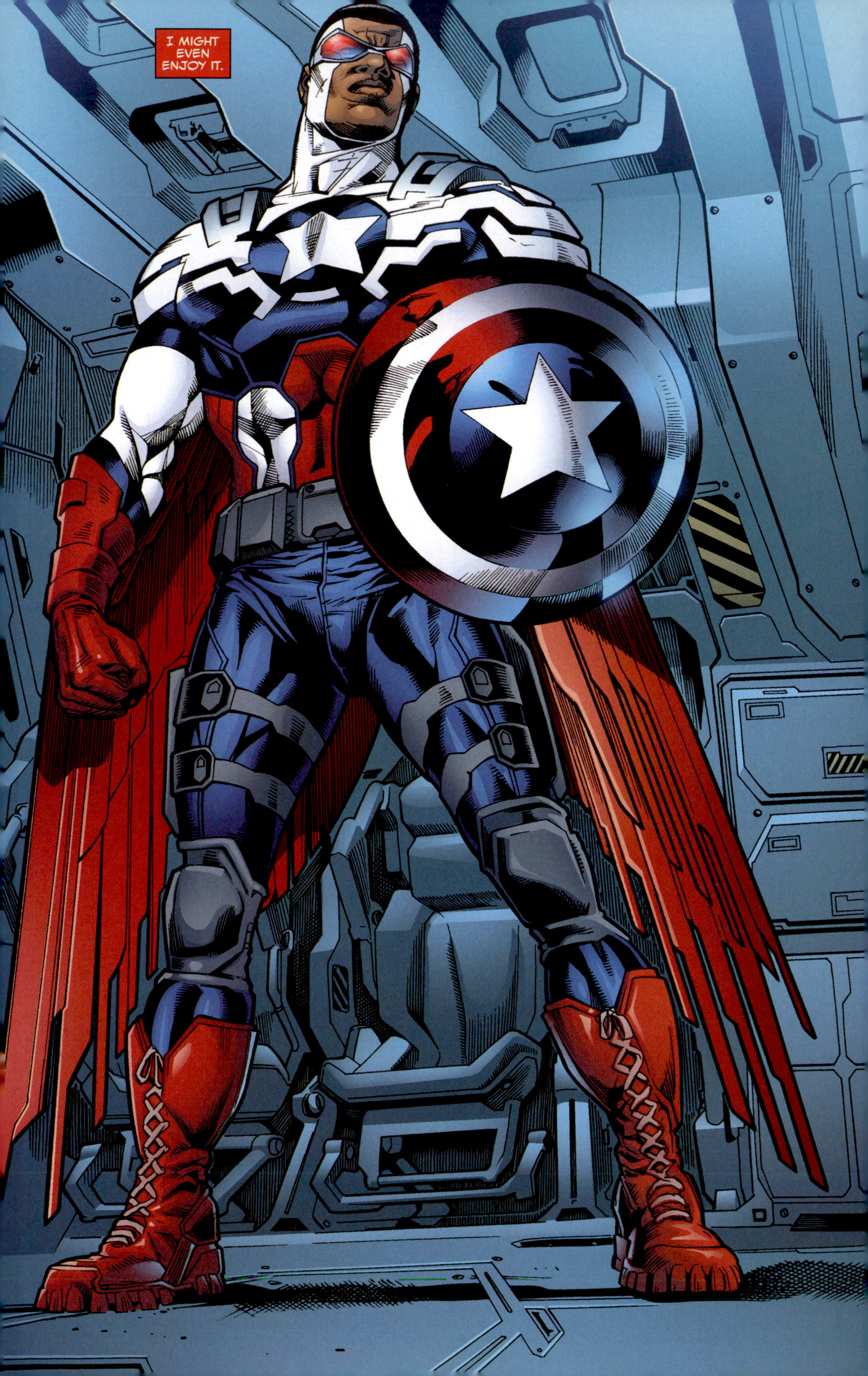
I MIGHT EVEN ENJOY IT.

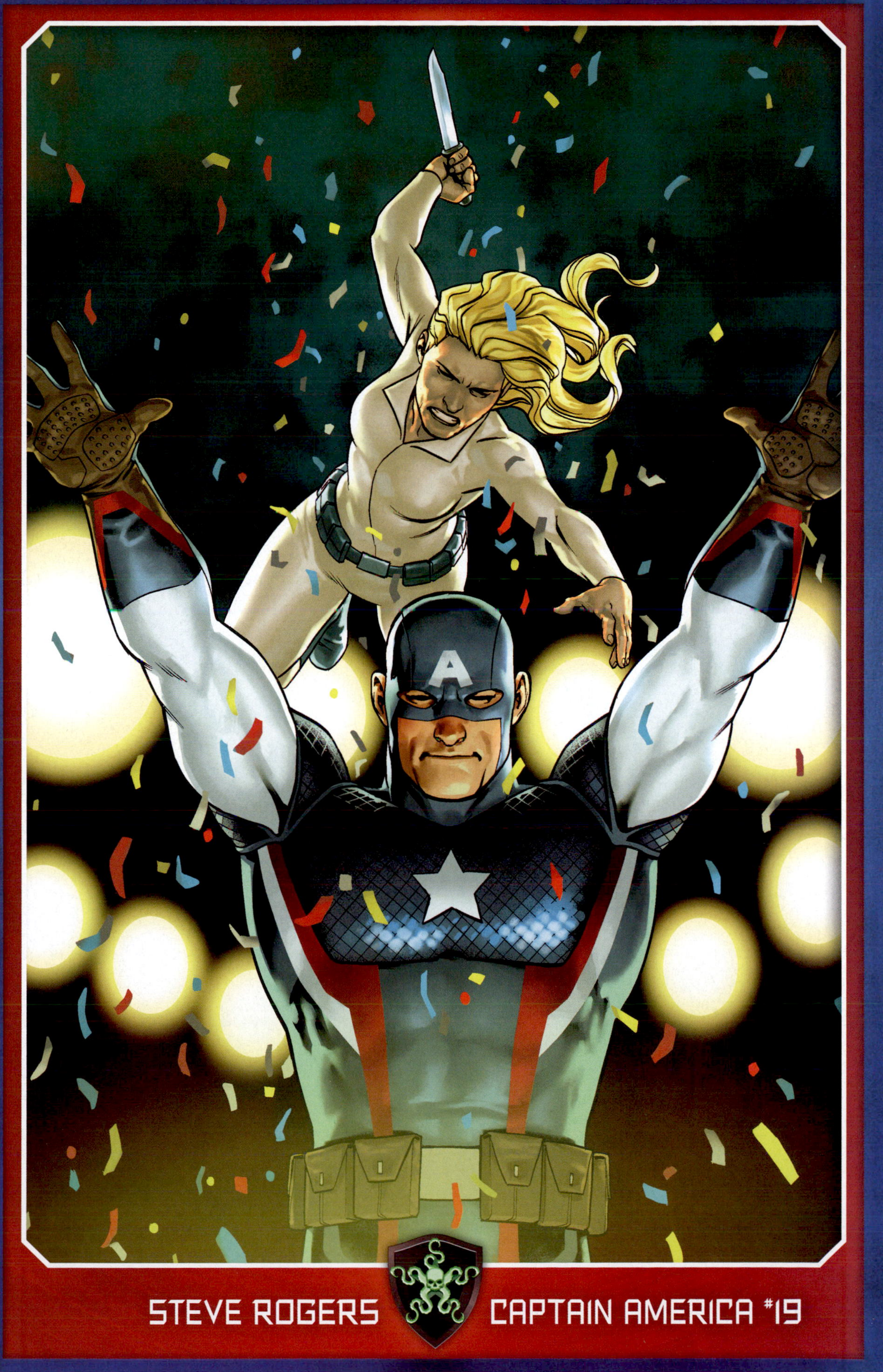
STEVE ROGERS
CAPTAIN AMERICA #19

Super-Soldier. Avenger. Agent of Hydra. He is...

Steve ★ Rogers
CAPTAIN AMERICA

WARNING! Read this issue AFTER SECRET EMPIRE #7

A Cosmic Cube transformed Steve Rogers, Captain America, into the ultimate Hydra sleeper agent. After months of careful manipulation, Steve Rogers took control of S.H.I.E.L.D. and used a moment of international crisis to claim the country for Hydra.

In the early days of his reign, Rogers ruled with an iron fist but tried to show mercy where he could, and pawned off the dirtiest work to trusted members of his inner circle. But after the death of Madame Hydra and an assassination attempt by Sharon Carter, the love of Steve's life, that's all about to change...

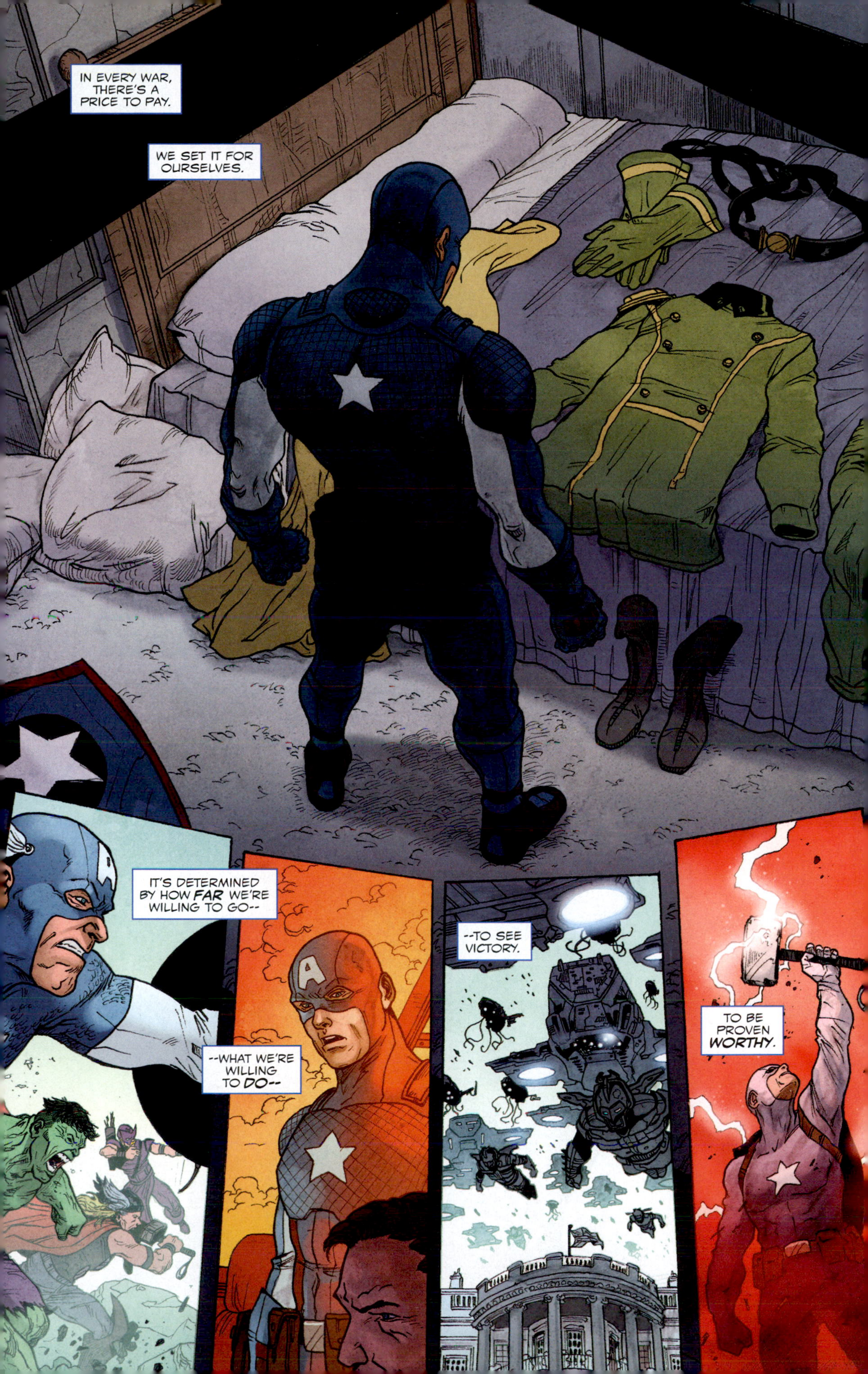
IN EVERY WAR, THERE'S A PRICE TO PAY.
WE SET IT FOR OURSELVES.
IT'S DETERMINED BY HOW FAR WE'RE WILLING TO GO--
--WHAT WE'RE WILLING TO DO--
--TO SEE VICTORY.
TO BE PROVEN WORTHY.

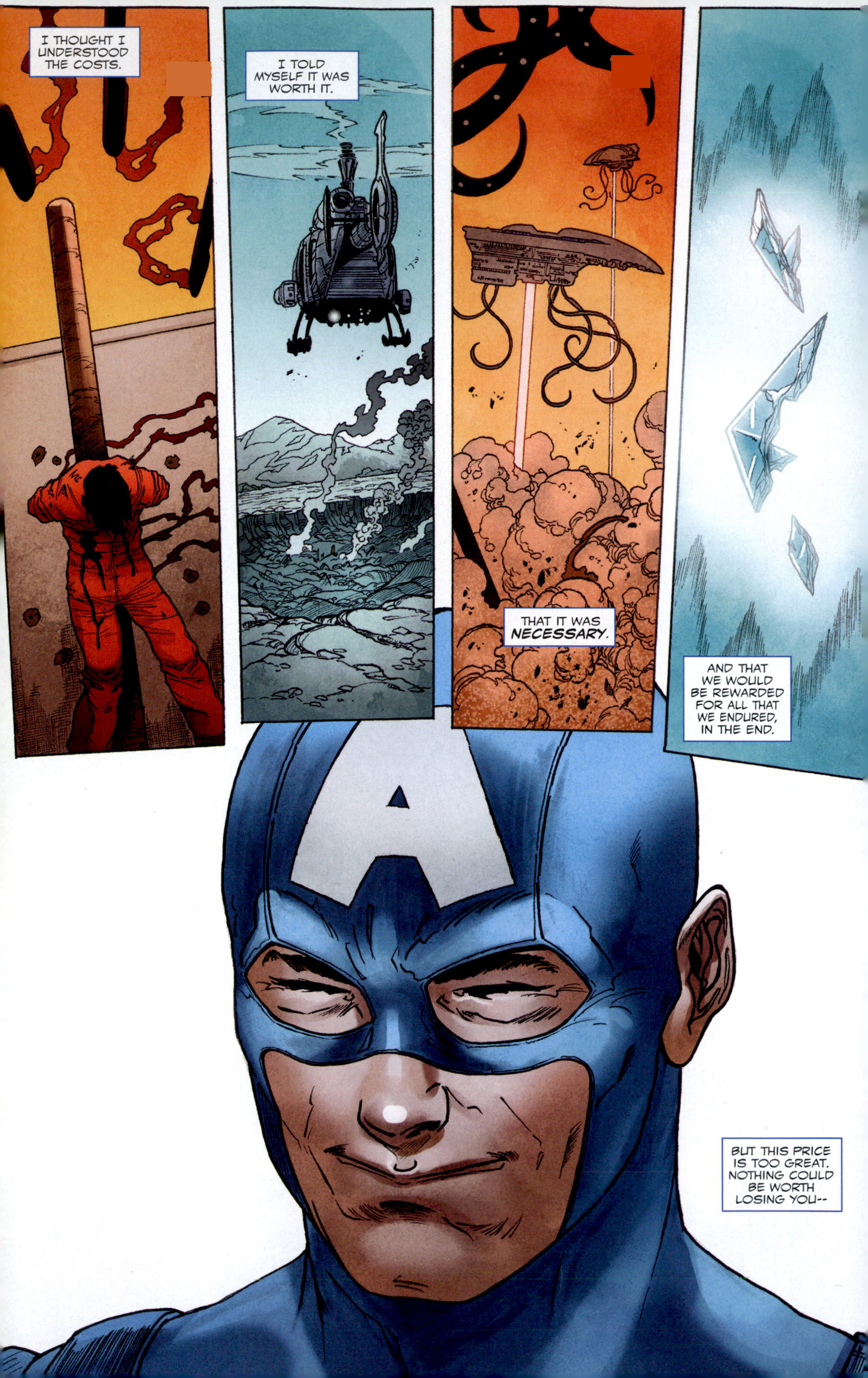
I THOUGHT I UNDERSTOOD THE COSTS.
I TOLD MYSELF IT WAS WORTH IT.
THAT IT WAS ***NECESSARY***.
AND THAT WE WOULD BE REWARDED FOR ALL THAT WE ENDURED, IN THE END.
BUT THIS PRICE IS TOO GREAT. NOTHING COULD BE WORTH LOSING YOU--

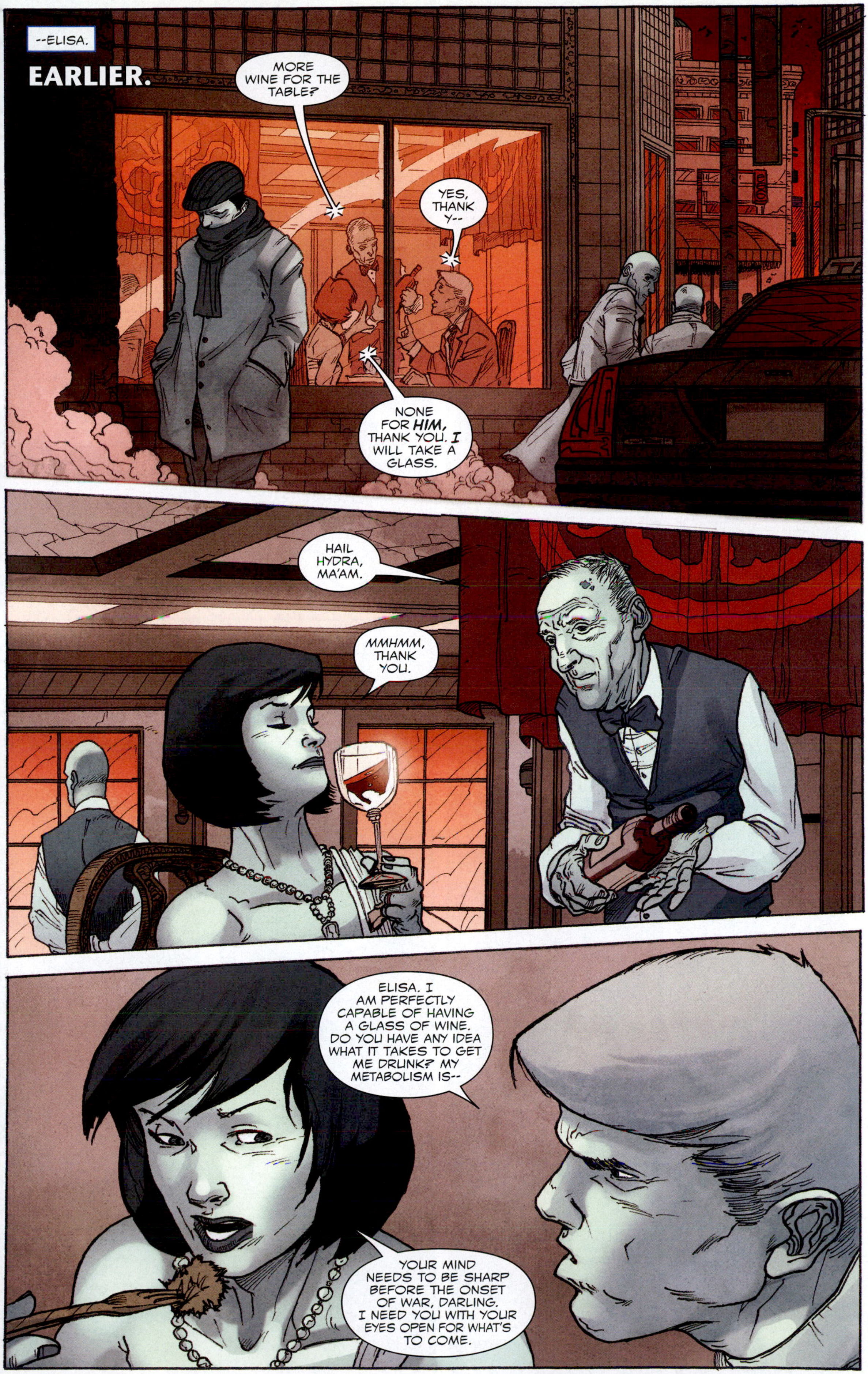
--ELISA.
EARLIER.
MORE WINE FOR THE TABLE?
YES, THANK Y--
NONE FOR **HIM,** THANK YOU. *I* WILL TAKE A GLASS.
HAIL HYDRA, MA'AM.
MMHMM, THANK YOU.
ELISA. I AM PERFECTLY CAPABLE OF HAVING A GLASS OF WINE. DO YOU HAVE ANY IDEA WHAT IT TAKES TO GET ME DRUNK? MY METABOLISM IS--
YOUR MIND NEEDS TO BE SHARP BEFORE THE ONSET OF WAR, DARLING. I NEED YOU WITH YOUR EYES OPEN FOR WHAT'S TO COME.

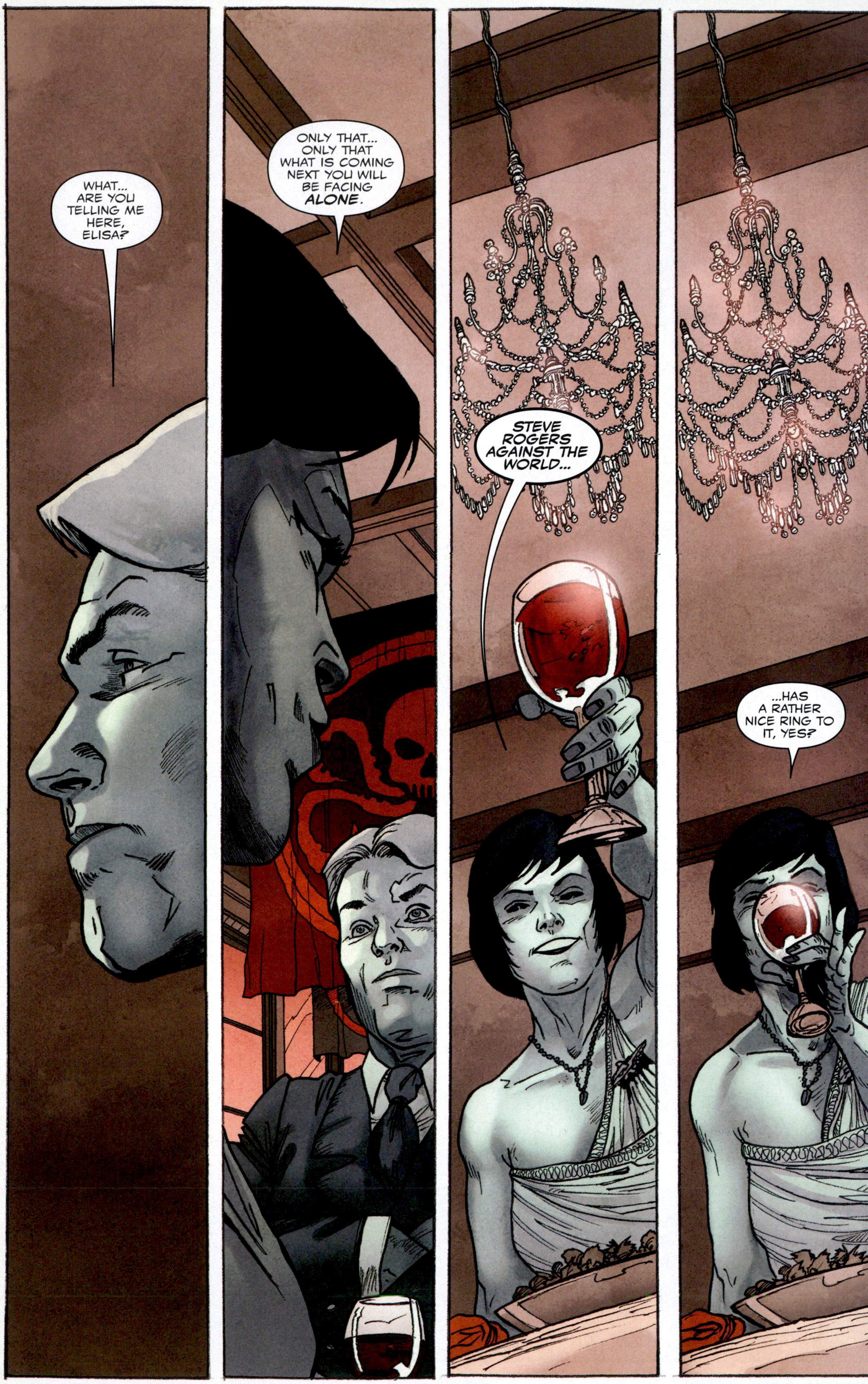
WHAT... ARE YOU TELLING ME HERE, ELISA?
ONLY THAT... ONLY THAT WHAT IS COMING NEXT YOU WILL BE FACING ALONE.
STEVE ROGERS AGAINST THE WORLD...
...HAS A RATHER NICE RING TO IT, YES?

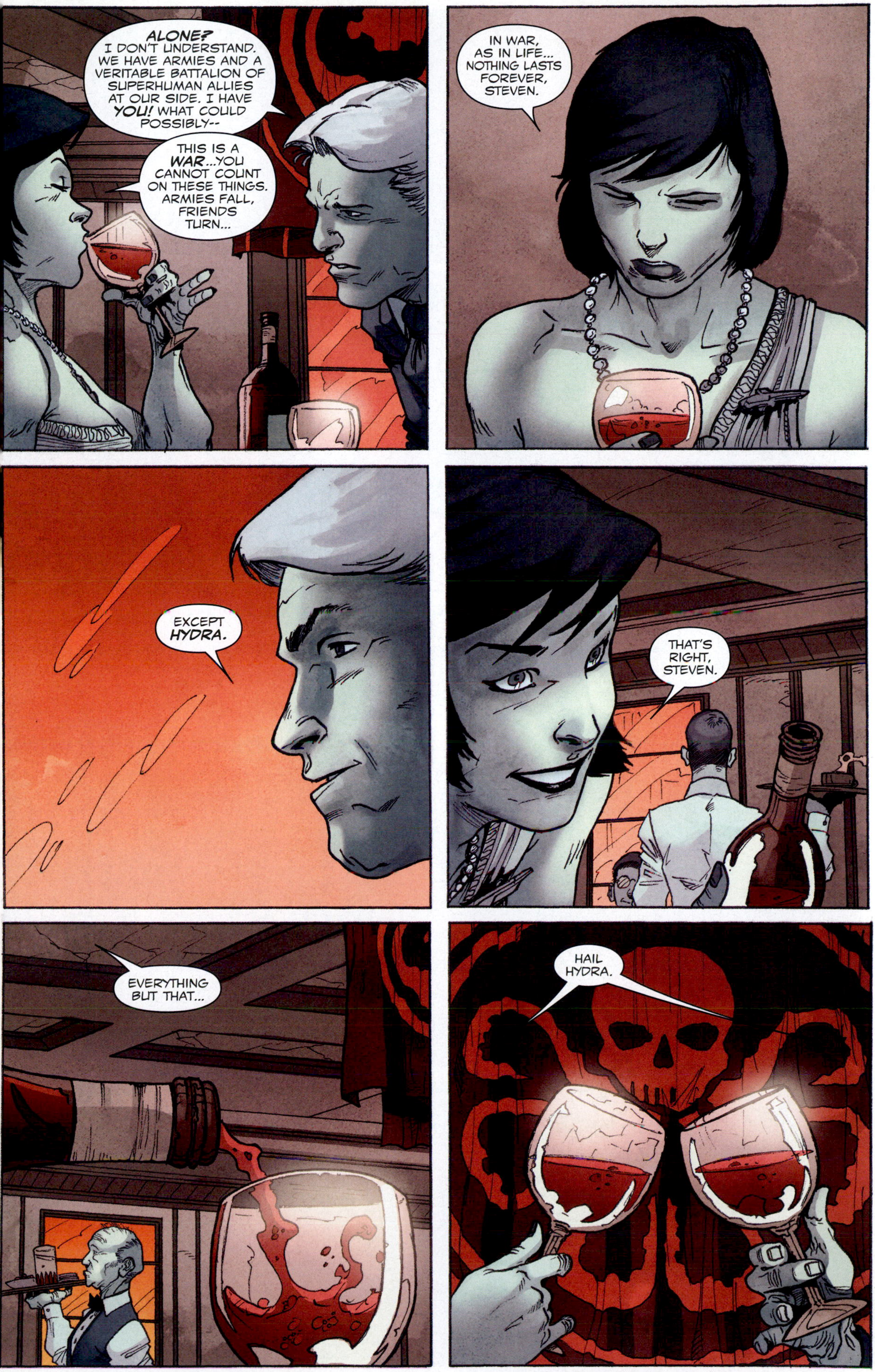
ALONE? I DON'T UNDERSTAND. WE HAVE ARMIES AND A VERITABLE BATTALION OF SUPERHUMAN ALLIES AT OUR SIDE. I HAVE YOU! WHAT COULD POSSIBLY--
THIS IS A WAR...YOU CANNOT COUNT ON THESE THINGS. ARMIES FALL, FRIENDS TURN...
IN WAR, AS IN LIFE... NOTHING LASTS FOREVER, STEVEN.
EXCEPT HYDRA.
THAT'S RIGHT, STEVEN.
EVERYTHING BUT THAT...
HAIL HYDRA.

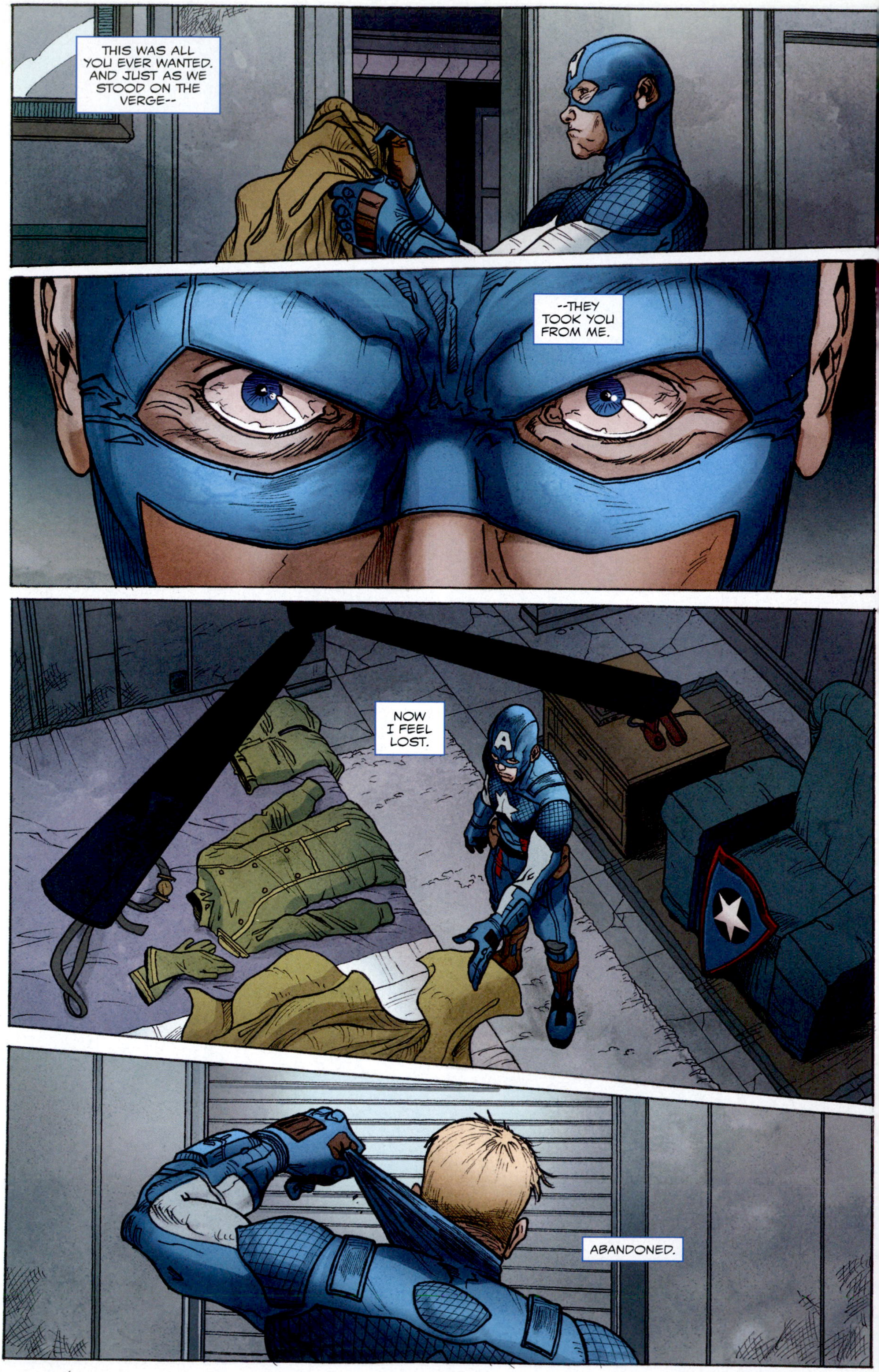
THIS WAS ALL YOU EVER WANTED. AND JUST AS WE STOOD ON THE VERGE--
--THEY TOOK YOU FROM ME.
NOW I FEEL LOST.
ABANDONED.

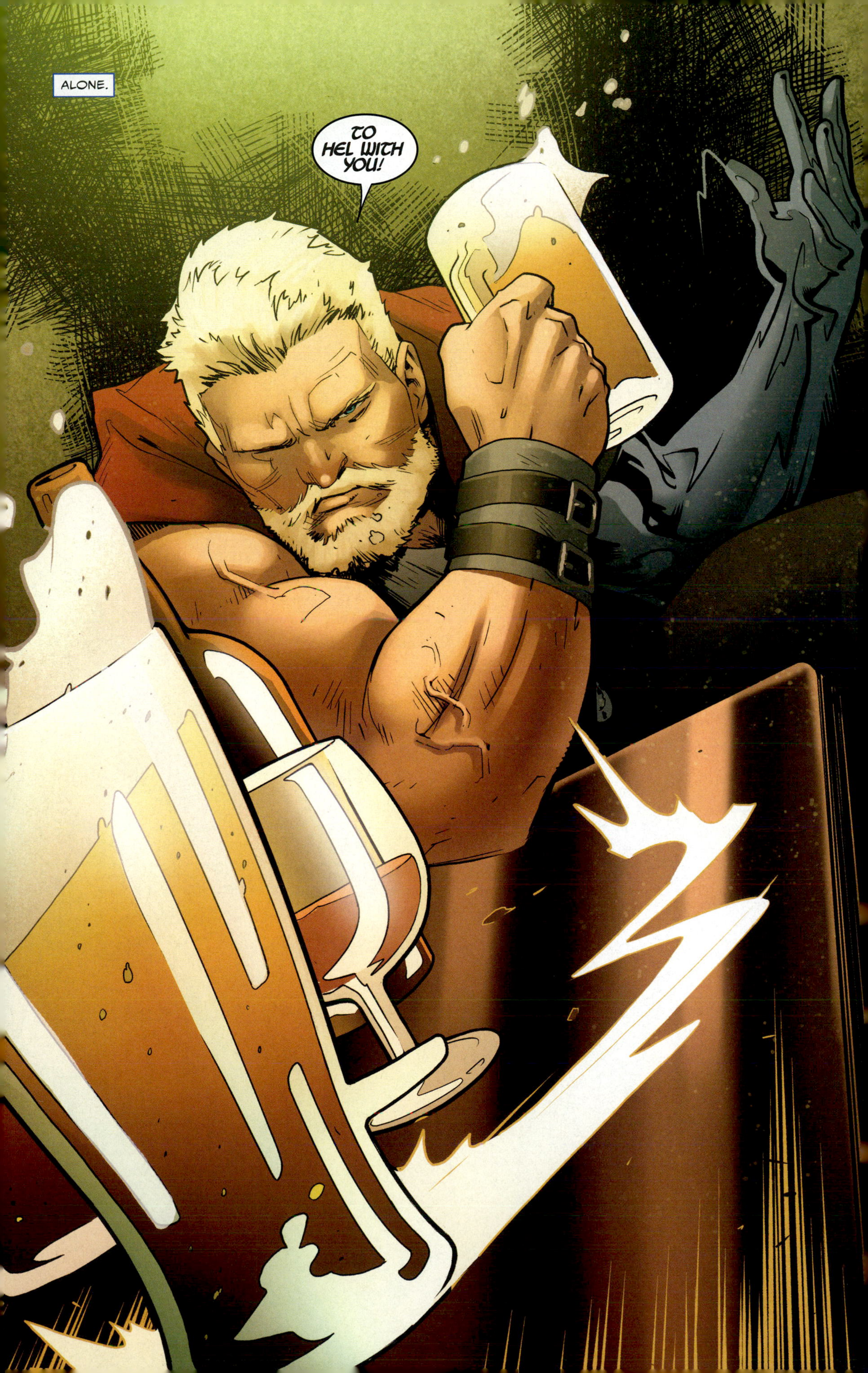
ALONE.
TO HEL WITH YOU!

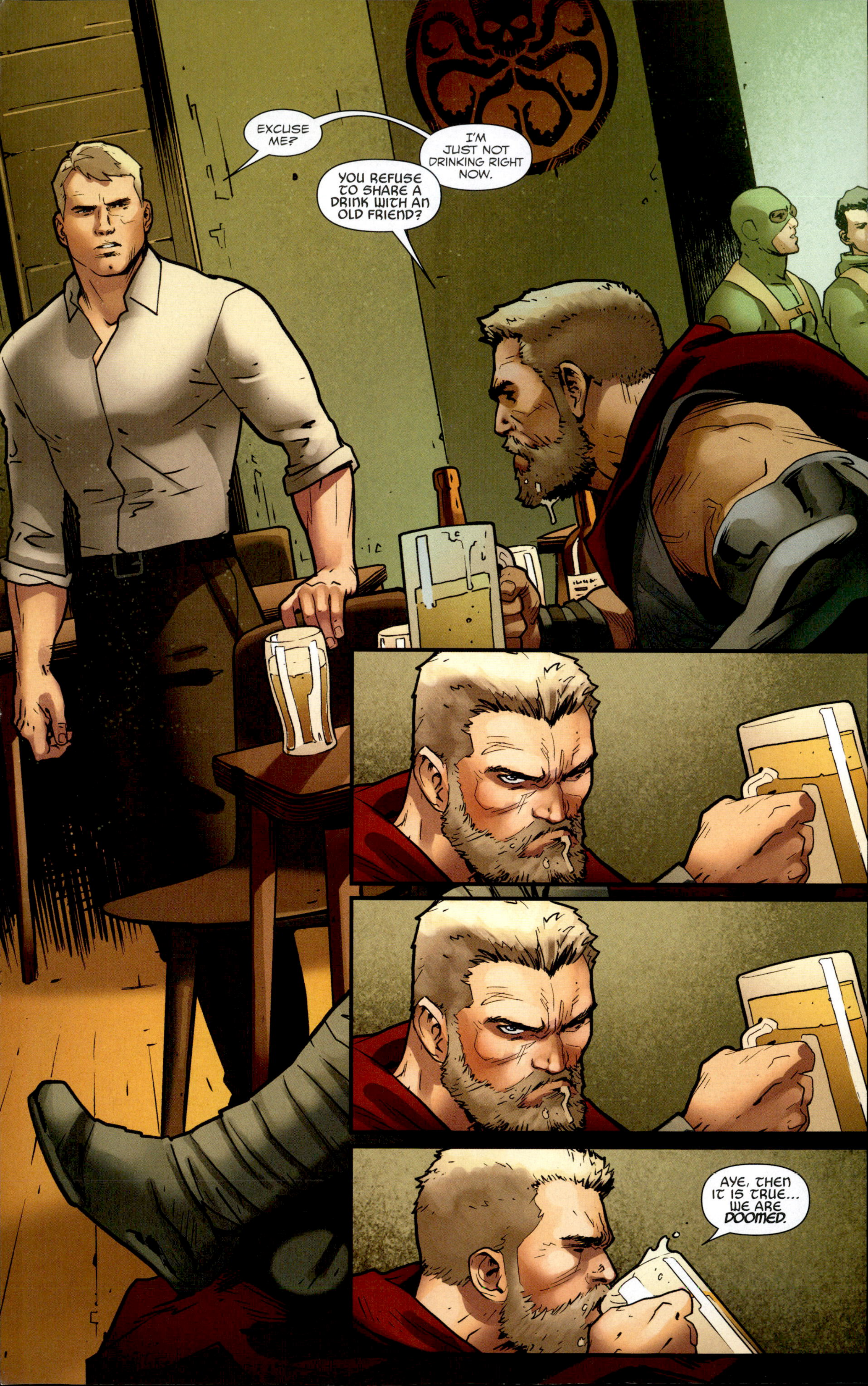
EXCUSE ME?
I'M JUST NOT DRINKING RIGHT NOW.
YOU REFUSE TO SHARE A DRINK WITH AN OLD FRIEND?
AYE, THEN IT IS TRUE... WE ARE DOOMED.

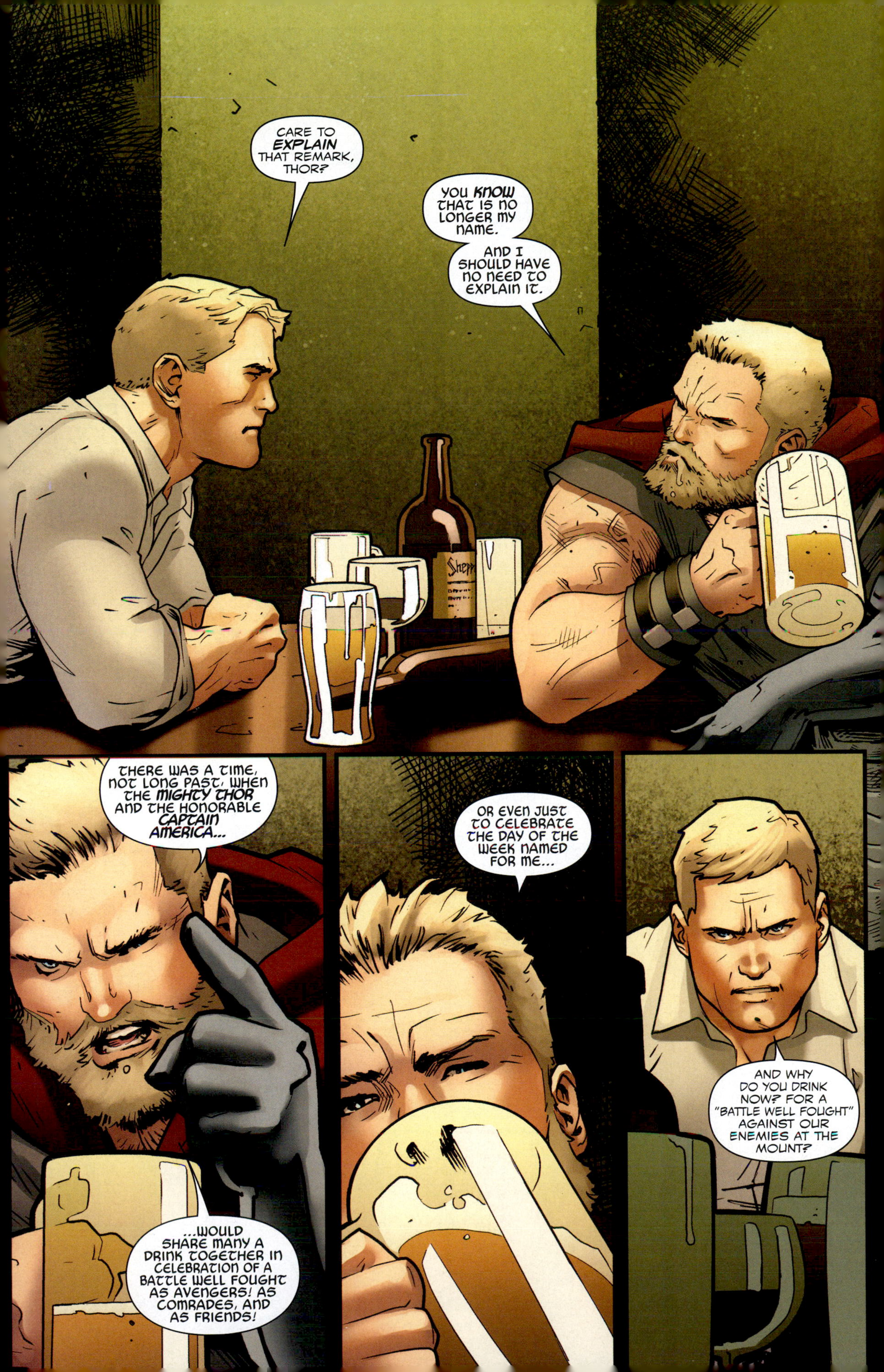
CARE TO EXPLAIN THAT REMARK, THOR?
YOU KNOW THAT IS NO LONGER MY NAME.
AND I SHOULD HAVE NO NEED TO EXPLAIN IT.
THERE WAS A TIME, NOT LONG PAST, WHEN THE MIGHTY THOR AND THE HONORABLE CAPTAIN AMERICA...
...WOULD SHARE MANY A DRINK TOGETHER IN CELEBRATION OF A BATTLE WELL FOUGHT AS AVENGERS! AS COMRADES, AND AS FRIENDS!
OR EVEN JUST TO CELEBRATE THE DAY OF THE WEEK NAMED FOR ME...
AND WHY DO YOU DRINK NOW? FOR A "BATTLE WELL FOUGHT" AGAINST OUR ENEMIES AT THE MOUNT?

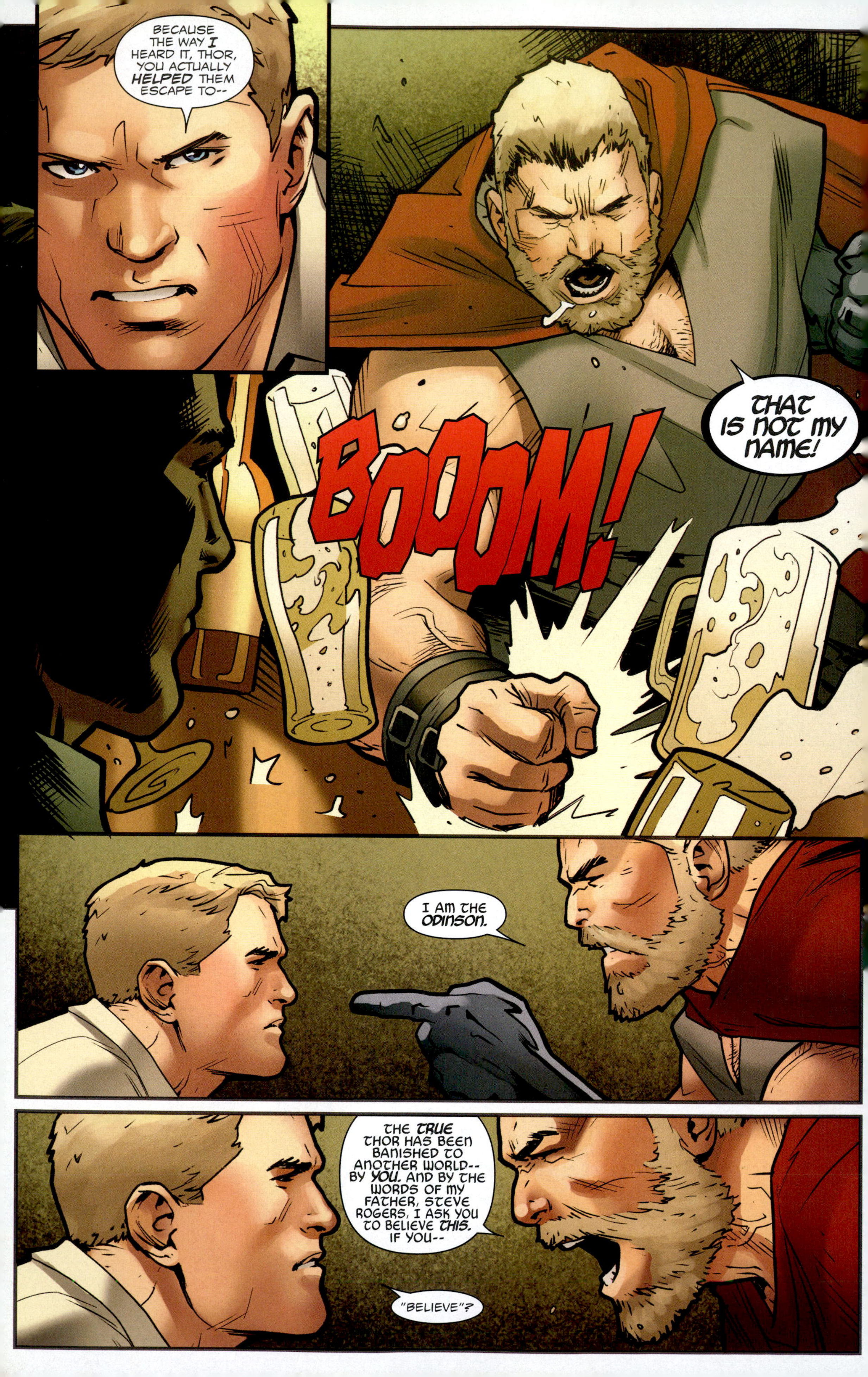

BECAUSE THE WAY I HEARD IT, THOR, YOU ACTUALLY HELPED THEM ESCAPE TO--
THAT IS NOT MY NAME!
BOOOM!
I AM THE ODINSON.
THE TRUE THOR HAS BEEN BANISHED TO ANOTHER WORLD-- BY YOU. AND BY THE WORDS OF MY FATHER, STEVE ROGERS, I ASK YOU TO BELIEVE THIS. IF YOU--
"BELIEVE"?

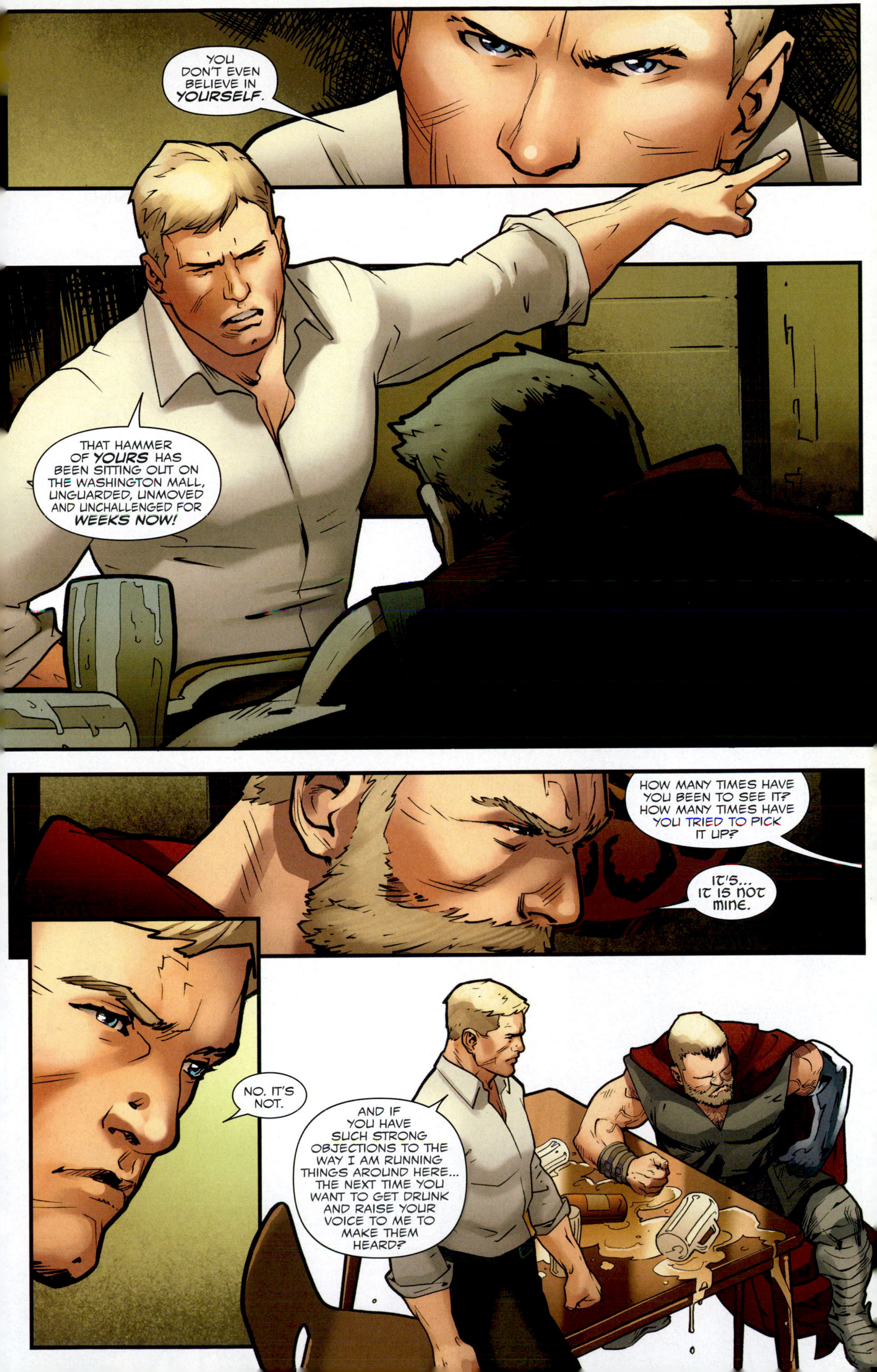

YOU DON'T EVEN BELIEVE IN *YOURSELF*.
THAT HAMMER OF *YOURS* HAS BEEN SITTING OUT ON THE WASHINGTON MALL, UNGUARDED, UNMOVED AND UNCHALLENGED FOR *WEEKS NOW!*
HOW MANY TIMES HAVE YOU BEEN TO SEE IT? HOW MANY TIMES HAVE YOU TRIED TO PICK IT UP?
IT'S... IT IS NOT MINE.
NO. IT'S NOT.
AND IF YOU HAVE SUCH STRONG OBJECTIONS TO THE WAY I AM RUNNING THINGS AROUND HERE... THE NEXT TIME YOU WANT TO GET DRUNK AND RAISE YOUR VOICE TO ME TO MAKE THEM HEARD?

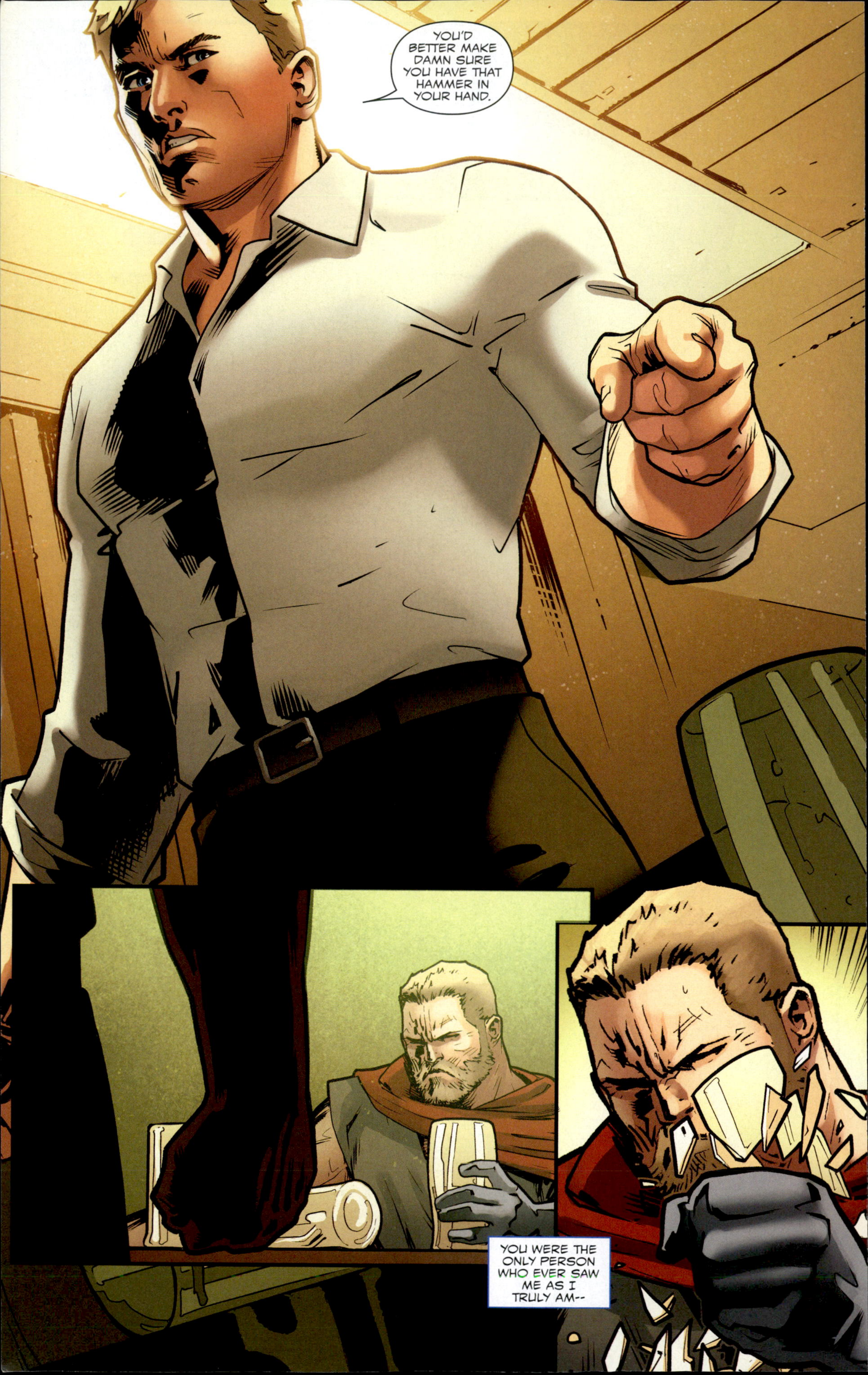
YOU'D BETTER MAKE DAMN SURE YOU HAVE THAT HAMMER IN YOUR HAND.
YOU WERE THE ONLY PERSON WHO EVER SAW ME AS I TRULY AM--

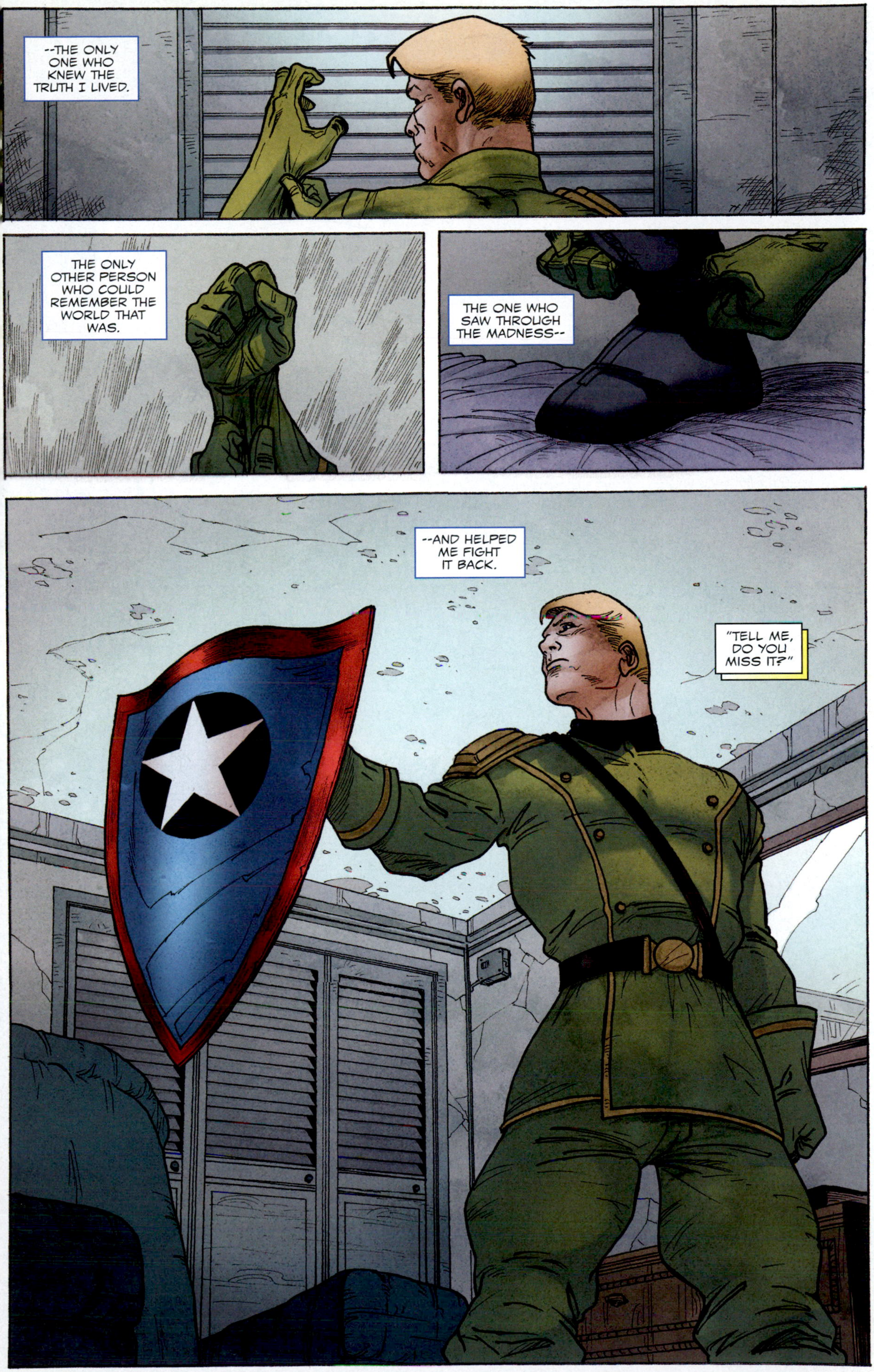
--THE ONLY ONE WHO KNEW THE TRUTH I LIVED.
THE ONLY OTHER PERSON WHO COULD REMEMBER THE WORLD THAT WAS.
THE ONE WHO SAW THROUGH THE MADNESS--
--AND HELPED ME FIGHT IT BACK.
"TELL ME, DO YOU MISS IT?"

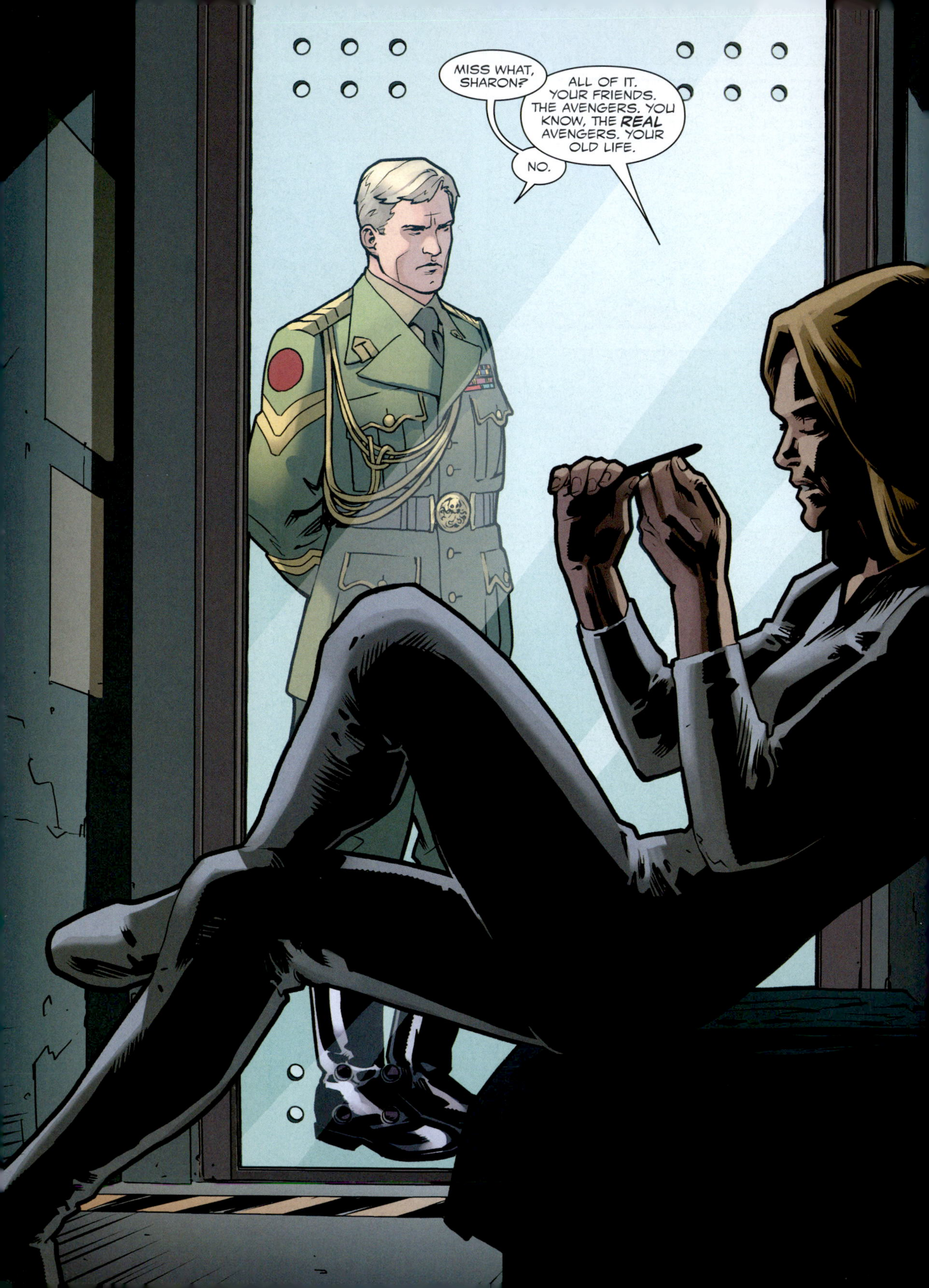
MISS WHAT, SHARON?
ALL OF IT. YOUR FRIENDS. THE AVENGERS. YOU KNOW, THE REAL AVENGERS. YOUR OLD LIFE.
NO.

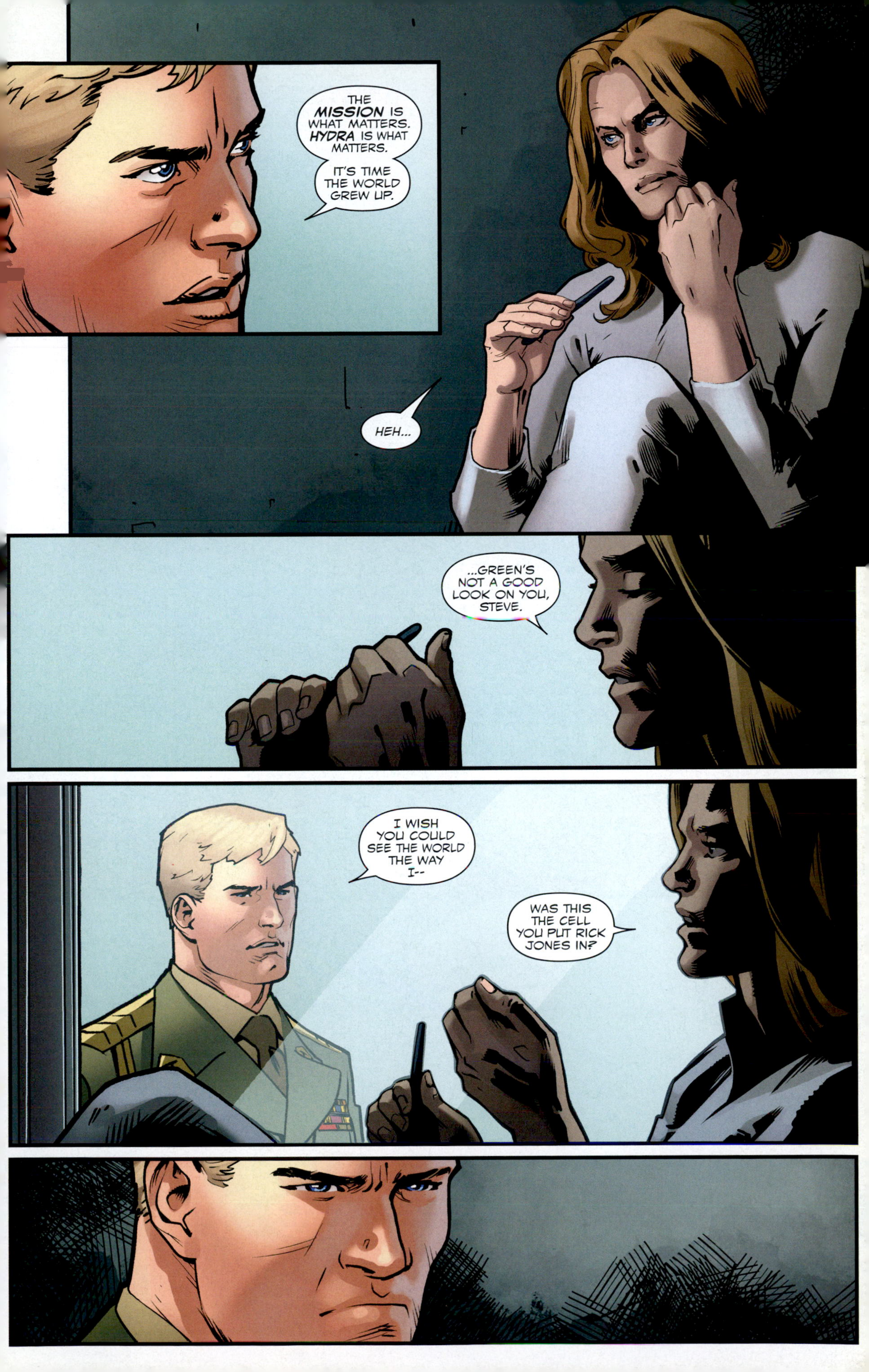
THE MISSION IS WHAT MATTERS. HYDRA IS WHAT MATTERS.
IT'S TIME THE WORLD GREW UP.
HEH...
...GREEN'S NOT A GOOD LOOK ON YOU, STEVE.
I WISH YOU COULD SEE THE WORLD THE WAY I--
WAS THIS THE CELL YOU PUT RICK JONES IN?

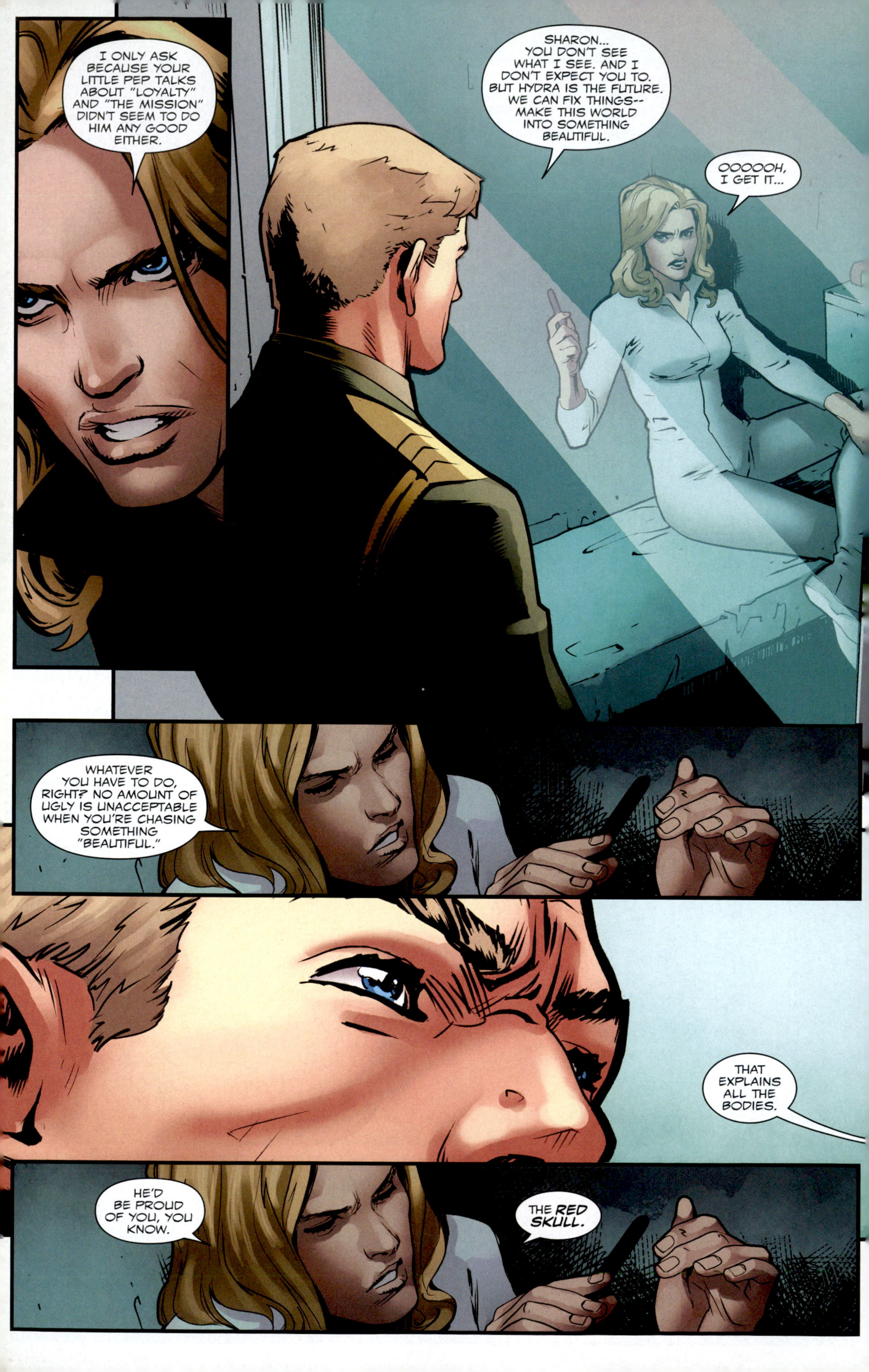
I ONLY ASK BECAUSE YOUR LITTLE PEP TALKS ABOUT "LOYALTY" AND "THE MISSION" DIDN'T SEEM TO DO HIM ANY GOOD EITHER.
SHARON... YOU DON'T SEE WHAT I SEE. AND I DON'T EXPECT YOU TO. BUT HYDRA IS THE FUTURE. WE CAN FIX THINGS--MAKE THIS WORLD INTO SOMETHING BEAUTIFUL.
OOOOOH, I GET IT...
WHATEVER YOU HAVE TO DO, RIGHT? NO AMOUNT OF UGLY IS UNACCEPTABLE WHEN YOU'RE CHASING SOMETHING "BEAUTIFUL."
THAT EXPLAINS ALL THE BODIES.
HE'D BE PROUD OF YOU, YOU KNOW.
THE **RED SKULL**.

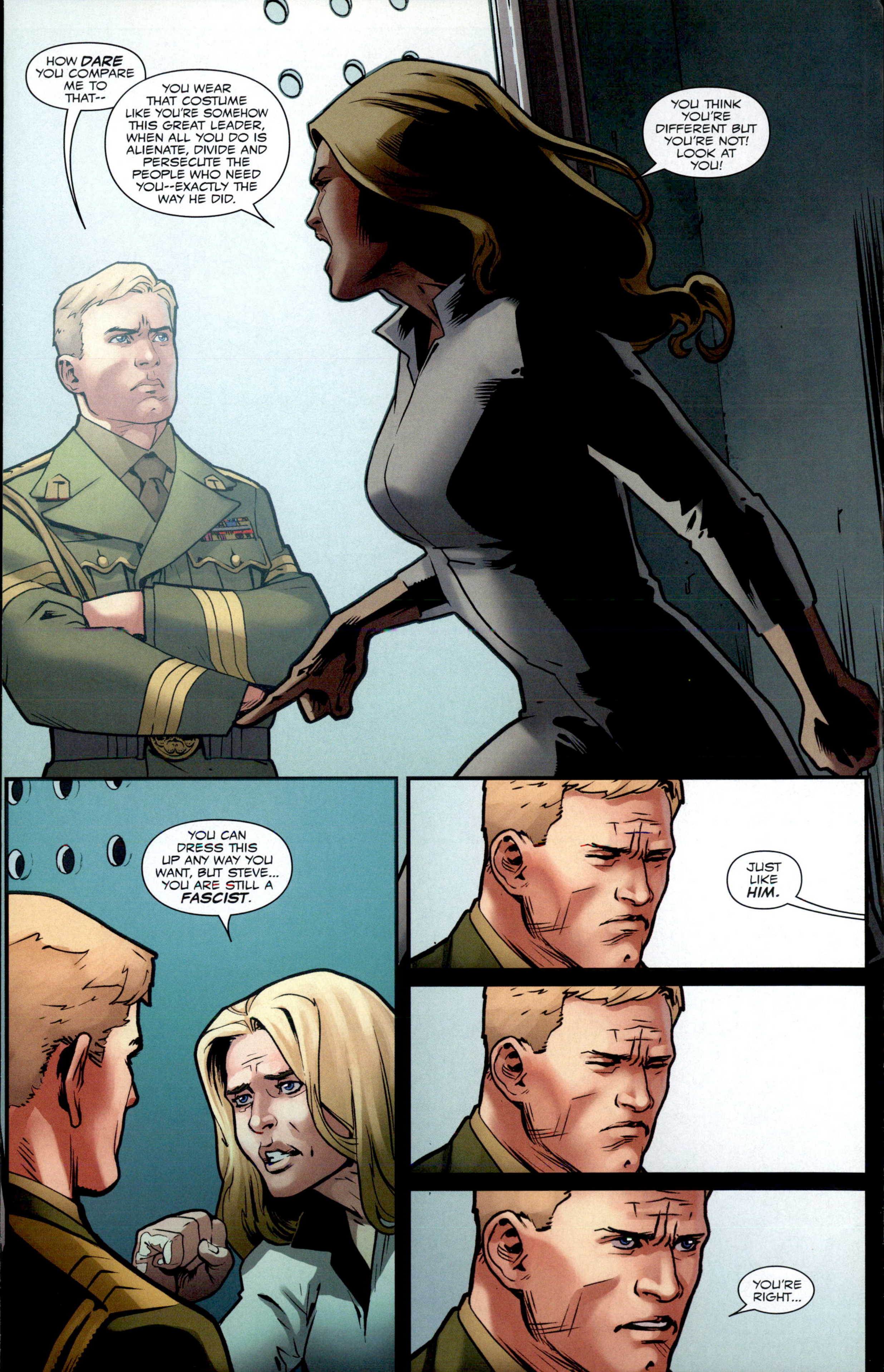
HOW DARE YOU COMPARE ME TO THAT--
YOU WEAR THAT COSTUME LIKE YOU'RE SOMEHOW THIS GREAT LEADER, WHEN ALL YOU DO IS ALIENATE, DIVIDE AND PERSECUTE THE PEOPLE WHO NEED YOU--EXACTLY THE WAY HE DID.
YOU THINK YOU'RE DIFFERENT BUT YOU'RE NOT! LOOK AT YOU!
YOU CAN DRESS THIS UP ANY WAY YOU WANT, BUT STEVE... YOU ARE STILL A FASCIST.
JUST LIKE HIM.
YOU'RE RIGHT...

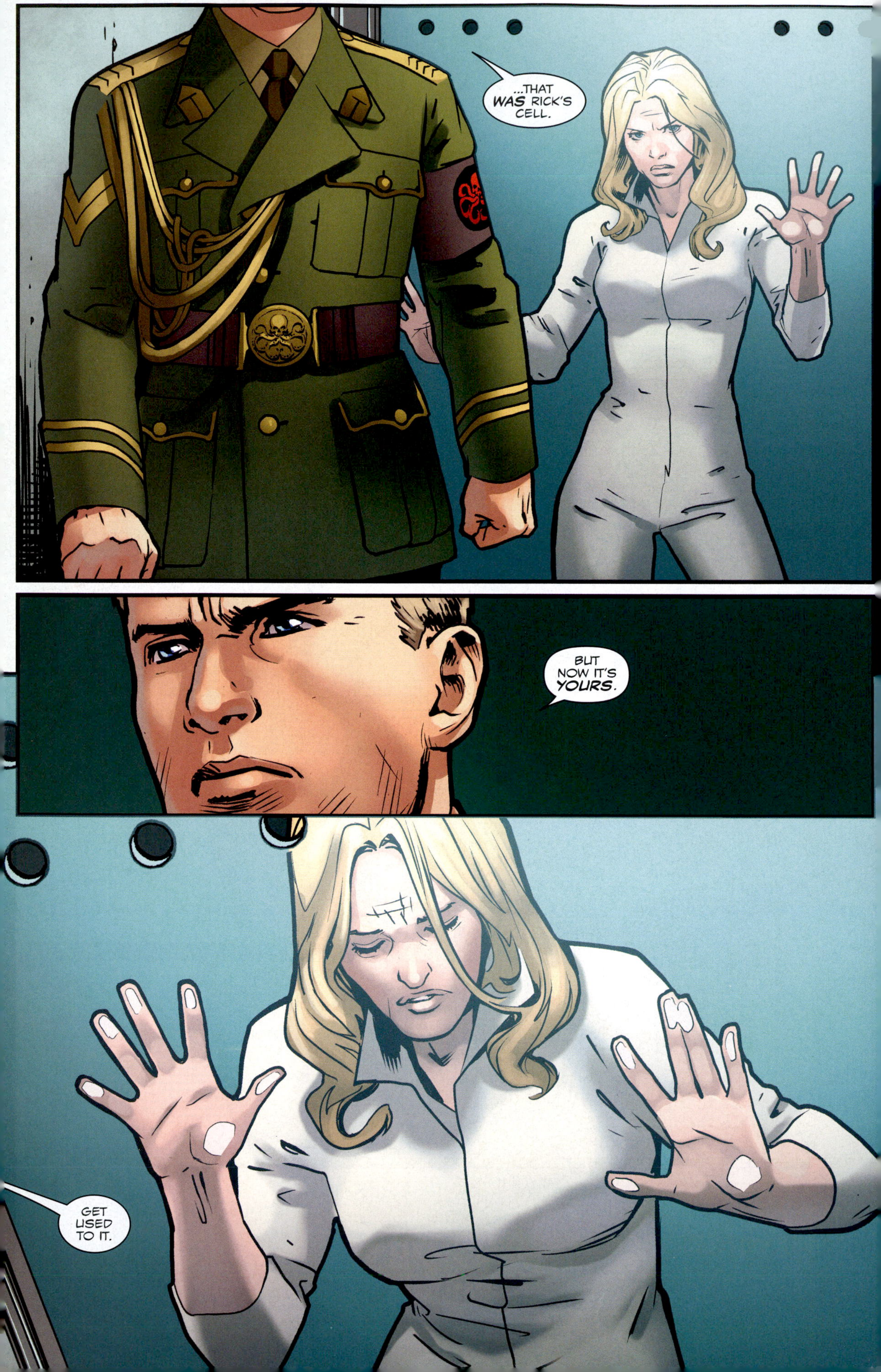
...THAT WAS RICK'S CELL.
BUT NOW IT'S YOURS.
GET USED TO IT.

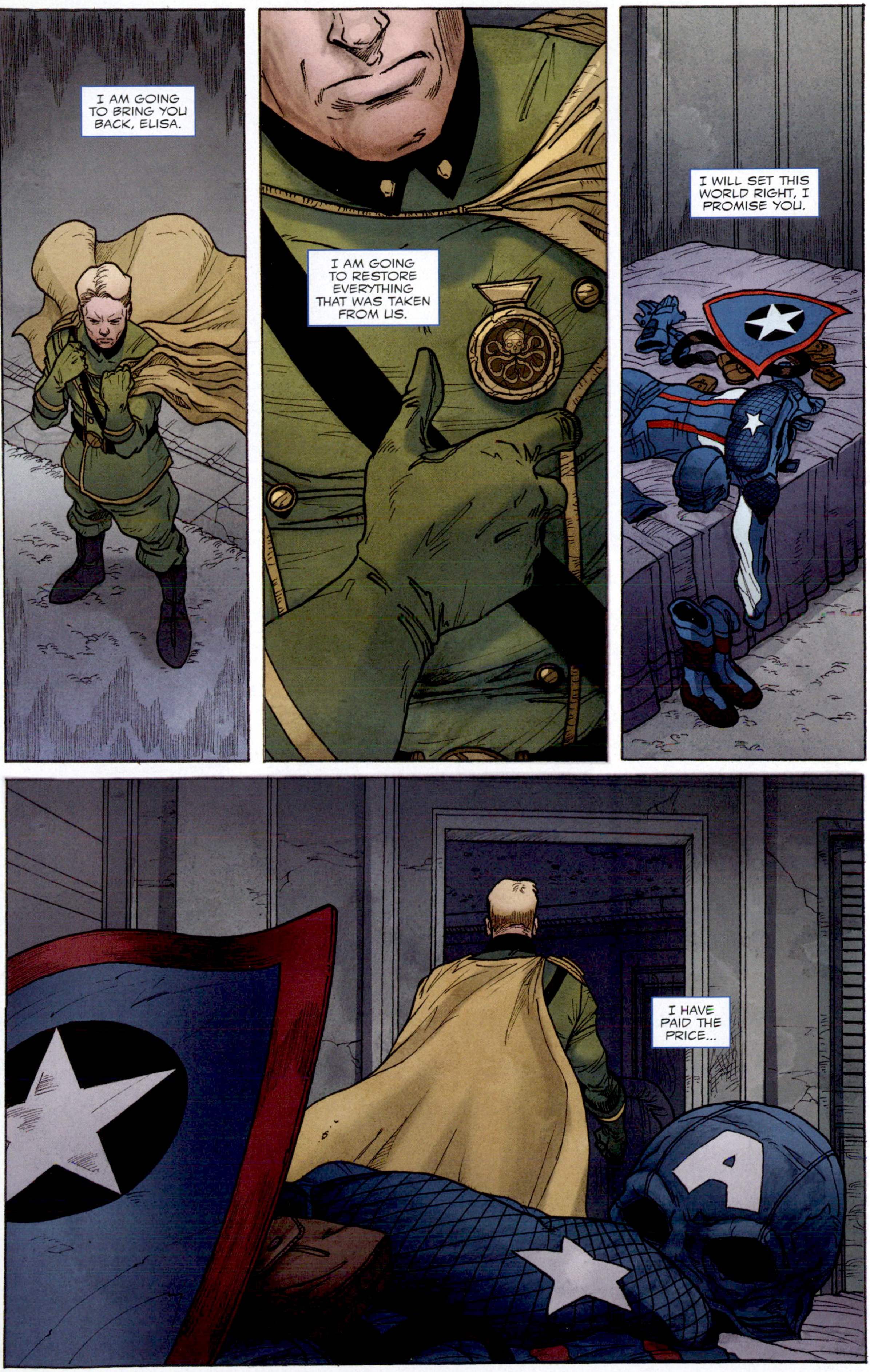
I AM GOING TO BRING YOU BACK, ELISA.
I AM GOING TO RESTORE EVERYTHING THAT WAS TAKEN FROM US.
I WILL SET THIS WORLD RIGHT, I PROMISE YOU.
I HAVE PAID THE PRICE...

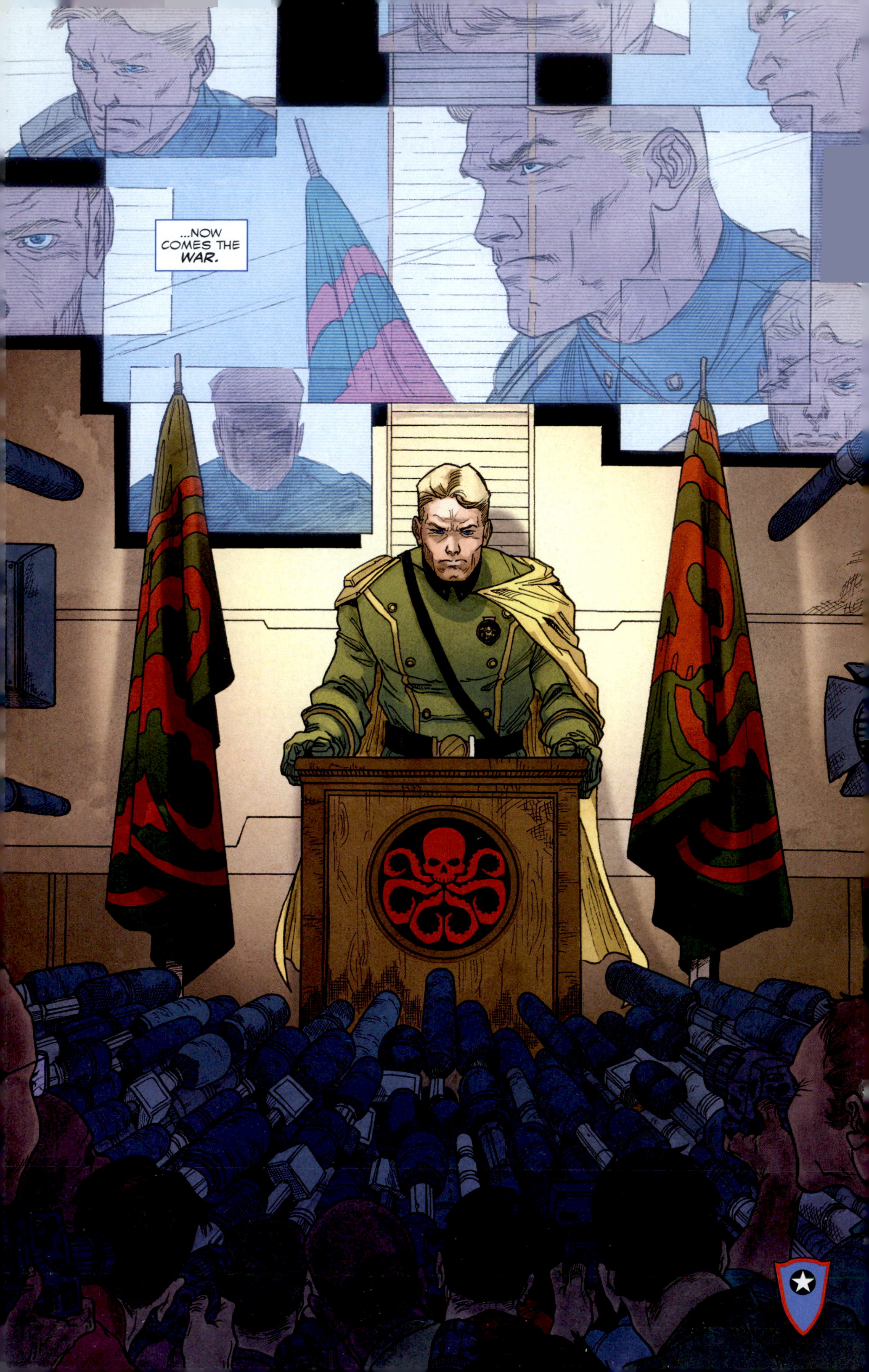
...NOW COMES THE WAR.